THE DAY CARE DILEMMA

Critical Concerns for
American Families

THE DAY CARE DILEMMA

Critical Concerns for American Families

Angela Browne Miller, M.P.H., D.S.W.
Schools of Social Welfare and Education
University of California at Berkeley
Berkeley, California

✸ **INSIGHT BOOKS**
PLENUM PRESS • NEW YORK AND LONDON

Library of Congress Cataloging-in-Publication Data

Browne Miller, Angela.
    The day care dilemma : critical concerns for American familes /
Angela Browne Miller.
        p.   cm.
    "Insight books (New York, N.Y.)"
    Includes bibliographical references.
    ISBN 0-306-43435-0
    1. Child care services--United States. 2. Day care centers-
-United States.   I. Title.
HQ778.7.U6B76 1990
362.7'12'0973--dc20   89-26664
                                                           CIP

Photographs and illustrations by Angela Browne Miller

© 1990 Plenum Press, New York
A Division of Plenum Publishing Corporation
233 Spring Street, New York, N.Y. 10013

An Insight Book

Printed in the United States of America

To Richard
and
to Evacheska
and all her "sisters":
Ryah,
Sarana,
Claudia,
Evelyn,
Giselda,
Irma,
Sarah,
Anna,
and in memory of my mother,
Luisa Francesca.

PREFACE

This book began as a social scientist's inquiry into a social problem. When I became a mother, this research took on heightened significance. During four of the last months of my work on this manuscript, my daughter was on three day care and preschool waiting lists and had twelve different full- and part-time babysitters. I was employed full time. So was my husband. I worked on this manuscript between 10 P.M. and midnight. I wish to thank my daughter, Evacheska, for being in my life; and her father and my wonderful husband, Richard Louis Miller, for his encouragement and faithful support of this project.

Among the many others whose devoted assistance has been invaluable are Susan Barrera, Nina Feldman, and Elizabeth Cunningham, who helped in manuscript preparation; Neil Gilbert, Ph. D., School of Social Welfare, University of California at Berkeley, for his valuable advice; Jack Haley, California Office of Legislative Research, for his wealth of information; and my father, Lee Winston Browne, whose wisdom filters into all my work.

Above all, I wish to thank the directors, parents, and children at the day care and preschool programs that I studied in writing this book. These people know the day care dilemma by heart.

*   *   *

This research was supported in part by a National Institute of Mental Health Postdoctoral Fellowship.

CONTENTS

Introduction

CHILDREN IN THE SEAWEED

There are children in the seaweed,
There are children in the morning,
They are leaning out for love,
They will lean that way forever.

—*Suzanne*
Leonard Cohen

There may or may not be enough love to go around. But there certainly is not enough child care. One of the most tragic indications of the lack of adequate child care services involves the 1987 death of two young boys aged three and four in Florida. They were left alone while their mother was at work. They crawled into a clothes dryer and closed the door. The heat cycle was automatically activated. They died in the machine.

The child care arrangements their mother had made had fallen through. The boys had been on a waiting list for admission to a publicly subsidized child care program for at least half a year. Hundreds of thousands of children around the nation are on waiting lists for admission into child care and preschool programs. Yet, many of their parents cannot afford to wait until they find suitable care for their children. These parents are economically driven to go to work and to leave their children wherever they can, regardless of the quality of care provided [1]. Their children, along with all of our young children, are being tossed about in a sea of massive economic, social, and political change. They are tangled in the seaweed. Their fates are uncertain. It is, therefore, essential that we ask how we as a society can best handle the tangled problem of child care. How can we meet human need in a responsible and humane way?

CONFRONTING COMPLEXITY

We must begin by facing the fact that child care is a complex problem. No single policy or program can provide the entire solution. We must form a larger picture of child care in order to confront its complexity. We must acknowledge many unknowns as we design child care programs and policies, the ultimate being what is best for our children. With this book, I aim to contribute to the formation of a larger picture of child care. I also aim to show that no single political point of view contains this larger picture.

The intricate process of caring for young children involves numerous levels of activity, including attention to the environmental, physical, social, educational, and psychological needs of these children. This process of directly caring for children is, in turn, deeply connected to the encompassing social system. Powerful historical, political, and economic forces have helped to shape the many forms of child day care that we have today. The day care dilemma did not evolve in a vacuum. Because of this, parents and policy makers must always examine day care in the encompassing societal context—in terms of the larger picture. We must not allow our political debates to distract us from the dangerous march of human care into the realm of the purely functional.

Children are not separate from the social environment. They exist amidst the tangled interactions of their parents, their families, their communities, the economy or "market," the public sector or "polity," and society as a whole. As our understanding of the child care problem evolves, so does the potential for its solution. In our complicated world, a narrow approach to child care is very confining. If we do not look at the issue on many levels, we are denying its complexity and its far-reaching implications.

The child care issue is hardly a neat package awaiting a simple solution. This is true of many social issues. Policymakers and analysts commit the "environmental" fallacy when they fail to consider the larger picture. Philosopher C. West Churchman has defined the "environmental fallacy" as being a fallacy in which the entirety of the societal environment encompassing a policy is overlooked. Our fallacious analyses of child care tend to focus on one or two of the items circled in Figure I.1, rather than on all of them. For example, legislation may be designed to encourage employers to sponsor child care programs, the effects of which only apply to employees of willing corporations. This is a very limited portion of society.

Environmental fallacy is a myopic tendency that frequently results in a host of undesigned and unexpected consequences, and in policies that often fail to bring about their originally intended outcomes [2]. Myopic views of social problems begin with our reluctance to integrate personal, social, economic, political, and scientific perspectives.

Let us now briefly examine the importance of unanswered social questions, human instincts, and personal and political diversities in our

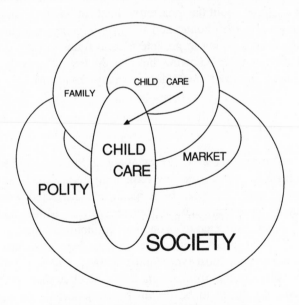

FIGURE I.1. Child care in societal context.

policy process. These are just some of the angles from which we must view child care.

UNANSWERED SOCIAL QUESTIONS

There is, at present, no centralized program to provide quality child day care to all children in the United States. This may be because of difficult questions that remain unanswered, such as: What is quality? Who is responsible for our children? How can women successfully integrate their changing family and workplace roles? What are families for? Perhaps it is that we already have an implicit national child care policy, an unspoken choice to maintain an informal, decentralized child-care capability instead of an explicit, formal, and centralized social program. Regardless, a lack of answers has never held this nation back from the explicit policy decisions it has wanted to make. For example, we have maintained a policy to provide special economic assistance to welfare mothers who meet specific economic criteria rather than to all mothers. This policy decision has been made without knowing anything about the long-term effects of having so many mothers working out of their homes and away from their young children. We have maintained a policy to provide federal funds to fight drug abuse and addiction without knowing how to do this effectively. Explicit public policies are often made despite many unknowns.

THE PULL OF INSTINCT

Let's turn to what we do know about child care. Motherhood, in its ideal form, is one of the few remaining unmediated experiences. Most human experience has been mediated, interfered with, or impinged upon by intermediate or outside forces. Motherhood is, of course, also being affected by economic, commercial, medical, institutional, and social forces. Yet, while we have legislated, institutionalized, and organized almost every human activity, intense parental bonding, especially in the form of motherhood (but also occurring in fatherhood), continues to be driven by deep-seated, time-tested instinct. This bonding provides the opportunity for female and male parents to feel and to act upon their unconditional, gut-level love and commitment to their young children.

Thanks to the power of this instinct, caring well for a young child in an intimate way is still possible. The intensity and beauty of true parental bonding have survived and have maybe even been enhanced in the modern world. However, the especially good care we associate with parenting does not always occur and is by no means restricted to mothers and fathers. In fact, both the ability and the inability to care well are found among both parental and nonparental caregivers.

The modern world provides many opportunities for nonparental caregiving. Driven by economic and social pressures, working parents' demands for help with the "job" of child caring invite nonparental care into children's lives. As child care has become a "job," many of its providers have become "workers," who count the paid hours that they "spend" caring, while parents, motivated by economic pressures, count the dollars that they earn during the hours that their children are in the care of others.

PERSONAL AND POLITICAL DIVERSITY

Child care is one of the strongest examples of the fact that social policy questions are both personal and political. A society cannot ask itself what to do with its children without hearing competing responses from its individual members. There is no single right answer. Each way that society answers or refrains from answering its child care questions will be an important and risky social experiment, performed by our hearts and our minds upon the next generation.

Child care shows us that when our society is called to recognize a profound need among its members, it does not necessarily respond in an organized manner. In fact, in the case of child care, the response is so disorganized that the unmet need persists. At best, there are only enough family day care and center-based child care slots available for one in every three children who have working mothers [3]. The demand is increasing faster than the supply. A close look at the child care supply in the United States reveals a growing need that cannot be adequately met by the existing patchwork of services and programs [4]. At the same time, we are taking no measures to provide economic support to parents who choose to stay home with their young children. There is no single right answer; there is no simple solution. Our hesitation as a nation may reflect this awareness.

IDENTIFYING SPECIFIC TRENDS

Several present-day trends have increased the perceived need for quality child care. The once shocking and now acceptable women's movement and the labor force changes of the 1960s and 1970s have brought large numbers of mothers of young children out of their homes and into American workplaces.

INCREASING EMPLOYMENT OF MOTHERS

Now, in the 1990s, as these developments become incorporated into our culture, the demand for child care is intensifying. An estimated 75% of all mothers with children under six will be employed outside their homes and there will be 11.5 million children under the age of six whose mothers will be working. This represents an increase of 2.5 million over the 9 million children under six with working mothers in 1984 [5]. Working mothers will require an increasing level of child care services. Each year sees more children enrolled in organized day care. In just the three years between 1982 and 1985, the number of preschool-age children in day care grew 60% [6]. This means that, in sheer numbers, the effects of nonparental care upon children, whether positive, negative, or both, are increasing.

GROWING CONCERNS OF PARENTS

And while this trend continues, another equally important trend has emerged in the attitudes parents hold about child care. Surveys of working parents show that parents feel that their young children may be paying a price for the increasing amount of time they spend in care outside the family. A 1987 Fortune 500 survey finds that over half of working parents (55.4% of the men surveyed and 58.2% of the women) think that their young children "suffer by not being given enough time and attention" [7]. The comments of parents participating in my Day Care Consumer Study further evidence this trend. They were asked what they would change about their child care services if they could. These parents provided a range of answers that, while revealing variations in their priorities and sensitivities as well as in the quality of care their children received, showed that they were dissatisfied with their child care services [8]. These parents said they would like to change many things about the quality of care their children receive. Their comments addressed the environmental, physical, social, educational, and psychological dimensions of their child care services.

Regarding the child care environment, parents wanted improvements such as these:

"Provide air conditioning in the rooms."
"Have a nicer, softer lawn for children to play on."
"Have more outside play in good weather. The indoors here is not pretty."
"Have more availability of space in the nursery."
"Upgrade this facility. It looks dingy instead of nice and bright."
"Fumigate the place for fleas."

Concerning the attention to their children's physical care and development, parents called for changes such as these:

"More one-to-one attention in the area of children's hygiene, e.g., changing clothes when wet, cleaning face if dirty, etc."
"Have a separate place for ill children."
"Healthier snacks."

About the social elements of their child care, parents said they wanted to see improvements such as:

"More parent-teacher interaction."
"Keep children from hitting each other too much."
"Let the children have some fun."
"Celebrate birthdays."

About the education provided to their children, most parents had this sort of comment:

"Upgrade the requirements for staff members."

"Have it be more towards learning."

"Teach my child how to say his name."

"Hire male teachers, not only women."

"Have formal training for teachers."

"Have better teacher-child ratio so children can be learning something."

"There is a holding back of older kids by combining all activities with younger kids. This is unfair to older and younger kids. It should be changed."

"Have fewer children in classes. Teach more fundamentals."

And, regarding the psychological qualities of the care their children receive, parents wanted improvements such as:

"I would like to see a little closer relationship between child and teacher. Being away from home twelve hours a day, a child needs a little extra attention."

"Hire more teachers and pay them more to improve the overall level of commitment to the children."

"More caring."

More care. This is the spoken and unspoken wish of parents who leave their children in organized child day care. More love. More care. Yet, parents' definitions of the term "care" are as diverse as the types and qualities of care available to their children.

My research also shows that parents want to change the cost and convenience of their child care services. In the area of cost, parents claim:

"It takes over half my income. I may have to find other care."

"Increase the pay of the caregivers. Decrease the clients' cost."

"Lower the cost and get it away from the management of the city. That's why the cost is so high."

In the area of convenience, parents say:

"I would prefer it opened earlier. I would also like it if there weren't so many holidays."

"Open it at 7:00 A.M."

"The program could meet my needs better. The hours I work are not constant but vary. There is not always a place for my kids. Having no back-up means I have to miss work. I can't afford to." "Responsiveness to parents who work varying hours." "Make it available twenty-four hours a day, seven days a week."

These comments reveal that parents devote mental and emotional energy to specific concerns about the child care that they have selected, and that they have good reasons for their discomfort over child care.

GROWING CONCERNS OF EMPLOYERS

Because the numbers of children in day care are increasing, and because of parents' discomfort with leaving their children in care, employer's perceptions of child care issues are changing. Employers are now struggling with the dilemma of whether or not to provide or subsidize child care services or benefits for their employees. Understandably, employers are reluctant to pay for unproductive work time. An anxious parent can become an unproductive employee [9]. Many potentially and actually productive employees are of childbearing age, and this "age range" is continuing to extend as a result of technological and cultural change. Ellen Galinsky, Director of Work and Family Life Studies at Bank Street College, underscored this trend, reporting that ". . . problems with child care are the most significant predictors of absenteeism and unproductive time at work" [10].

INCREASING DISPARITY AND DIVERSITY

Perhaps the most critical trend is the growing socioeconomic disparity surrounding child care. Some parents receive social assistance in locating and paying for their child care services while others, who may also need it, do not. The United States is one of the few Western developed countries without a public support system for working parents of all preschool-age children. American parents are facing vast disparity in the characteristics of the care that they are able to obtain. On the other hand, it could be pointed out that disparity in the characteristics of child care can also mean diversity. Disparity is grossly unequal, but it means that every child is not unnecessarily subjected to the same form of child care. In the United States, there are diverse answers to child care needs, and this diversity leaves room for the individual desires of different families to be addressed by a variety of alternatives.

The diversity of services arises, in part, out of the fact that both our public and private sectors and a broad mix of unrelated organizations within them are involved in providing child care. The provision of social services in this "mixed economy of care" offers several advantages, including freedom of consumer choice and the responsiveness of diversity to individuals' needs.

The free enterprise typical of the market sector suggests that there will be an improved quality of service as a result of competition among entrepreneurial providers. But this view is challenged by those who question the extent to which the production and distribution of social services responds to what the theoreticians claim is the basic operation of the market economy. When day care is available for a price, it is a commodity. If the laws of supply and demand worked in a straightforward manner and in a vacuum, parents could "demand" day care services in sufficient quantity, with reasonable quality, at affordable prices, in convenient locations, and have it available during particular hours. Private-sector care merchants would establish programs in response to these demands and would satisfy consumers, or they would lose money when their competitors offered better choices. Unfortunately, this simple economic process has not had this effect on child care services. Parents often find that they have to choose from among programs of questionable quality, at high prices, in difficult locations, with undesirable hours. Moreover, the consequences of poor choices are often more critical in the selection of care services than in the purchase of goods in the market economy. The purchase of a bad refrigerator is of much less consequence than the selection of poor child care.

Although limited in their power, supply and demand, the forces which motivate the market, are creating impetus for the development of day care services by employers, entrepreneurs, and nonprofit organizations. A day care program comes into existence because families need a day care service. When a family cannot afford to buy what it needs, or when the market does not offer the good or service needed, the public sector may respond [11].

Day care services are becoming more and more diversified and this diversity presents numerous problems. Day care is financed and delivered by families, nonprofit agencies, individual entrepreneurs and large-scale profit-making bodies, government agencies, and combinations of these units [12]. Public policies which encourage diversity invite fragmentation, as a mix of public, private for-profit, private nonprofit, and informal agencies fashion numerous responses to a private and public need. This conglomeration of effort does not provide uniform care; it does not guarantee universal entitlement to care; and it makes regulation of the quality of care difficult to achieve. This is not necessarily all bad; because the meaning of and need for care vary among families, a centralized, unified response may be unable to satisfy quality-of-care criteria as defined by different consumer groups.

In the private sector, only if parents know how to discriminate among many different child care options will children benefit from the diverse offerings available in the mixed economy of care. And in the public sector, only if public agencies can control the quality of care will children be well cared for. Unfortunately, even when child care settings are licensed and thus subject to regulatory control, the cost and time involved in inspecting the care provided by the myriad day care programs that cover a large geographical area impede effective enforcement. Quality is difficult to legislate and enforce.

Although society offers a wide range of preschool-age experiences to young children, society does not offer equal preschool opportunity to all children. In the public sector, the highly successful, federally sponsored Head Start Program has made preschool education available to children from qualifying low- and no-income families, but it has not become universally available to all children or even to all children of low-income families. In the private sector, some highly innovative models for intensive early childhood education have been developed. In these programs, very young children have the opportunity to learn music, computer operation, mathematics, geometry, reading, and languages. If this form of intensive early childhood education proves beneficial, these children will enter kindergarten with heavy advantages. Unfortunately, innovative educational programs are only available in some geographic areas and to some of the families who can afford the often high tuition.

This means that some children get this form of "head start" in their early childhood educations while others do not. Furthermore, some children get a different head start or more of a head start than others. However easy this is to explain, the problem of inequity is actually complicated by a professional debate about exactly what forms of child care provide a head start and how any form of nonparental care stacks up against parental care. Neither the definition of nor the solution to inequity is clear. Because of this, society cannot always provide legislation that will ameliorate inequity even when it chooses to. Thus the trends toward increasing diversity and disparity are accompanied by growing debate about the meaning of quality in the child care field.

These trends will stay with us as the face of the labor force changes and as modern economic and cultural pressures emerge and continue to apply. Social pressure is building, leading to an increased focus on the child care issues in the United States. It is essential that we incorporate several new and forward-looking perspectives into our policymaking process as we respond to this pressure.

GENERATING CRITICAL POLICY PERSPECTIVES

We must respect the complexity of child care as a personal, social, and even political activity, and as an issue which has not only present-day implications but great implications for the future. There are many important perspectives which must be addressed by policymakers when making specific decisions about child day care. Let's examine some of these.

MULTIPLE CONTEXTS

The first perspective that policymakers must acknowledge is that any policy decision regarding child care is set within several societal contexts: the context of each individual child's development, the context of the family, the context of the marketplace (which both motivates and enables the family to "purchase" child care), and the context of the polity or the society at large. The complexity of the child care problem, however, does not stop here.

IMPLEMENTATION PROBLEMS

Public policies often highlight promises that are easy to make but hard to keep. Whether it originates locally, regionally, or nationally, child care policy must learn from the problems encountered during the implementation of other types of policy. For example, the guarantee of equal opportunity in education provided by Public Law 94–142 ensured that all handicapped children would receive a free and equal public education. Yet, the environment, or, in this case, environments (individual schools), in which the law was implemented affected the extent of equal opportunity actually achieved. In the end, each instance of bringing children with special needs into the regular classroom (mainstreaming) was "ultimately no better than the vision of the handicapped child that informed its implementation" [13]. As mandated, children were "mainstreamed" into regular classrooms. In some cases, this proved advantageous to all children involved. But in other cases, the mainstreaming of children with special needs resulted in their not receiving the special care and instruction they required or in their being stigmatized by their classmates. The policy perspective which gave rise to mainstreaming was a narrow one. It failed to consider the larger environment, such as teachers' abilities and children's understandings of disabilities, in which the policy was to be implemented. This is one example of how the effects of many social policies are unforeseen.

Court-ordered school desegregation is another example of a well-intended policy that failed to consider the larger picture. Busing was used as a means of moving children from one part of a school district to another in order to integrate the schools. In many areas, what occurred instead has been described as "white flight," in which white families moved away from desegregating school districts [14]. Some social scientists claim that this white flight was the result of regional economic and employment pressures and that it was not an undesigned consequence of a poorly designed public policy. Nevertheless, white flight demonstrates that policymakers went ahead with implementation even though they had not considered the possibility that undesigned consequences or events, regardless of their cause, would affect the desired outcome of the busing policy.

Some of the unplanned effects of policies are difficult to avoid and many of them appear to be almost inevitable. Perhaps this explains why these unplanned effects are not carefully considered when our nation is in the process of either making or refraining from making important policy decisions. Consider the problem of illegal immigration. Every effort to control the influx of illegal aliens has met with a mix of some success and an immeasurable level of failure [15]. Many questions about immigration policy remain unanswered. Do stiff immigration laws drive illegal aliens further underground rather than sending them home or keeping them out? What are the global pressures driving underground migration? How can we know what policies will work best until we try them? Unfortunately, this question suggests that public policy often takes the form of social experimentation, with undesirable outcomes becoming an inevitable part of the policy formation process.

In the case of child care policy, social experimentation is risky because the subjects are our children. While we may not be able to control all undesigned consequences, policymakers must maintain a continuous regard for the larger picture. This will at least introduce an ethical respect for the risks of policy decisions. This is especially important when those most affected by policy decisions are our children.

THE THREAT OF DEHUMANIZATION

These are only some of the largest, most expansive policy issues encompassing child care. Let us journey still further beyond what seem to be the commonly accepted boundaries of the child care discussion to some other essential perspectives. I have already referred to an almost invisible trend toward depersonalization and dehumanization in our highly technological and heavily populated world. When large numbers of people are to be moved, counted, and cared for, their individual needs are not of primary concern. How can they be? It takes time and energy and money to focus on each person being impacted by a particular social policy. Caring about individuals is expensive.

That we keep this in mind is critical to child care policy development. In child care, we find evidence that we are in need of a solution to an immensely threatening and complex problem. This problem is the dangerous trend toward dehumanization of the care of large numbers of dependents. To find alternatives, we must be able to clearly define one of the most important aspects of caring for people. Specifically, we must define what we mean by "quality care." The range of this definition must be broad enough to specify everything from the quality of hand washing to prevent massive contagion when child caregivers change large quantities of diapers, to the naming of the specific ingredients of touching and affection involved in caring for young children. "What truly is quality care?" is a question of our times. As the number of children in institutionalized day care increases, do we risk the dehumanization of childrearing?

This change is actually a change in our tolerance for and perception of dehumanization in our social services. As a society, we advocate the idea of "quality" care but we often substitute mass-produced "institutional" care for this quality. This is particularly evident in the way the elderly and the mentally ill are cared for in low caregiver-to-patient-ratio settings, which frequently involve the drugging of dependent people to control them. The message found in the form of care we select says that we prefer to save money by warehousing and medicating people in institutions rather than paying for additional caregivers to provide more labor-intensive and thus more humane care. Stated more succinctly, it is less expensive to institutionalize, to *warehouse,* people who are dependent than to provide real human care for them.

As we dehumanize, as our population grows, we find large political bodies interested in controlling large numbers of people for both political and economic reasons. Dependents, whether they are adults or children, are especially subject to this form of control. Perhaps this subtle but ever-present trend toward dehumanization is one reason why there is such a frantic emphasis on individuality in our society. The fate of being a dependent is, in all too many cases, horrible.

In order to care for an ever-growing population of dependents in a cost-effective manner, the humane element of care, the "feeling," is losing out to the more mechanical element of care, the "function." And while this state of affairs continues to develop, there is a confusing undercurrent in policy development. The confusion stems from the increasing desire to institutionalize care while the federal government makes no explicit and comprehensive policy provisions to provide day care to all children. Certainly these seem to be countertrends. Massive social programs to provide day care to young children may press us to recognize how economic pressures transform care from a feeling, humane process to an inhumane process. Society tends to look the other way when the disabled, the elderly, and the mentally ill are warehoused and even drugged to store them at the least social cost in dollars and energy. However, we might not be so indifferent if the dependents "in care" were our children. Imagine massive child care institutions where hundreds of children are stored for eight to ten, even twelve hours a day, while their parents work. Locked rooms, understaffed programs, sick children in with well children, sporadic violence and abuse, and prevalent neglect could result. Would we tolerate this? (Are we now tolerating this without realizing it?) When the dependents in care are children, some instinctual or emotional drive surfaces and alerts us to our humanity. Perhaps our innate desire to preserve our species is the source of our discomfort with the idea of poor care for children. We do not believe we would tolerate this.

The question remains, if a centralized, government-sponsored form of child care for all children is not adequately funded or well supervised, will the dehumanization of child care result? Let us not restrict our concerns about such a development to the public sector. Ironically, this scenario is appearing in some private- as well as some public-sector child care programs even now. In my research I visited a number of child care settings in which large numbers of children were being cared for by few adults. The children played or cried alone or sat on the floor doing nothing for hours. Their dirty and sad faces, the caked-over mucus on their noses that had not been wiped for hours, the stench of their dirty diapers, sometimes leaking and unchanged all day, stays with me. I am relieved that I do not have to leave my child in these settings. I am deeply saddened to know that many other parents feel that they have no choice but to leave their children where I do not have to leave mine.

I have been told that I am too finicky. I demand too much quality for my child. Perhaps I should settle for less. On the other hand, we as a society are already settling for less. In order to counteract the possibility of this subtle yet pervasive change in our orientation toward child care, we must keep a watchful eye on ourselves. We must analyze our present and future child care policies and develop humane and holistic means of doing so. We must always remember that care is more than an administrative, organizational, and social function; it must be governed by feelings that involve love, affection, tenderness, protectiveness, and nurturing.

THE NEED TO SENSITIZE RESEARCH

Social policy analysis suffers a deep schism between its methods of research and its issues of concern. This predicament is especially visible in the case of child care policy analysis. Consider our limited understanding of the task of child care policy analysis. How do we evaluate our child care services? And how do we analyze the demand for child care services? What childrearing values do we adopt as models? The research methodology we employ will play a very important role in the conclusions of our research.

Analysis of child care policies must be personally involving. There are some aspects of child care which can be best understood on a feeling level. Take, for example, quality of care. What is quality? Can it be analyzed? Can our personal feelings help us understand what quality care really is? I believe that they can. Imagine studying child day care settings in which children are being neglected or abused. Objective research requires nonintervention. However, it is difficult for the customary detachment of research to continue when the sensitivities of researchers are offended, especially when the offense involves children. The temptation researchers feel is to avoid seeing the pain of the parents and the children who are not receiving quality care. Yet on some level, the researcher cannot be blind to this information. Honest and well-informed research will admit and even make use of subjectivity in these instances. Our feelings about what we study can teach us a lot about how people feel about poor care.

Research must be done with this level of personal involvement. Consider the topic of child abuse. Reports of child abuse in day care centers continue to appear in the media. Children have been locked in closets, hit and beaten, force-fed, shocked with cattle prods, and sometimes even raped and photographed nude while in the "care" of adults. In child care, children are regularly subjected to a range of environmental, physical, and emotional health hazards. We cannot estimate how many cases of abuse go unreported by children and by parents and go untried in the courts and unpunished by law. We also cannot tell how much the media magnifies such issues.

The Lori Nathan case in California is an example of abuse in day care. Lori Nathan was a day care center operator who seemed to have good references and had cared for some 400 children. In 1983, she was sentenced to a forty-four-year-to-life imprisonment for murder in the first degree, eight counts of felonious child abuse entailing bodily injury, and twelve counts of child-abuse-with-bodily-injury misdemeanors [16]. Her crimes had gone undetected for years. This and similar cases suggest that there are other undetected instances of child abuse and neglect in day care. Decide for yourself what the possibilities are. In California, state investigators manage to pay unannounced visits to only one third of all licensed day care centers each year. There are only 102 investigators to monitor the activities of the over 40,000 day care centers in California. This means that in California alone, at least half a million children are receiving care which is unmonitored [17]. These numbers speak strongly to our sense of morality. But the true stories about what specific children experience wrench the heart.

It is important to note here, however, that this discussion does not intend to incriminate child care workers as an occupational class. We must keep in mind that less than 2% of all child abuse cases reported involve day care workers or babysitters [18]. Instead, the majority of the cases involve family members. The quality of parental care is perhaps even more deserving of scrutiny than the quality of child care outside the family. Most child care workers are loving, caring, and hardly capable of cruelty or violence. If anything, they go unapplauded and underpaid for their good work. When there *is* a problem, it is usually neglect or inattention to children's behaviors, needs, hygiene, and safety. This can be the result of lack of training or knowledge, overworking or overburdening of child care workers, or lack of funds to make child care environments safe. Keep in mind that this can also be true for parents who care for their own children in their own homes.

ANALYZING AND MEASURING QUALITY

My research has shown me that there are, indeed, difficulties in analyzing and measuring the quality of child care. We do not know how to calibrate the quality of care. Do we simply count the number of children per caregiver, the number of years of education each caregiver has had, the square footage per child indoors and outdoors, or the number of hugs and kisses received by each child? No. Good care is difficult to quantify. It must be measured in other ways. My research included extensive interviews and a survey of parents, observations and photographs of children, and many visits to child care and preschool sites. Based upon these experiences I formed a strong commitment to better understanding and improving the child care world. My work stems from this commitment, and my methods seek to join personal involvement with analytic procedure. I believe that this is the only way to study child care and to learn about the feelings of parents and children that are so critical to the study. The first step in creating viable child care policy is methodological. We must recognize the wide range of influences inherent in child care issues, and we must seek to learn what good care means to us as well as what it costs us as a society. And our research methods must include subjective observation.

PUBLIC RESPECT FOR PARENTING

This respect for the role of sensitivity in research brings us to another critical perspective in child care policy development. Policy analysis must demonstrate its respect for the fact that the bonds of parenting are profound, involving the instinctual drives to (1) care well for one's offspring and then to (2) ensure the success of one's parental investment. How can public policy, barely prepared to grapple successfully with less personal issues such as air traffic patterns and the economy, begin to cater to the fierce calls of parental instinct? Policy is in over its head. This situation can afford us critical insight into policy research and into the whole policymaking process. In its inability to grapple with the child care issue, the ultimate weakness of our policy-making methodology is revealed: the inability to see child care as one very human issue interlinked with many other human and pressing social issues, including welfare, mechanization, and feminism.

The women's movement has resulted in the opening of many doors otherwise closed to women. Opportunity appears to have moved in the direction of equality. Young women now enjoy their choice of role models. Not many years ago, mothers were generally viewed as being directly responsible for children while fathers were economically responsible. These role definitions have undergone and continue to undergo modification. Recently I encountered a six-year-old girl whose mother is employed as a full-time physicist and whose father is employed part-time as a mathematician—part-time, so that he can care for his daughter after school. I asked the girl what she wanted to be when she grew up. She replied, "A physicist." "Why not a mathematician?" I wondered aloud. She answered quite seriously, "Because math is for boys!"

A girl can almost be anything she wants to be when she grows up. But no matter how liberated she becomes, a woman cannot yet entirely escape traditional role modeling. And she cannot entirely escape the biological claim of motherhood. Many women feel deeply torn when they must leave their babies and young children in the care of someone else during the working day. This is not an easy separation. This painful experience is something to which one may eventually become accustomed. After several separations, the pain may be somewhat diminished, but many women report that it never dies away.

COST, CONVENIENCE, AND CHOICE

In conscious or subconscious hopes of feeling better in the situation, working parents seek suitable child care. Frequently, child care options are limited by cost, convenience, and choice. Cost: Quality child care must be affordable for parents to use it. Convenience: Child care sites must be easy to drive to and they must be open at least during working and commuting hours. Choice: The characteristics of the caregiver(s) and the care setting(s) must be of the quality each parent would want for his or her child, and a child care consumer must have several care options to choose from in order to be free to choose quality care.

Unfortunately, parents are rarely ensured convenience or affordability or guaranteed a choice from among several quality care options. Instead, child care is often inconvenient, expensive, or not what a parent would select if he or she actually had a choice and could afford that choice. Income is always a limiting factor. As a mother in cartoonist Cathy Guisewite's comic strip is told in a personnel department, "No one's saying only rich people can have children. Only rich people can have jobs" [19]. An average single mother with one child under two years of age spends 49% of her income on child care. Child care costs are a sizable chunk out of the family income even for lower-middle-income, two-parent families, who typically spend 26% of a $24,000 annual income on child care [20].

The absence of national support for well-functioning, high-quality child care whispers some of our saddest societal secrets: that we as a nation place a low priority on our children and have little reverence for parenthood, especially motherhood. Perhaps we keep such a secret because it is not a pleasant admission for us to make.

Reverence for motherhood? What is that? Have we traveled so far away from an appreciation for our humanity and a respect for the generation of new offspring that we have omitted reverence for motherhood from our consciousnesses? Or have we not yet developed the capacity to truly *revere* motherhood?

It is obvious that in the United States we do not maintain a policy that subsidizes motherhood (supports mothers who choose to stay home with their children). At the same time, we do not subsidize high quality child care for all children whose mothers participate in the labor force. Social policy has other priorities. Reverence for motherhood is low on the waiting list. And although we pay lip service to our reverence for children, evidence suggests a deficit in this area as well.

MERGING PUBLIC AND PRIVATE ISSUES

It is essential that we turn both our civic and our spiritual eyes to these issues. Public policy and private heart meet head on when it comes to child care. What are these two forces? Public policy is a measure of society's sensitivity. Private heart reflects the individual's sensitivity within that society. These forces must be aligned to better direct us in resolving social problems.

Today we have the capacity to affect more individuals with the presence and absence of social programs and policies than ever before. Large numbers of elderly individuals are ill and dying in poorly managed and unloving nursing homes. Large numbers of consumers are at risk when they purchase foods with new and inadequately tested additives. And all of us are legally required to accept impersonal labels such as Social Security numbers and license and other identification numbers.

MOTHERHOOD AS A LAST STRONGHOLD

In an era in which dehumanization, mechanization, and depersonalization are sweeping our psyches, almost unbeknownst to us, the profoundly instinctive connection that a mother can still feel for her baby is one of the last reminders of the powerful essence of our humanity. Many other expressions of our humanity are fading away. As a society, we make no substantive expression of gut level caring about the homeless, the hungry, the dying, or even our elderly dependents. The one exception is in caring for our children. But even this expression of care is watered down or translated into diaper commercials by the media, while budget cutbacks have resulted in the lowering of child care quality standards in at least thirty-three states [21] and no effort has been made to develop policies that clearly subsidize parenthood. To be unconscious of, and then to look away from, this connection, this heartstring, on a societal level is to place the preservation of the humane aspects of our existence low on our list of social priorities, thus sacrificing one of our last bastions of humanity.

Women as well as men share responsibility for this sad trend. Fortunately, the feminist movement is now turning around, under the guise of "neofeminism," and taking back the appreciation for motherhood that it had almost sacrificed in its haste to move into what once appeared to be a man's labor force and a male-dominated economic system. And fortunately, many men are joining women as they take a second look at the larger picture. Nancy Chodorow observes that,

> Women come to mother because they have been mothered by women. . . . Women's mothering has created daughters as maternal, and this has ensured that parenting gets done. . . . Many men are coming to regret their lack of extended connection with children. They feel that they are missing what remains one of the few deep personal experiences our society leaves us. [22]

Perhaps the development of a new reverence for childbearing and parenthood may preserve the remaining light in a darkly clouding sky—a human, personal light that may enable us to see how clouded, inhumane, mechanical, and impersonal—how utterly functional—the world is becoming.

One thing that modern parents are learning is that it is costly in dollars and cents and in personal energy to care well. While the pocket-books of parents cringe, many parents report that their hearts do the same for emotional reasons. Again, the guilt reported by many parents who leave their children in child care facilities does not necessarily disappear over time.

INTELLECTUAL AND EMOTIONAL CROSSFIRE

Parents are caught in a confusing intellectual and emotional crossfire between day care advocates and day care opponents. Should parents relinquish their role of providing direct and intensive care in their homes in favor of an institutional experience which may be coun-terdevelopmental, or at least less than optimal, for a young child? Should parents keep their children at home, causing the children to miss out on the possibility of heightened developmental stimulation in child day care which may enable them to succeed decades later in their adulthood? What is better for children: subsidized day care or sub-sidized parenthood? On these questions, the jury is still out, and it may remain so for at least another generation.

My research interviews revealed that parents' concerns about the quality of care that their children received often went unstated, later surfacing as guilt, split attention on the job, and high stress levels. All of this suggests that the bonds of parenting, the instinctual drive to care for offspring and to ensure the success of the parental investment, are indeed profound.

DISTINCTIONS BETWEEN PARENTING AND CHILD CARE

The range of awareness that must go into the formulation of day care policy extends far beyond the economic issue of cost and the instinctual issue of parental care. One of the ironies that emerges during a close examination of child day care issues is that the process of caring for one's own child in one's own home is called "parenting," but when someone or ones *outside* the family and outside the family's own home care for that family's child, common parlance dubs this process "child care" or "day care" or "child day care." ("Babysitting" is usually an intermediate and less formal operation, somewhere between parenting and child day care.)

Parents "parent" all the time, at great reward and at great cost to themselves in terms of time, energy, earnings, and career opportunities. The usually unspoken belief is that the parents should not be paid for their child caring hours and that nonparental, unrelated child care workers should be paid very little for their professional parenting hours, but that they should be paid.

Familial caring is a very personal process. Modern pressures to translate it into a more explicitly functional social process may steal some of its humanity. This is not to argue that all familial care is quality care and that all nonfamilial care is not quality care. But family care offers a greater chance that a continuity of highly personal love, fueled by the drives of parental investment and bonding, will be provided to a child. As social child care grows, these chances are diminished. And while legislators, acting in response to reports of unsatisfactory, neglectful, and even abusive child care programs, enact a scattering of laws attempting to ensure quality child care, the truth is that love cannot be legislated. The definition of quality care is highly personal, subjective, and painfully difficult to standardize.

Attempt to write a few sentences on paper clearly describing the characteristics of feeling that one human being must demonstrate in order to be taking good care of another. This exercise quickly reveals the complexity of trying to standardize quality. Legislation may be able to control the functional elements of care but has no ethical place in the realm of feelings and no method of controlling feelings even if it could ethically justify doing so. Moreover, once legislation settles on acceptable parameters of even administrative and functional quality, there are problems in checking programs to see if they meet regulated standards. As suggested earlier, the sheer cost of hiring enough personnel to visit every child care program, large or small, even once a year, may become prohibitive as the number of programs expands to meet the ever-growing demand. It may prove very difficult for the public sector to provide child care to all citizens who need it, to adequately monitor its quality, and to staff the programs across the nation with large numbers of well-trained people who love children, all with public support and at public expense.

PARENTAL LOVE VS. PUBLIC POLICY

When I first began my research, I thought that a socialized system of extrafamilial day care service, for all citizens who had children, was the best answer. Now, I am less sold on the idea of a simple socialism being the solution to the child day care issue. There are a number of reasons for my change of mind, one of which is the birth of my own daughter, who has taught me so much about the chasm between parental love and public policy. I can personally feel this division now, rather than simply knowing about it. I now feel directly, as well as know, the effects of parental bonding and instinct and the joy and love and pressures of being a mother. This is genuine expertise. It is also instinct. Now I know firsthand that the parental investment in care is one which accrues immediate as well as long-term rewards. Modern views of family life are challenging the immediacy of parenthood and usurping the long-term parental investment that parents can make during early childhood. We must remember that the state can never replace the parent. Public policy is not parental instinct. Instead, the state can either serve or fail to serve the parent.

A child's total dependence and naivete evoke deep sympathy and affection. The energy, purity, and sheer youthful vibrance of a child are qualities that are hard to find in a world where very little seems uncontaminated by media role models, commercial values, and pollution. And simply the speed at which children change can hold parents riveted upon their child's monthly, daily, and even hourly development. Now I know firsthand what instinctual feelings are involved when balancing freedom and responsibility in making child care choices. I also know that social privileges such as education and a reasonable income help to balance the freedom and responsibility that our existing policy approach toward child care offers parents. Not all parents have these advantages.

CONFUSION IN DIVERSITY

It is very hard to choose the right program when there are countless differences among child care programs. Some of these are formal and others are informal or unplanned differences in program policy.

Take for example the variation in how child care programs handle children who are sick. Only one site in my study of six child care programs had a sick room with a crib, a bed, blankets, and toys. Another site maintained a policy stating that "Children who fall ill during the day are sent home with no exceptions." One of the sites preferred not to have sick children attend but was, as the director stated, "stuck with them." The director complained about this but felt that she could not enforce a no-sick-children rule. She stated that she was willing to take children with colds, but not with the flu; she said, however, that she "gets them all anyway."

Clearly, asking a parent, "Do you feel good about the place where and the person with whom you leave your child while you work?" is a loaded question. There is a hidden but stinging double bind compelling many parents to reply "yes" and even to bring themselves to believe that they mean "yes" when they actually mean "no." If parents do not feel good about the child care environment and the caregiver they selected for their child, they may feel they are doing poor jobs as parents. To alleviate feelings of guilt, parents may force themselves to believe that their child is in good hands. These feelings of guilt and denial gnaw at parents' hearts.

SEEKING THE PATH OF THE HEART

A philosophy of multilevel, holistic analysis shapes the structure of the following investigation. Several analytic perspectives are employed here. While it is only a beginning, this book lays the foundation for an examination of the child care picture with a wide-angle lens. Chapters 1 through 4 contain an analysis of the many levels involved in child care issues, organizing the relevant concepts and issues into three categories: the polity, the market, and the primary or direct care category. Chapters 5 through 7 present my empirical study of child care programs, along with parents' and my own ratings of these programs. A dialectic between data provided by numbers and data provided by pictures and parents' comments is at work in this research.

Chapter 1 reviews a set of philosophical issues which are germane to most forms of care, inquiring, "Who cares and for what reason?" Chapter 2 looks at care from the perspective of the polity, outlining the obstacles to a national response to families' needs for care. This is followed by a look at economically motivated marketplace responses to the need for care in Chapter 3. Next, Chapter 4 considers the basic ingredients of both familial and extrafamilial care, whether it is considered from the point of view of the polity, the market, the first-line child care provider, or the familial, usually parental, caregiver. An "investment" of money, time, energy, or emotion in care differs in each of these "investment realms"—the polity, the market, and the primary (first-line familial) spheres. These spheres often overlap; in fact, anytime direct child care is provided, in a shared-care or even an institutional setting, by the polity or by the marketplace, all dimensions of primary care are evident in expanded, amended, or abbreviated forms. Chapter 4 suggests that all caregiving activities reiterate the dimensions of primary care: social, psychological, educational, physical, and environmental. These dimensions are addressed each time care, the feeling, and care, the function, are delivered to a dependent.

Persuaded by the notion that families invest time and money in the care of their dependents, parents are herein viewed as both home economists and day care consumers. The consumer's evaluation of his or her investment in each of the dimensions of care (delineated in Chapter 4) is influenced by a myriad of informal, political, and market factors. Chapters 5, 6, and 7 present an empirical analysis which compares characteristics of day care programs to parents' (consumers') ratings of these programs. This analysis examines the extent to which auspice and cost, as well as consumer characteristics, affect consumer ratings, and then it asks whether consumers are actually knowledgeable enough to choose if and when they find themselves free to do so.

Three characteristics of the mixed economy of child care delineated by the empirical study are presented in Chapters 5, 6, and 7:

1. There are broad structural and substantive variations in services available to child care consumers.
2. Child care consumers as a group demonstrate a diminished capacity to exert a regulatory influence upon the quality of the child care services that are available to them.
3. Child care consumers, as individuals, are relatively unable to evaluate the quality of their child care services when their

objectivity is obscured by both the complexity of care and the moral implications of their choices.

What can be done? In the "Conclusion," I suggest a public day care rating scheme which would not only ensure a baseline of quality care for children but would enable consumers to intelligently use child care for their children. Public subsidy of any form could be made contingent upon programs' achieving scores that do not fall below a nationally defined baseline of quality. Day care programs could be required to display their ratings to provide consumers with a basis for making comparative judgments and with an objective indicator against which they might check their intuitive assessments of program quality.

Although it is a comparison of the characteristics of child care programs and parents' perceptions of them, I have designed this study and defined the dimensions of care so that they are applicable to any "care" service. With a few changes in detail, consumer evaluation of the quality of many forms of care can be measured and compared by program and consumer characteristics, according to the method defined in Chapters 5 through 7. It is because this research design is intended to be a prototype for similar policy studies of child day and other care services that the first four chapters of this book bring together philosophical, political, economic, and psychological issues relevant to most types of care.

In deciding upon a coherent national child day care policy, it is important to consider the short- and long-term effects of our response to parents' needs. The effects of the existing laissez-faire policy approach are numerous. On the negative side, many working parents will be without adequate care for their children:

- Quality of care is not ensured.
- Future inequality is fostered as the disparity in early childhood education magnifies differences in later educational achievement and adulthood earnings.
- Present-day inequality is fostered because only parents who have access to and can afford quality care or any form of care at all tend to be more successful will succeed in occupational competition in the workforce.
- Women, who continue to be the majority of caregivers, will continue to bear more direct responsibility for childrearing and

child caring and will continue to feel the stressful and often limiting effects of parenting upon their occupational and economic viability, as will their dependents.

- Women, who will continue to be compelled by economic necessity to enter and remain in the workforce, will continue to feel the stressful and often limiting effects of working upon their parenting, as will their children.
- Child care workers will continue to be predominantly women, and child care will continue to be underpaid, undertrained, and underrated as a profession.

On the positive side:

- The mixed economy of child care offers diverse responses to the diverse needs of American families.
- Massive institutionalization of children, depersonalization of their care on the broad societal level, is not occurring.
- Public costs for child care programs do not soar.
- The massive public sector problems of implementation and guaranteeing quality in social services and education are not expanded further in the child care field.

Again, the stance of public policy in the United States regarding families' needs for assistance with child care must be considered in terms of the larger picture. We will return to this notion in the "Conclusion." Every effort must be made to see the whole picture, the societal context in which the child care problem is occurring. Child care has left the almost exclusive domain of the family and now exists amidst the combined spheres of family, market, polity, and society (see Figure I.1).

It is clear that the child is no longer the sole responsibility of his or her parents. American families are blending with the highly organizational society around them. Family members are increasingly affected by the society in which the family lives. Young children once lived primarily within their families. Today, many children live at least half their lives, often five days a week, sometimes ten hours a day, in institutional settings. This change in the way our society handles its children has a deep meaning and profound effects. The meaning and the effects may not be immediately evident. It is our responsibility to interrogate this transition in child caring as it evolves, and to be watchful for the ramifications of personal and political child care decisions on many levels. My intention is to call attention to the need for watchfulness.

At present, in the United States, many forms of care are provided in a laissez-faire fashion. This means that, on a societal level, the provision of care is characterized by fragmentation and diversity. From the experimental side of this laissez-faire process may come the models uniquely suited to the standardization of quality care. The scattered and uneven availability of care services, including day care, in part reflects a societal preference for experimentation and variety. This societal preference places the freedoms as well as the burdens of choice upon day care consumers.

Public policy which desires to promote consumer choice should aim to teach consumers how to choose wisely [23]. It should also teach society as a whole to choose wisely. Again, we must all be watchful. We must compare carefully what it means to warehouse our children as opposed to what it means to provide them with feeling care—heartful and developmentally geared experiences that will preserve their humanity. Our children are the carriers of our souls. They are the future of the species of the human heart.

In our complicated world, a narrow and partisan approach to social issues is far too confining. In an age of rapidly advancing technology and highly organizational society, a narrow focus is encouraged in the name of precision and mechanical forthrightness. Yet the mind without the heart can never see the whole of the social problem. Together, it is possible for mind and heart to confront complexity, identify trends, generate critical policy perspectives, and then merge public and private issues, with a commitment to seeking the path of the heart.

We can preserve the human element by guaranteeing that the heart will accompany the mind in exploring social issues, rejecting the single-minded viewpoints of particular professions or political parties, and always seeking the larger picture. This must be a perpetual endeavor. We are all tangled in economic, political, and social change. We are all leaning out for love in a world of massive institutions and impersonal public policies. We are all children in the seaweed.

Chapter 1

WHO PROVIDES CARE AND WHY?

> *What'll we do with the baby-o?*
> *Wrap him up in calico,*
> *Send him to his mammy-o.*
>
> *What'll we do with the baby-o?*
> *Wrap him up in a table-cloth,*
> *Throw him up in the fodder loft.*
>
> —American Folksong

Infant and toddler care can try the patience of even the most dedicated and loving parents. I remember visiting friends when their first child was sixteen months old. They seemed at first glance to have it easy. They both worked, but they had different schedules. Their daughter had what seemed to be the benefit of one parent present and totally focused on her at almost every hour of the day.

I stayed with them for several days. After a while, I saw the exhaustion in both parents' faces and realized that their child was crying fitfully much of the time. She was teething, continually screaming for mommy, and turning down most of the food that her father tried to feed her. Finally, the father turned to me and said, "My business is falling apart, my career is suffering, I never see my wife, we never talk, my baby daughter doesn't want me around and she is never quiet. I'm on the edge. I *know* why people hit their children. I'm not going to, but I sure feel like doing it."

Several years and two children later, this family has survived early childhood, dual careers, grandparent illnesses, and many other stressful demands experienced by the "sandwich generation." I asked them how they made it, why they stayed together through all the pain and anguish. They replied, "Because we care so very much."

Caring, when it comes from the heart, can make all kinds of impossible things possible. Yet sometimes all of the heartfelt caring in the world is not enough to give children or any other dependents all that they need. Time, money, and knowledge are also involved in providing quality care. Unfortunately these assets cannot be guaranteed by a caring heart. There is a larger social context that determines much of the basic groundwork on which child care, and all forms of human care, is built. We would do well to ask ourselves who it is that provides care and what their motivations are.

To begin our analysis it is important to stand back from the specific problems of child care for the time being and to look at the larger picture. The first questions we must ask are: Who provides care? And why do they provide care? An understanding of the social, economic, and moral contexts in which *any* form of care is given and received will set the stage for the discussion of child care that I develop in the chapters which follow.

This chapter provides an overview of selected characteristics of care, placing basic child care issues in the general context of human care. Some of the questions germane to the examination of the many forms of care are: Is care a function or a feeling? What are the catalysts of care? What are the implications of allocating care informally, politically, and according to market principles? What are the characteristics of dependence? What are the settings for care delivery? And, finally, what are the parameters of care? The last two sections of this chapter diagram the parameters of care. Readers who choose to avoid the theoretical discussion at the end of this chapter would do well to briefly consider the material in Figures 1.1 and 1.2 and Tables 1.1 and 1.2, before moving into Chapters 2 through 7, which deal specifically with child care.

THE TWO FACES OF CARE: FUNCTION AND FEELING

In an age of high technology and professionalism, there are facets of human experience that still remain intuitive and personal. In most of its forms, care depends upon these intuitive and personal facets of experience. Yet even care is being engulfed by a sort of scientific and administrative imperative. A growing army of professionals dispenses various forms of care, such as therapeutic counseling, legal representation, and medical treatment, in exchange for fees. Organizational settings, designed to deliver care to increasing numbers of people, proliferate. In every dimension of care, special services are being developed.

These services are designed not only to meet needs, but to *suggest* a need, to create a demand for the services themselves. This supplier-induced demand is especially apparent in the field of health care, where professionals, such as physicians, define people's needs and prescribe the medical treatments which address them [1]. Thus professional judgments and interests influence the price of, distribution of, and demand for health care more than do consumer decisions or governmental allocations [2].

But supplier-induced demand and the powers of professional and institutional suggestion are not unique to medical care. While many services, including those which provide some form of care, have originated in response to consumer needs, once they exist they tend to perpetuate a dependence upon them [3]. The unprecedented growth of the service industry is indicative of its ability to perpetuate demand. The service industry employs an increasing percentage of the labor force [4]. The United States spends at least 30% of its GNP on public and private services, reducing the dollars available for investment in what have been called the more "productive industries" [5]. Of course, not all of this expenditure is on services which provide care. Service industries include services such as auto and computer repair, mailing services, amusement, and recreation. Still, human care services are among the most important services produced and consumed. These services draw a significant portion of the GNP. In 1977 about 19.7% of the GNP was spent on government-sponsored social services, including education. Although, by some calculations, this decreased to about 10% at the federal level in 1986, state and local spending in this category increased markedly [6]. Beyond this high level of public spending, over half of all health care expenditures and about one-fourth of all welfare and education expenditures are made by consumers rather than government agencies [7].

Consumers who purchase and taxpayers who support social services maintain unstated expectations that a care service will provide more than a function—that it will convey a feeling of human commitment and concern. Users of care services are looking for the warmth and commitment associated with family care in a world where human care is becoming an increasingly institutional, professional, and administrative function.

It can be argued that there is a clear distinction between a care service and personal care, between the function and the feeling of care, and that these should not be confused. However, many critics of care services, especially of medical care, suggest that a service delivered without feeling is an inferior service. Even the "most sophisticated schemes of planners and 'experts' may founder if the intimate personal needs of distressed individuals are neglected" [8].

When in distress, a patient is not impressed by technological devices or professional behavior. He or she "requires intimate, time consuming personal care and human involvement" [9]. In many cases, the intrusion of time-saving technology and expertise-oriented professionalism into the physician-patient relationship, or into any caregiver–care-receiver relationship, strips away the personal quality of this interaction. The *intimacy* of caring has been transformed into the *practice* of care, of medical care, of dental care, and of child care.

However, even the most highly specialized care professional cannot completely ignore the human concern associated with care. In prescribing treatment, he or she "scarcely ever makes a decision that is justifiable on strictly scientific grounds" [10]. The practice of good medical care is both a science and an art [11]. In treating patients, the physician's personal feelings may interfere with his or her technical practice. The difficulty of becoming overinvolved with patient's pains and problems has therefore led to the sanction of "detached concern" [12]. Yet even when the explicit purpose of professional care is that of a function, the feeling associated with care may still emerge in the relationship. This dual character of good care lends it an elusive quality which confounds both professionals' and laypersons' efforts to measure and judge its essence. The day care consumer study presented in Chapter 7 offers an example of this problem. This study reveals that parents have difficulty accurately evaluating the quality of their child care services.

CATALYSTS OF CARE: INSTINCT, SOCIAL OBLIGATION, AND ECONOMIC GAIN

The transition from total dependence in infancy to relative independence in adulthood is the product of a wide range of social and biological forces. Whoever provides care to dependents must orchestrate these forces. This caregiver shelters, protects, nourishes, and encourages development; the caregiver gives care.

Caregivers are not all the same—their motivations vary. For some, the provision of care is driven by feeling, instinct, and culturally inherited roles. Others are compelled by societal norms and a sense of duty or justice, perceiving care to be a birthright. And some care providers sell care, because it is a marketable commodity that is in demand. Thus the provision of care is variously inspired by instinct, a sense of social obligation, and hopes of commercial gain.

INSTINCT

Caregivers provided by nature are special. They are usually parents and their "parenting" is inspired by a combination of feeling, instinct and culturally inherited behavior. What distinguishes most parental caregiving from professional caregiving is the amount of feeling involved, or its "affective intensity."

To better understand this "affective" mode of behavior, recall the difference between feeling and function. The affective mode of behavior can be similarly distinguished from the instrumental mode of behavior [13]. The affective mode deals with the expression of feeling, and the instrumental mode deals with the expression of function. This general division of forms of behavior suggests a separation between love and work. Work, in the instrumental mode, is a disciplined, goal-oriented type of task. Love, in the affective mode, is an expression of attachment and involvement. Love's goals, such as the desire for gratification, may be vague and unspecified [14], and love's outcomes will be difficult to measure. These are the affective elements of caring which make it difficult to define care simply in functional terms. Care is more than providing food and shelter; it is an affective behavior. Especially in the case of parental caregiving, it involves some sort of personal touch, compassion, and emotional involvement. A parent develops affective bonds through a continuous interaction with his or her children. There is no formula for generating between a caregiver and a care receiver the affective bond that occurs between a parent and a child. Child care workers can do their work well, but they may not feel the same affect that parents can feel for their own children. No pay check can guarantee that biological instinct. In this sense, instinct is the most abstract and intractable motivation for care.

SOCIAL OBLIGATION

As an instinct, care is an interpersonal activity, the biopsychological product of love and commitment between individuals. By great contrast, care as a social obligation is a public responsibility, expressed through governmental mechanisms such as constitutional guarantees, court rulings, legislation, public policies, and publicly funded social programs. The explication of public responsibility to an individual in a dependency relationship is especially difficult when the dependent is a child. Throughout history, childrearing practices have been influenced by changing perceptions of what a child's social, economic, and political position is within society. It has been argued that the United States has exhibited "a cultural recalcitrance toward assuming public responsibility for children's needs" [15], and that children have been deprived of the rights naturally accorded adults in this society. According to this view, our children exist in a political limbo without either full responsibility or full privilege of citizenship.

The political limbo of childhood is mitigated by the role of the family as a mediating institution [16]. The family stands between the child and the political world, representing the child and protecting him or her from the world. The family has remained an independent entity, serving as a buffer between the state, the market, and the individual.

The family secures for its children and its elderly dependents most of what they need from the polity and the market. Parents vote and buy, one assumes, on behalf of their children. When the family fails to care for its dependents, the state intervenes, in what may be called the best interests of the child, aiming to secure all of the dependent's birthrights for him or her.

Of course, as John Holt has noted in his discourse on children's rights, "There is no use telling the state to guarantee what it does not have and cannot provide . . . the state cannot guarantee every child a good home and a good family. It does not have these things and it cannot make or get them" [17]. At best, the state can make an effort to provide children the social and physical supports necessary for development and to protect them from harm.

During the past 100 years public and private organizations have demonstrated growing concern for children. The first federal program to actually include both the words "child" and "development" in its name did not appear until 1963. This was the National Institute of Child Health and Human Development, an arm of the National Institute of Health. Its focus was research and training in the field of maternal and child health. The next year, in 1964, the Economic Opportunity Act initiated the Head Start (or Comprehensive Child Development) Program. This was later placed under the Office of Child Development (OCD), created in 1969 [18]. The OCD promoted the child development concept over child protection and nondevelopmental approaches to child care, throwing into bold relief the problem of defining the limit of public responsibility. The resulting debate included these questions: If every child does indeed have a right to child care, does he or she have a right to any more than custodial care or maintenance? Is developmentally oriented care, such as early childhood education for all preschool-age children, a luxury that the public cannot afford? Where does the responsibility of the public sector end?

ECONOMIC GAIN

In addition to private family and public sector provisions, care is supplied through the market economy. When treated as a commodity, care is bought and sold in the marketplace. Imagine buying packages for ten dollars apiece, each of which say "love and affection, just add water."

The costs of care are mediated by consumer demand and competition among caregivers. To the degree that consumers maintain their "sovereignty," they can control market activities. Producers are motivated to produce more or less in response to consumer pressure on prices [19]. When consumer demand for a new product develops, producers move to meet this demand. For example, the 14% increase in the number of working mothers during the 1970s created a demand for child day care services [20]. The inadequate development of this service industry was in effect a "market hole," an area of unrealized potential in the market. Child care did not remain a market hole for long because of the opportunity for economic gain that it provided.

In more recent years the burgeoning demand for day care has met with an energetic market response. By 1977, of the 18,310 day care centers in the United States, 7,500, or 41%, were private, for-profit centers [21]. Some 80% of these for-profit centers were independently owned and operated. However, day care chains, rather than independently owned centers, are the fastest growing sector of the child care market. Consider Kinder-Care. In 1986, seven years after the Kinder-Care Learning Center business opened its doors in Montgomery, Alabama, it had expanded to 1,100 centers in forty states in the United States and in Canada, serving 100,000 children and employing 14,000 people, with a revenue approaching $200 million. Also in 1986, the founder of Kinder-Care, Perry Mendel, anticipated that he would operate some 2,000 centers by the mid-1990s [22]. The growth of proprietary child care has also been stimulated by the public sector. In fact, proprietary organizations have become "the single largest source of child day care financed with public funds" [23]. And by 1986, over half of the women in the labor force had children age six and under, and many of them wanted child care [24]. This presented a marked opportunity for economic gain. All of these developments have fueled the astoundingly rapid growth of the child care industry.

ALLOCATIONS OF CARE: MARKET, POLITICAL, AND INFORMAL

The economics that drive the provision of child care and other care services are complex. The dollar is not the sole motivation for the provision of care. The heart and the society interact with the dollar to tangle and to mix the economy of care. This mixed economy of care includes the market economy, the political economy, and the informal economy. In each of these systems the allocation of care responds to different considerations.

THE MARKET ECONOMY

The quality of care provided in the marketplace may fluctuate as consumer demands and provider competition press for improved techniques as well as for lower costs. When care is a commodity, those who are most dependent are, by virtue of their condition, rarely responsible for the actual purchase of care. Children, for example, do not pay their child care bills.

Primary caregivers, usually family members, become the purchasers of care. Market forces, if they are at all responsive to consumers, reflect the tastes of these primary caregivers. This means that the quality of proprietary care is determined more by those who pay for it than by those who receive it, i.e., children, severely disabled or ill persons, and the infirm elderly. Of course, in the case of day care, the dependents, the children who receive the purchased care, can affect family preferences if they return home ill, unruly, or unhappy. Parents will seek other child care services if their children drive them to do so, given that they can afford the time and money to do so.

THE POLITICAL ECONOMY

In the social market of the political economy, consumer's choices do not determine the distribution of goods. Instead resources are allocated by government decisions. The political distribution of care functions according to the logic of "externality" [25]: If Person A does not require care but contributes to the cost of B's required care, B benefits directly but A also benefits "externally" or indirectly (because the world will be a better place for both A and B). Person A is most apt to agree with this logic if, for example, B has a highly contagious disease and cannot afford to pay for his or her own treatment. Of course, when

A is unwilling to contribute to the welfare of B or when B's needs are shared by a large number of people and A cannot manage the burden alone, the political economy model of resource allocation is applied. Taxes are called for from the As and then redistributed, often in the form of services, to the Bs.

THE INFORMAL ECONOMY

The informal allocation of care is not fueled by the exchange of dollars or by the distribution of social benefits by the public sector. In its purest form, informal economy has been defined as the exchange of goods and services which takes place without the intervening medium of currency. This includes trading and bartering and doing favors. The informal economy of care often involves kith and kin. Informal care arrangements offer the possibility of more individualized and responsive forms of small-scale care than do their formal counterparts on a larger scale. Families and friends are often able to provide care for the members of their circles without formal arrangements for payment or distribution. They are the all-important yet informal members of the informal economy.

THE DELIVERY OF CARE: FROM FAMILIAL TO INSTITUTIONAL SETTINGS

Whether provided through political, market, or informal arrangements, the cost and requirements of care are heavily influenced by the types of dependence characterizing the individuals to whom care is delivered. Children have different needs at different ages, and the infirm and elderly have other specific needs.

As in the case of housewives, society tends to disregard the hard work that is done within the domain of the informal economy, because it is unpaid labor, and usually labor of love. Despite increasing demands for care services, families continue to retain primary responsibility for their dependent members. In the United States about 80% of home health care services for the elderly are provided by their own family members, and 67% of all severely mentally handicapped children live with their families [26]. Among these families who continue to provide home-based care, many share this responsibility for care with some form of extrafamilial or nonfamily care.

Sometimes, however, the degree and duration of care required by a severely ill, disabled, or disturbed member is entirely beyond the family's capacity. In their landmark analysis of institutional populations in the early 1980s, Martin Wolins and Yochanan Wozner found that of infants and preschool children, some 37,000 were in short-stay hospitals, 7,000 in institutions for the retarded, and 6,000 in institutions for the dependent, neglected, and disturbed. Of school-age children, some 35,000 were in short-stay hospitals, 45,000 in institutions housing retarded children, and 31,000 in institutions for the dependent, neglected, and disturbed. (The numbers in many of these categories are greater for adolescent and adult populations.) School-age children and adolescents are also found in boarding schools, and adolescents and adults may also be institutionalized in prisons, jails, and drug addiction treatment centers [27].

Foster care is a transfer of full-time care from a child's original family to a foster family or to an institution. In March 1977, half a million children were in foster care. Compared with 175,000 in 1961, this is an increase of almost 200%. Of the half million in foster care in 1977, 395,000 were in foster family care, 73,000 were in institutions and residential treatment centers, and 34,000 were in group homes. Each of the foster family, institutional, and group home populations increased dramatically during the 1960s and 1970s and has continued to increase in the 1980s, although less dramatically [28].

The range of alternative settings for delivery of care to family members can be viewed according to the *degree of familial and extrafamilial care* in each setting. This is illustrated in the spectrum in Table 1.1.

If, for the moment, the two ends of this spectrum are defined in terms of small versus large organizational care settings, then the family and the institution are characteristically opposite settings for the provision of care. In keeping with this view, some families may be completely independent ("A" in Table 1.1). They provide all of the necessary psychological, social, educational, physical, and environmental elements of care to their members, and they do so without informal or formal assistance from outside. But this archetype of the entirely self-

TABLE 1.1
SPECTRUM OF SETTINGS FOR THE PROVISION OF CARE

A Family care	B Family care with informal assistance	C Family care with formal assistance	D Shared care between family and formal care setting	E Group care with some independent or family living	F Total institutional care

sufficient clan is a rare breed in modern industrial society. Most families depend upon outside assistance regularly. Relatives, friends, and neighbors are sources of informal outside help ("B" in Table 1.1). Once the head of the household participates in the labor force in order to support the family, children leave home to go to school, or someone falls ill and is taken to a doctor, family care has been supplemented with some formal assistance ("C" in Table 1.1).

When the supplementing organization assumes a significant share of the responsibility for highly dependent family members, the work of care is shared ("D" in Table 1.1). Child day and night care is within this definition of shared care, as are day care programs for dependent adults (retarded, ill, infirm, and elderly). These are shared care programs which provide assistance to individuals who can manage some degree of independent or family living. For instance, organizational assistance supplements independent living for adults who can work at regular jobs or in sheltered workshops during the day, but who need to return to a care setting at night ("E" in Table 1.1). This is one form of group care, usually provided within the community. In its extreme, group care becomes total institutional care ("F" in Table 1.1). Dependents live within the walls of relatively self-sufficient institutions. Theoretically, the most closed institution, self-sufficient in every way, resembles the archetype of the closed and self-sufficient family clan. Every dimension of care is addressed from within its boundaries [29].

From this perspective, the range of settings for the provision of care may be conceived of in a circular form, where the closed family and closed institution meet, and where shared care is the opposite of both closed familial and total institutional care (see Figure 1.1).

The categories in Table 1.1 encompass many specific forms of

Shared
care

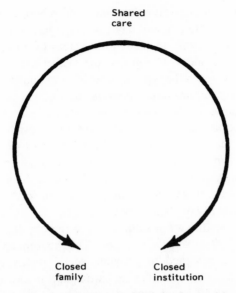

Closed   Closed
family   institution

FIGURE 1.1. Circular spectrum of settings for the provision of care.

care. Because isolated and completely closed families and institutions
are rare, there are few examples in this category. Most American
families supplement their caregiving with at least some type of informal
and formal assistance, including involvement in outside organizations
such as school, workplaces, churches, and public programs. Although
most modern families participate in outside organizations and receive
outside assistance, they remain relatively intact and their dependents
can be said to be in *familial care*. Extrafamilial care can be found in
several forms, the purest being total institutional care. When institutional care is defined as *total*, full-time, out-of-home custody, treatment, or training, it includes orphanages, residential treatment centers,
mental institutions, hospitals, nursing homes, boarding schools, military training programs, prisons, monasteries, and some modern-day
communes [30].

The current increase in the number of working mothers has drawn
the public's attention to the various divisions in *child* day care. Child
care programs are, naturally, age-specific. These programs divide the
early childhood and school years into a least four groups: infants under
eighteen months, toddlers between eighteen months and two and one-

half years, three- through five-year-olds, and school-age children who may be enrolled in after-school day care. Age-based divisions such as these correspond roughly to recognized stages of child development. From the care providers' standpoint, the age of the child also corresponds to differences in the type and cost of care required. For example, infants obviously require more supervision, a higher adult-child ratio, than do five-year-olds. And children in diapers require a different concentration of effort than children who have been toilet-trained.

Although the other chapters in this book focus on child day care issues, keep in mind that day care is not provided only to children. Adult day care is designed for adults who are incapable of full-time independent living. These programs take several forms. Geriatric day care can be medically or socially oriented. The "day hospital" is usually connected to a health care institution, with the objective of providing health care and physical rehabilitation. The "multipurpose" adult day care program is designed to generate social interaction among its clients, who are in better health than participants in day hospitals. Such a program is not affiliated with a hospital and rehabilitation is not emphasized [31]. Other developmental and rehabilitative day care programs serve disabled adults with the goal of aiding participants in their development of professional and general living skills. The current focus in child day care needs must not overshadow the greater need that all families experience: the need for assistance in caring for their dependents of all ages.

DEPENDENCE AND CHARACTERISTICS OF CARE

During a lifetime, we are all dependent, at some point, upon sources beyond ourselves for care and attention. The greater this need for care, the higher one's *degree of dependence*. Degrees of dependence may range from the need for partial assistance in the daily affairs of life to the need for total or comprehensive care.

Just as the degree of dependence may vary, so does its duration. During some stages of life such as childhood, one is necessarily more dependent than during other stages, but childhood has a predictably finite *duration*. Certain dependencies, such as those caused by illness, are of limited but uncertain duration. Other dependencies may be of lifelong duration, such as those of severely retarded persons. *Limited dependence* is usually attributable to developmental conditions: the need for care often reflects an individual's stage of psychological, social, cognitive, and physical development. As a child matures, a high degree of dependence is normally diminished.

When an individual's dependent position is of a limited degree *and* duration, the typical locus of response to his or her particular need for care can be broadly anticipated. For example, *the normal type of dependence found in childhood is self-limiting in duration and decreasing in degree.* Most families manage to provide care for their children, either alone, with the help of relatives or friends, or by paying someone to assist, such as a babysitter or a day care program. When care is provided from within the family or informally by relatives and friends, it falls within what can be described as the *primary response sphere.* When the care is purchased, it is found within the realm of the *market response sphere.*

Sometimes, when dependence is lifelong, very severe, and uncommon, families may need extra help in providing care. Relatives and friends may not be able to provide sufficient assistance. The market may not supply this special care because of the absence of demand (when this type of dependence is rare). More frequently, a dependence is normal, such as that of childhood, but a family's capacity to provide all of the care required is diminished, as in the case of a single mother who has to work. A family may not be able to afford to purchase substitute care in the market. In both of these instances, the need for care may be within the *public response sphere.* The general relationship between these response spheres and the characteristics of dependence is illustrated in Figure 1.2.

The characteristics of care previously discussed in this chapter are summarized in Table 1.2. These facets of care—its impetus, its function and feeling, its mode of allocation, the types of dependence it serves, and the settings in which it is provided—are differently combined and evaluated in each response sphere. The following chapters examine the major child care issues from the perspective of these alternate spheres, each sphere representing a particular level of social organization. It is from the perspective of this *multilevel analysis* that we will seek out the role of child care in our modern world.

With population and economic pressures bringing about the deper-

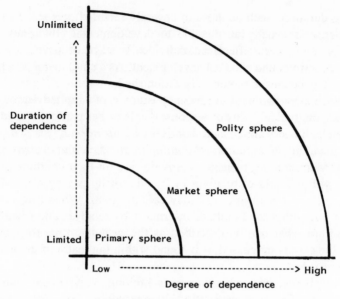

FIGURE 1.2. Response spheres.

TABLE 1.2
CHARACTERISTICS OF CARE

Quality of care		
Feeling		Function

Impetus (catalyst) of care		
Instinct and commitment	Economic gain	Social obligation

Allocation of care		
Familial and informal	Market	Political

Setting for care delivery		
Family care	Day care	Institutional care

sonalization and institutionalization of care services, we must always monitor ourselves for signs that we are turning away from our own humanity. In caring for our dependents, the functional side of care may win over the feeling side of care. Do we recognize when we have swayed too far in the direction of function and too far away from the heart? Are there forms of functionally expedient and functionally convenient care that are actually neglectful and even cruel? In my years of studying child care and other forms of care, I have often been reminded of Bruno Bettleheim's comments regarding the psychological abuse of human beings:

> Our actions have been changed for the better; however, our thinking and our unconscious motivation may have remained the same, and that is why we must now concern ourselves with the psychological abuse of human beings, which is still widespread. Though the method is less crude than physical abuse, the resulting damage to the psyche can be utterly devastating. This is why I believe we have to understand completely the unconscious causes of the cruelty, and to uncover the disguise behind which it tries to hide. [32]

Bettleheim was not referring to anything as innocuous as child care here. He is instead reflecting upon the problems occurring when human beings are in prison camps and in mental institutions. Yet he claims that human cruelty has unconscious causes and that it disguises itself. Our actions may have changed for the better, but what about our unconscious motivations? Who really cares and why? As we interrogate our motivations for and methods of child care, we must look closely at our actions and inactions, at the development of our policies and nonpolicies. Anything less than a close monitoring of what we do with our children is neglectful and potentially cruel.

Chapter 2

THE POLITY SPHERE

Obstacles to a National Child Care Program

> *Sleep, my child, sleep.*
> *When my little baby's grown,*
> *You'll soon see which is which.*
> *Like the rest of us you'll know*
> *The difference between poor and rich.*
> —"Sleep, My Child,"
> Yiddish Folksong

The United States entered the 1980s without a national child care program for all children and with a hodgepodge of solutions to the need for day care. Tax incentives were created to encourage employers to sponsor programs for their employees, and tax credits were awarded to working parents for their day care expenditures. Government subsidized programs for low-income families on a limited basis. Private nonprofit and profit-making day care centers proliferated. Family day care homes opened their doors all over the country. Some parents left their young children with family members; others left their children home alone. These developments occurred in the absence of any centrally planned response to the growing need for child care. However, they might also have occurred in the presence of a centralized child care policy.

Day care has become a political issue. One of the most critical issues in the evolution of the welfare state is the means of funding social services such as child care [1]. Should child care be publicly or privately funded or both? Also inherent in the debate over the development of a national child care policy is the question of the relationships between government and families and between families and the social expectations placed upon them. What are a family's obligations toward its preschool-age children? Should a family be entirely responsible for child care? In a society such as ours, can a family fulfill its obligations for the direct care of its young children and, at the same time, respond to economic pressures for employment? Or does the direct care of young children take a back seat to the indirect, economic, and practical care which parents must also somehow provide? Does feeling lose out to the demands of function?

What it boils down to is that many parents feel that they cannot afford to stay home with their children. In each working day, therefore, several hours of direct attention to children are surrendered by working parents. This is more than a private, personal predicament. If these hours are multiplied by the number of children under five in dually employed, two-parent families (at least 8 million children) and employed single-parent families (over 3 million children), we can estimate that some 20 trillion hours a year of direct, in-home parental care for preschool children are lost to the apparent economic necessity of parental employment [2].

As a society, we have somehow agreed that this loss of direct parenting time is acceptable and that it is more important to have these would-be parenting hours spent on labor force participation. We have made a general societal agreement that the family, not the public sector (the polity), should handle the problem of caring for its young children. But this agreement is hardly firm. There is a growing political dissensus regarding the duties of working parents and the role of the family in the provision of care: Some politicians claim that the polity should assist parents more; others suggest that it should share the burden equally with parents; and a few argue that the polity should assume total responsibility for all children. Ultimately, the day care issue is part of a broader controversy over the development of any form of family policy, directed at any facet of a family's need for assistance. For this reason, I begin my discussion of the political perspective on child care with a look at family policy in general.

Many observers are busy reading the American family for signs of social change [3]. The increasing instability of families is evident in the extraordinary rise in the incidence of divorce, which began in the late 1960s and leveled off in the late 1980s [4]. The growing number of low-income households headed by single females suggests that, based on the rate of increase from 1967 to 1978, the poverty population will be "composed solely of women and their children before the year 2000" [5].

During the 1970s, the interest in the development of a national family policy in order to assist and "protect the family" was led by the liberal wing of the Democratic party. This interest clashed with the demand by conservative Republicans for "profamily" legislation to protect families from "government intrusion." For advocates on either side of the debate, something was troubling families: they were finding it difficult to provide direct and indirect care to their members. And, from the standpoint of families, there was an apparent absence of any form of family policy: government was just not helping families very much.

Traditionally, American families in the United States have not expected a great deal of help from their government, but they do sense the difference between governmental support and the absence of it. This absence is a passive stand by the polity against government involvement in family life and may be thought of as an "active" statement of what I call family "nonpolicy."

FAMILY POLICY AS A SOCIAL RESPONSE TO THE NEED FOR CARE

There are at least 60 million families in the United States today [6]. Many get along well enough without the direct governmental aid of an explicit and comprehensive family policy. But they do not manage without difficulties. Increasing divorce rates, economic pressures, the growing participation of mothers in the labor force, and the prevalence of social problems such as domestic violence, teenage pregnancy, and drug and alcohol abuse challenge the well-being of families. These and other problems have engendered an interest in concern and a controversy over government intervention to strengthen family life through some type of public family policy.

Opponents of government involvement in family life argue that families do not need, and may even be harmed by, government designs in favor of an official family policy [7]. However, the fact remains that both the absence of "family" policies and the presence of policies in other sectors may intrude upon family life as much as any official family policy. While there are no explicit family policies, public policies that are designed for other purposes affect families. These may be thought of as unarticulated family policies. For example, the structure of personal income tax is such that married couples with two incomes pay more than an out-of-wedlock household [8]. This tax policy provides an economic disincentive for marriage and it works against families.

The absence of explicit profamily policies may be thought of as a policy *not* to help families. The absence of a comprehensive child care policy may be viewed similarly. In the 1970s and 1980s, the absence of federally sponsored child care in the face of widespread female participation in the labor force, for example, reflects the policy stance taken by President Nixon when he vetoed the Child Development Act of 1971. At that time, he stated, "Good public policy requires that we enhance rather than diminish both parental authority and parental involvement with children, particularly in their decisive early years when social attitudes and a conscience are formed and religious and moral principles are first inculcated" [9]. The view expressed by Nixon was that it is a good policy not to provide young children with care outside their homes, and to therefore encourage parental authority and involvement. This was a clear policy not to do anything. Nixon viewed his policy decision as a profamily decision.

In the years following Nixon's decision, government attention to family problems increased; however, this show of concern yielded few concrete results. The Republican administrations of Nixon and Ford were followed by the Democratic Carter administration. Carter spent $3 million on the White House Conference on Families from 1979 to 1981. One might claim that this $3-million White House Conference on Families was ineffective in that it failed to result in tangible changes and innovations in policy [10]. However, the conference provided a valuable forum for a national discussion of the issues. Its results have not been groundbreaking, but there has been an increased sensitivity to the impact of public and private policies upon families since the conference.

From the start, the White House Conference was limited in what it might accomplish because of several obstacles to public and private action in the arena of family life. These obstacles are expressed in the following questions:

1. *Who should be served by family policy?* There is little definitional clarity in the description of the family and its purpose.
2. *What problems should be addressed by family policy?* The myriad of problems confronting families cannot be separated from encompassing social problems such as drug abuse, crime, and economic woes. The problem of child care is inseparable from other social issues, yet existing child care policy is not explicitly related even to family policy. When child care policy exists but is not considered a family policy issue, children may be viewed as something other than the responsibility of their families. Should family policy speak to such political and philosophical child care issues?
3. *Who should benefit from family policy?* The motivation for family policy remains vague because policymakers are unclear about the extent to which family policy should serve the interests of the family, the state, or the market economy. And if families should benefit from family policy, should all families or only those with the most need for assistance benefit?

WHO SHOULD BE SERVED BY FAMILY POLICY? THE PROBLEM OF DEFINITIONAL CLARITY

It is difficult to gain an agreement on a comprehensive definition of family because there are countless variations in its form, all of which are influenced by economic and historical developments [11]. Tribal, feudal, communal, patriarchal, companionate, single-parent, and other modes of family life have emerged during the lengthy evolution of the family. For many years the nuclear family was considered to be the basic unit of society, and it was credited with performing the vital economic, reproductive, and socializing functions. In recent times, however, the idea of the universality of the nuclear family has been accused of being a "misguided application of Western family patterns to other cultures" [12].

Accompanying this rethinking of the family is a revision from family homogeneity to heterogeneity within the American society. Different types of families are going to care for children and conduct other family activities differently. Popular family typologies have been constructed around dichotomized aspects of families such as extended vs. nuclear, asymmetrical vs. symmetrical, and functional vs. dysfunctional families [13]. Distinctions based upon socioeconomic status, ethnic background, and stages in the family life cycle are also common [14].

Another approach to the definition of the family is to delineate its parameters. The family may be an elaborately networked web of internal and external relationships or a loosely knit group of relatively independent and unconnected individuals, who may be living together in what Margaret Mead describes as a "black box" of isolation [15]. This range of relationships delimits a parameter of family life which I call the *"dependence parameter."* It is bounded at one end by a high degree of *intradependence* and at the other end by a high degree of *extradependence,* with *interdependence* somewhere in between (see Table 2.1). A high degree of intradependence signifies that immediate family members are highly dependent upon each other. A high degree

TABLE 2.1
DEFINITIONAL PARAMETERS

	Dependence	
←——→		
Intradependence, isolated family	Interdependence	Extradependence, isolated individual
	Entitivity	
←——→		
High entitivity		Low entitivity
	Adherence to conventional form	
←——→		
Deviance	Conventional family	Deviance

of interdependence reflects a family's codependence upon other families, the neighborhood, and the community. Extreme extradependence occurs when an individual receives no support from the family unit, maintains little social codependence within the community, and depends solely upon formal extrafamilial organizations for care and support.

The present lack of clarity about the purpose of the family stems in part from mixed perceptions regarding the proper balance and degrees of these forms of dependence in American family life. With the advent of modern industrial society, traditional family ties have been supplanted; basic social functions have been increasingly taken over by extrafamilial bodies. These basic functions include (1) production, distribution, and consumption; (2) socialization; (3) social control; (4) social integration; and (5) mutual support [16].

The expertise and authority of the church, the various helping and healing professions, and the government loom much larger than those of the head of a household and his or her spouse. Marriage and parenting skills are not certified or licensed; parenthood is, in a sense, the last untrained profession. There are few guarantees of expertise, efficacy, or success in this domain. While the family may be expected to serve a particular purpose, its ability to do so is implicitly questioned by the world around it. Books and special courses (such as those provided by the Parent Effectiveness Training and Better Baby Institutes) train parents to care for their young children. Directions for mental and physical health care are provided by professionals; formal education is obtained from the schools; food is purchased at a store; income is earned in the workplace; morality is directed by the church; and laws are written by the government. Moreover, when the family or its members have problems which are perceived to affect society, outside organizations or the state may intervene.

The Marxists explain that, with the advent of the industrial revolution, the locus of economic production shifted from the home to the market and that, under industrial production, the workers were alienated from their labor [17]. Christopher Lasch suggests that this "socialization of production" has been followed by a "socialization of reproduction." If the primary task of the family is to care for its offspring, the delegation of parental authority, responsibility, and expertise to extrafamilial institutions constitutes the beginning of Lasch's second phase, the "assertion of social control over activities once left to individuals or their families" [18]. Consequently, the modern working parent may be experiencing an alienation not only from his or her labor in the work force, but also from the parental role. With the popularization of surrogate motherhood in the 1980s, even the once-essential role of the family in producing offspring is questioned [19].

In modern society many extrafamilial organizations assist the family in its effort to serve its members. However, some say that the family's domain of expertise and responsibility is obscured, if not undermined, by this trend [20]. The intradependence of its members is diminished or at least altered by the support and the intervention of outside organizations [21]. And, as professional facilitators seek to strengthen traditional networking and interdependencies, these relationships are transformed to extradependencies upon professionals and public programs. In this way, bit by bit, the family's basic functions are assumed by external institutions. The family's power and significance are eroded and degraded.

The dependence parameter of family life, bounded by extreme intradependence and extreme extradependence, thus interacts with the clarity of a family's self-definition and the degree of its wholeness or unity. In systems terminology, this wholeness or self-integration might also be described as the degree of "systemness" or "entitivity" [22] (see Table 2.1).

But there is one level upon which entitivity remains relatively unthreatened and unquestioned—the level of the individual. It is conceivable that the evolution of the family could ultimately result in an isolated, highly extradependent individual, surrounded by professional and technological supports, his or her own modern version of the single-person family unit. Perhaps the brave new world will even spawn this new being in a test tube. One can even find some acceptance of this trend in public policies. For example, the Department of Housing and Urban Development recognizes a *single-person family* as a category of recipients eligible for low-income housing, and the New York Metropolitan Museum offers "family memberships" to any two people who live apart as long as they agree to have membership forms sent to one address [23]. However, the biological urges for reproduction and parent-child bonds show little evidence of disappearing. The needs of young children, perhaps more than those of any other age group, help to perpetuate family life. Childrearing may emerge as the ultimate *raison d'être* of the family. Or childrearing may instead become increasingly socialized as parents delegate their responsibilities to professionals and policymakers. What we do about child care may well be a turning point in the evolution of the modern family.

So what is family for? Confusion over the definition of the family was prominent during President Carter's White House Conference on Families. Some participants argued that the conference should address only the needs of traditional families, while others contended that the only fair definition would include single-parent families, families who do not cohabit, and unrelated individuals who do cohabit. In addition, various advocacy groups claimed that the needs of minorities and disabled people as well as social problems such as unemployment and drug abuse should be addressed in the context of family policy. The accompanying controversy over the issue of homosexual parents provided evidence that although a variety of nontraditional lifestyles have emerged, there is no consensus as to their relation to the history and evolution of the modern mainstream American family. Based upon current social perceptions of the traditional family, a third definitional parameter can therefore be identified, indicating the degree to which a living arrangement resembles or deviates from the currently perceived "conventional" family form. (The three definitional parameters described here are illustrated in Table 2.1.)

Many policies affect families who live at all points along these parameters. The degree to which a policymaker can specify the consequences of a policy within selected parameters represents the amount of definitional clarity in the formulation of a policy. It is essential that public policies be evaluated in terms of their potential impact on families along these parameters.

Issues of dependence, entitivity, and adherence to traditional form are representative of only a few of our unanswered questions regarding the characteristics of the modern family. The definition of "family" remains unsettled, because perceptions of the family are embedded in broader political and social trends.

With respect to early child care, families who can retain relative control over this domain tend to be located at the center of the parameters of dependence, entitivity, and adherence to conventional form. Families outside the middle definitional range may be aided by certain types of policies that might have little bearing or even a negative impact on other families. For example, it has often been argued that Aid to Families with Dependent Children (AFDC) grants, which provide desperately needed support to single-parent families, also encourage a slackening of support or even desertion by unemployed fathers in two-parent families [24].

WHAT PROBLEMS ARE FAMILY PROBLEMS?
A DICTIONARY OF SOCIAL ILLS

It is often difficult to separate the myriad of problems confronting families from the encompassing body of social problems in the larger social system. Because the family is to some extent an "open system," it is affected by many factors in its environment; family difficulties can be described in terms of broader social problems. Although symptom-based diagnosis such as this rarely pinpoints causes, it can serve as a classificatory device in policy analysis.

Various classificatory schemes have been utilized in the discussion of family policy. Gilbert Steiner suggests three groups of "intractable problems" which a family policy orientation must somehow address: (1) problems which relate to moral issues, such as abortion and teenage pregnancy; (2) problems of care and support enforcement; and (3) neglect and abuse problems which incur the need for programs such as foster care and domestic violence programs [25]. These problem areas are marked by substantive differences in the types of troubles they contain as well as varying degrees of social urgency.

Steiner's first category, that of moral issues, consists of problems which are social problems because a large number of people perceive them to be so. A woman's (and her family's) right to determine what happens to her own body must contend with moral beliefs supported primarily by conservative social groups that a fetus has a "right to life." These beliefs touch upon the quintessential issue of our era—the threatened diminishment of our respect for life and for humanity. We hedge our bets, arguing about the exact number of weeks of age at which a fetus becomes a human being with a right to life. On some level, we remain uncertain. At the same time, it is clear that a woman has a right to decide the course of her own life, and part of that decision is a very personal decision about giving birth. Because abortion is not performed by the family in the home, it has become one of the many "services" for which outside expertise and thus social consent are required. Here the public and private domains continue to interact and conflict.

By contrast, problems of care and support, listed in Steiner's second problem set, have not drawn the same high level of ethical controversy. The care and support of children have traditionally been considered parental responsibilities. Only recently, when a growing number of mothers in conventional families have gone to work, or have found themselves divorced, have these needs been attracting public attention. Families' needs for care and support are increasingly viewed as moral dilemmas for society. Powerful controversies have emerged regarding societal responses to families' needs for assistance with child care. The title of a 1988 article by Karl Zinsmeister of the American Enterprise Institute captures the feeling of these controversies: "Brave New World: How Day Care Harms Children." Zinsmeister quotes a prominent mother:

> While I—and most of my friends—were saying our minds were "too good" to stay at home and raise our children, none of us ever asked the question, "Then what sorts of minds *should* be raising our children—minds that were not very good?" [26]

Sylvia Ann Hewlett of the Economic Policy Council captured another angle on these controversies in her 1983 article "Child Carelessness." She explains that in our society, having a child "is a strictly private matter," that "America neglects its women and children," and that the "cult of motherhood continues to haunt policymakers and millions of American women." As a result, nothing satisfactory is done to resolve continuing child care program inadequacies [27].

Steiner's third problem set, that of neglect and abuse, tends to require ameliorative or corrective social intervention. Some of the most glaring abuses of human rights, such as child abuse, occur in this domain. Although there is great alarm over child abuse in families and in child care, the problem has not commanded as great a sense of social urgency as advocates of ameliorative intervention would like.

There are other ways to categorize families' problems. Rather than dividing policy issues along abstract conceptual lines, the Carter White House Conference on Families grouped family problems and issues based upon their apparent substantive relationships. The conference held 500 state hearings and forums, heard the testimonies of 2,000 members of American families (generating thousands of pages of otherwise unheeded transcripts), commissioned a Gallup Poll, and organized a national forum and three national conventions. All of this activity boiled down to the identification of twenty issues for family policy, which were incorporated into four general topic areas. Keep in mind that these categories were conceptualized in the early 1980s [28]:

Families and Economic Well-Being

1. Economic pressures
2. Families and the workplace
3. Tax policies
4. Income security
5. Status of homemakers

Families: Challenges and Responsibilities

6. Preparation for marriage and family life
7. Specific supports for families
8. Parents and children
9. Family violence
10. Substance abuse
11. Aging and families

Families and Human Needs

12. Education
13. Health
14. Housing
15. Child care
16. Handicapped conditions

Families and Major Institutions

17. Government
18. Media
19. Community institutions
20. Law

Each of the twenty issue areas represented a set of problems being experienced by families. Indeed, the majority of contemporary social problems are represented on this list. Child care is Number 15 on the list, in the category of families and human needs. It could as easily fit into the economic well-being category, as the need for child care is intimately related to growing female labor force participation. It could also have been placed among challenges and responsibilities, as the child care issue speaks directly to the question of parental responsibility and represents a major challenge to our society. The Conference on Families' issue list was, in essence, a compendium of social problems. However, as the questionable categorization of child care issues suggests, it was not necessarily a strong conceptual aid to the analysis of family policy.

A third approach to the analysis of family problems may be derived from Urie Bronfenbrenner's "structure of the ecological environment" in which human development occurs. This structure can be described as a set of five concentric circles. From the inner circle outward these are: Circle 1—At the heart of this structure is the "immediate situation directly affecting the developing person," which includes the objects and people he or she relates to firsthand. Circle 2—On the second level is the "microsystem," which is a set of interconnections between persons related to the immediate setting who have "an indirect influence upon the developing person." Circle 3—The "mesosystem" further elaborates this interconnectedness in its set of linkages, not within the primary setting, but among the settings in which the developing individual participates, such as the workplace. Circle 4—Beyond the mesosystem is the "exosystem," composed of settings which the developing individual may never enter but which nonetheless affect his or her development. Circle 5—The "overarching" system is, naturally, the "macrosystem," in which the ideology and organization of social institutions produce "generalized patterns" which affect all individuals within a culture or subculture [29].

A policy-related analysis of family problems may be conducted by mapping family problems into this hierarchy of systems. Problems and potential solutions can be delineated in each of these systems. Some problems originate in one or more systems and are manifested in still another system. Some policies are formulated in one sphere, implemented in another, and impact still another. In this light, family problems are tied to many other problems and therefore may not be successfully treated by "family" policy per se.

This systems approach to the conceptualization of family problems tends to merge the specific goals of family policy with numerous other social goals. For example, the increasing number of teenage pregnancies leads to both high abortion rates and the creation of families which, some argue, "should never have been formed" [30]. Either way, the problem of pregnancy for the adolescent spreads to other levels. Her family must cope with the issue. Her high school may struggle with excruciating decisions regarding on-campus child care and breastfeeding in the classroom. Religious and political groups will debate the morality of abortion. Society may have to cover the cost of maintaining the young mother and child. In 1981, there were 1.1 million teenage pregnancies, 75% of which were unintended. Half resulted in live births. Of the over 500,000 infants born to teenagers each year, 300,000 have mothers who have not completed high school. They lack the job skills and earning power which would enable them to support their infants [31]. When a child is born to a teenage mother, the problems of that individual become the problems of that child, and they threaten to spill over into the next generation of children.

Of all the ties between the family and surrounding systems, the relationship between the family and the workplace have drawn increasing attention, because of the universal effects of work upon all families in their microsystems, and across all levels of the social system.

On the microlevel, it is obvious that parents need to work. In the early 1980s the expenses of raising a child to age eighteen were estimated to be from $52,000 to some $140,000, depending upon family income. The projected cost had already increased by 30% from 1977 to 1980 and it continues to rise [32].

On the mesolevel, we find the workplace. There are approximately 8,000 women who lose time from work each month because of failures in child care arrangements. The rate is almost the same for married women as for single women [33]. Employers find that female employees have a higher absenteeism rate than men [34]. Although absence rates for women are higher than those for men within all age groups, the difference is greatest during the peak reproductive years. Some workplace policies have been formulated in order to adapt to this trend. Public policies have encouraged the development of private family-oriented policies via tax incentives, such as the revised depreciation provisions of the Economic Recovery Act of 1981. This act enabled employers to "recover the costs of capital improvement, such as day care facilities, more effectively and more conveniently" [35].

Since World War II, the labor force participation rate for married women has overtaken that for single women. Still, there has been a rapid increase in the number of "female family households" in which there is no husband to share the burden of the costs of raising a child. Out of the 8.2 million female heads of households in 1978, 1.3 million had never been married and thus were doubly compelled to work [36]. These trends have extensive implications in all systems of social organization.

More than half of the 12 million children who live in families headed by women are living in poverty. More than half of the black and Hispanic families headed by women are poor. In 1981, 59% of white children under six in families headed by women were poor, while the rate for black children was 74% and for Hispanic children was 75% [37]. Seven out of eight black women who head families have children in their households compared with three out of eight white women who head families. Unemployment is much higher among these black women, increasing by 200% between 1970 and 1978, compared with an increase of 63% for white women in the same category [38]. In 1986, 25% of all black women and 20% of all Hispanic women were unemployed, compared with 14% of all white women [39]. Clearly, the trends in employment and family life vary by race. Should the disparity be addressed by redistributive macropolicies or should it be left, unaided, to evolve at the microlevel? Family policies seeking to address this problem may appear in the form of "affirmative action," developed to serve particular social groups. They may also take the form of labor or workforce policies which seek to improve employment rates as a means of fighting poverty. Children's welfare becomes secondary to the goals of such policies.

Bronfenbrenner's hierarchy is useful in determining the parameters of the family environment and in tracing social problems and policies. Still, the obstacles to the development of family and child care policy go beyond adequate conceptualization of the problem to the question of whose interests are being served by such policies.

WHO BENEFITS FROM FAMILY AND DAY CARE POLICY? THE STATE AND THE MARKET VS. FAMILY INTERESTS

While relationships between the family and the workplace have undergone similar changes in most industrialized countries, the policy responses of these countries vary. According to analysts Sheila Kamerman and Alfred Kahn, the determinants of these varying policy responses include labor force participation rates of women, per capita GNP, the availability of resources to support alternative policy choices, population trends, and social emphasis upon issues such as equality between the sexes [40].

However, there is another determinant that has a powerful influence upon the speed and comprehensiveness of public policy responses to social changes which affect children and families. That determinant is the extent to which family policy is seen as having an instrumental value to the state.

The degree to which the family is considered to be an instrument of "the state" is associated with several factors that bear on the development of family and child day care policy. As depicted in Table 2.2, these factors include (1) *the degree of definitional clarity;* (2) *the perceived instrumentality or utility of the family;* (3) *the degree of unity in*

TABLE 2.2
RELATIONSHIP BETWEEN INSTRUMENTALITY OF FAMILY POLICY
AND RELATED FACTORS

Definitional clarity		
←		→
Low		High
	Instrumentality of family	
←		→
The state serves the family	The family as its own service provider	The family serves state
	Unity in perceived goals	
←		→
Pluralist goals		Unified goals
	Centrality of planning	
←		→
Decentralized approach		Central planning

the perceived goals of family policy; and (4) *the degree to which social planning is centralized.*

At the center of the instrumentality continuum in Table 2.2 is the situation in which the family is self-sufficient. Family "self-help" may be inspired by policies which define the family as being in this position. The notion of family empowerment implies that programs and policies should enable families to serve themselves. While the public provision of child care is a case of the state serving the family, it can also be interpreted as an effort to enable families to become economically self-sufficient.

A high degree of definitional clarity about what constitutes a family often exists in societies where families serve the state. However arbitrary, definitional clarity facilitates the development of family policy. In a society undergoing rapid and unplanned social change (such as the increase in the number of working mothers of preschool children during the 1970s and 1980s), conventional definitions are muddled by nascent perceptions and pressures.

Clarity regarding acceptable and expected degrees of *dependence, entitivity,* and *adherence to or deviance from conventional form* (see Table 2.1) facilitates a policy response to family needs. Such clarity is likely to be highest in countries where the family serves the state. In China, for example, where family policy dictates the number of children a married couple is allowed to have, the form and size of families are sharply defined in response to state needs for population management.

The evolution of family policy in twentieth-century Russia reflects a changing definition of family functions. During the 1920s the family was officially viewed as an anachronism and a hindrance to the new social order. Deliberate policy-invoked manipulations of the family were performed to remove this "bourgeois institution" called "family." Divorce and abortion laws were liberalized, unmarried mothers and their offspring were delegated new rights, and major goals of Soviet policy included equality of the sexes, economic independence, and labor force participation for women. Policy proposals for public dining halls, domestic services, and child care institutions were designed to "free women" for "more productive" work.

Today many of these early Soviet efforts sound like familiar policy options for providing supportive services to working people and their families. Yet the explicit intention of these Soviet policies was to "weaken the family by eliminating its functions," rather than to cater to its needs [41]. Child care, for example, was perceived as one of the family functions which, if eliminated, would dilute the cement of family life.

During the 1930s, it became apparent to the Soviets that these policies were failing. The people were reacting negatively, and social problems were on the increase. Policymakers responded by changing their tack: now the family was to be strengthened. It would serve as "an agent of social control," a medium for development of public support, and a means of increasing the birthrate.

By the mid-1940s the antifamily policy of the 1920s had been completely reversed. Abortion, and then divorce, became almost impossible to obtain in Russia. Pronatalist policies were initiated in response to abrupt drops in population growth. But the promotion, via family policy, of fertility and female employment equally among all Soviet families may not have been the goal of the state. Geographical and racial variations in population distribution inspired what appear to be population-specific family policies. Although not conclusive, there is some evidence that pre-Gorbachev Soviet family policy was indeed discriminatory along racial and ethnic lines [42].

In recent decades, Soviet family policy has been confronted with a dilemma. Should it encourage increased birthrates or increased and sustained female labor force participation? And are these goals incompatible? The essential design of Soviet family policies has been motivated by the view that the family can serve as an agent of the state to help achieve overarching societal goals.

Regardless of its justification, a high degree of definitional clarity and a consensus regarding the societal goals of family policy lend impetus to policy formulation. A dissensus serves to diffuse that force. A unified vision of the societal goals of family and accompanying child care policy is more likely to be imposed in systems where the family is seen as serving the state, because this view serves as strong motivation for policy development.

The results of central planning and socialism have received mixed reports. For years, Sweden was touted as a model of a state with laudable social benefits. However, in 1984, a survey of Swedish citizens reported that 81% of the respondents agreed that, "The state has become increasingly despotic at the expense of its individual citizens."

Although the Swedish state lavishly subsidizes day care up to $9,000 per child, citizens with average earnings are taxed 62% [43]. The family is frequently perceived as an instrument of the state in democratically socialized systems as well as in authoritarian and totalitarian settings. Family policy is usually an arm of economic, labor, and population policy in these states. Policy planning is centrally controlled. A high degree of central control facilitates the design of a unified family policy mandate, such as those developed in Russia and Sweden. A decentralized system may allow for and even encourage heterogeneity and erratic action in the design and implementation of family policy, as has occurred in the United States. Both centralized and decentralized systems have difficulties as a result of their policy approaches.

Modern political systems, regardless of their orientations, are in the process of learning. After years of concentrated debate, the Canadian government unveiled a national child care plan in 1987. Among its components was one providing low-income families with a subsidy for the purchase of public or private child care. Heated criticism resulted, with opponents arguing that marked influx of funds into the child care market would attract entrepreneurs from the United States, who were described as "less likely to provide high-quality care than are non-profit services" [44]. While this reaction may seem nationalistic, it is primarily one of apprehension regarding free enterprise: Can the profit motive ensure quality care?

At the same time, the United States was learning that government regulation does not ensure quality in child care. Public Law 98–473 became active in October 1985, requiring the Department of Health and Human Services to provide Child Care Standards. These guidelines failed to prevent the existance and spread of poor-quality child care. Psychologist Edward Zigler reported:

> We are finding children strapped to chairs, we are finding senile and alcoholic people taking care of children, we are finding many children who are simply neglected. [45]

This situation existed in a year in which the federal government spent $7 billion on child care and had little effect [46]. Even the best laws and guidelines do not guarantee the realization of their intended outcomes. The authors of child care legislation are still learning how to affect the implementation of their words by improving their words.

In an entirely or even partially capitalist society, answers to the questions of who benefits from family policy extend beyond the family and state to the market economy. Public family policy initiatives may be stimulated by the needs of the market economy. In the United States, many industries are feeling the effects of the relationship between work and families [47]. Industrial motivations for the development of family-oriented workplace policies are clear: the goal of profit maximization provides a rationale for the development of employee services and programs such as child care [48].

Economic pressures yield a concern not just for the competitive value of the product, but for the economy in its production. Human productivity, measured in terms of "output per man-hour," is affected by administrative efficiency, rates of absenteeism and turnover, the physical health of employees, and other less tangible factors such as job satisfaction, identification with the employing organization, and morale [49]. The relationship between the home environment of the employee and the employee's workplace behavior is among the less tangible factors affecting productivity. During the 1980s this relationship became a matter of increasing public and private concern.

In lieu of developing an explicit family policy, the American federal government appears to have laid responsibilities for family-related provisions at the doorstep of the private sector. Public forums and public funds have been used to bring the issue into the limelight, through efforts such as those of the White House Conference on Families in the early 1980s, which generated several initiatives aimed to increase employer awareness of the needs of working parents. Indeed, the top recommendation of the conference was that family-oriented workplace policies be instituted [50]. The formation of the Conference on Families Corporate Task Force, which was headed by a private sector representative from the J. C. Penney Company, encouraged an increased sensitivity to family issues, at least among participating corporations [51].

During its implementation phase, the White House Conference on Families held a "business briefing" in which attending employers were informed of the recommendations made by the corporate task force and the conference. Participants at this briefing were asked to complete a questionnaire regarding their current family-oriented benefits and workplace practices, as well as their desires for more information about options for family policy in the workplace. The questionnaire listed seven major categories of work-related family policy: (1) flextime, which is especially helpful for parents with children in day care or on school schedules that conflict with working hours; (2) permanent part-time, which is useful for parents who have only half a day free from parenting in which to hold a job; (3) job sharing, another creative allocation of working hours to two people who may both need time for family responsibilities such as child care; (4) a flexible benefits plan, presenting employees with the option to substitute for or add to their traditional employee benefit plans a service or benefit tailored to family needs such as a child care benefit; (5) flexible leave and transfer policies, for expecting and new parents and for dually employed spouses, respectively; (6) child care, which may be provided in a variety of forms, either in the workplace or in the community, via benefit plans, employee compensation, vouchers, referral services, or employer contributions to the development of community child care programs; and (7) employee assistance and counseling programs, including parent, family, teen, and retirement counseling; alcoholism and drug abuse programs, and mental health programs [52].

Forty-six of the business-briefing questionnaire respondents represented a sample of large corporations. While over half of them reported that they were currently offering some form of employee assistance and counseling programs, less than half utilized flexible scheduling or flexible leave and transfer policies. Only three offered any form of child care service at that time. However, some corporations reported that they were experimenting with family-related practices, and at least half of them indicated an interest in developing a child care program. Since that "briefing," numerous work-related family policy conferences, with and without public funding, have been convened by research groups, local governments, and businesses, including those by the Conference Board (the research arm of the Fortune 500 companies). However inseparable its effects are from current trends, Carter's White House Conference on Families clearly contributed to the growing sensitivity of employers to the need for family and child care policy development in the private sector.

The conference also helped to draw bipartisan attention to child care issues in the public sector. By 1987, politicians, both left and right, were addressing the need for child care. Utah Senator Orrin Hatch, a conservative Republican by reputation, explained his perspective on child care as follows:

My reputation as a fiscal conservative has apparently caused some to wonder why I have become so involved in the child care issue—having just introduced my own child care legislation in the U.S. Senate. It is true that I try to be tight with taxpayers' dollars and it is also true that I approach any new federal program proposals with a somewhat jaundiced eye. But I have supported and sponsored several measures over the last few years with the goal of minimizing the risk to children in our rapidly changing and confusing society. I was supported in these previous efforts by both liberals and conservatives, because child welfare is not a partisan concern. It is not surprising that a conservative would propose child care legislation. Conservatives have always been among the first to acknowledge reality. While I personally believe that children benefit much more from having a full-time parent, I realize it is wishful thinking to expect a return to "Ozzie and Harriet" style families. [53]

The idealization of the American family as one similar to the Ozzie and Harriet television family is something that most politicians have said goodbye to. While appearing idyllic and easy on the screen, it is far from achievable in the 1980s. Many mothers feel that they cannot afford to stay home and take care of their children and households full-time. What is the answer to the demise of the American myth about family life? Again, who should be caring for the children if not the parent? The federal government? Politicians are split on this topic. As is the traditional conservative stance, Senator Hatch argued that a massive federal policy which would impose a "federally designed program in every town" will swell the bureaucracy, discourage local responses to the need for care, and create "insoluble funding problems" [54]. Senator Hatch therefore argued in favor of leaving the child care solution to local government and families.

As was expressed in his Child Care Services Improvement Act of 1987 (Senate Bill 1678), Senator Hatch favored a policy approach that "plants the seeds" for diverse local child care projects [55]. This was intended to protect American families from the intrusion of the biggest brother, the federal government, into family life. It was also intended to allow for diversity and local control, which are viewed by political conservatives as being necessary alternatives to centralized socialism.

To the contrary, California Democratic Senator Alan Cranston in the same session of Congress (100th Congress, 1st Session) proposed a bill to "ensure economic equity for American women" by making a number of federal policy changes including the enactment of a program that would make "quality dependent care" available to all those who need it [56].

The stated premise behind this dependent child care component of the Cranston bill was that women are the primary caretakers of all dependents—children, handicapped adults, or the elderly—and are therefore at an economic disadvantage [57]. Their participation in the labor force and the sequential building of their incomes as a result of their uninterrupted participation in the labor force are affected by their traditional roles as primary caretakers in their families. The increased respect for women who work has coupled with the increased need of women (whether single or married, with or without work) to work. These social trends have not reduced the responsibility that women bear for dependents, especially their children.

Senator Cranston was therefore one of the original sponsors of the Act for Better Child Care, or ABC (Senate Bill 1885 and House Bill 3660). This was the first comprehensive child care legislation to go before Congress since 1971. This bill proposed an initial cost of $2.5 million for the first three years with a 20% matching fund provision to encourage states to improve their child care services [58]. The required involvement of the states (via matching funds) departs from the traditional liberal view that all citizens have a right to equal economic opportunity and that it is the responsibility of the federal rather than the state or local government to protect this right.

This liberal support for state involvement is an acknowledgment that the federal government cannot do it alone. Child care is a federal, state, and local problem. The solution must arrive on all those levels.

With some amendments, the ABC Bill was passed in the Senate on June 23, 1989. Interestingly, Republican Senator Orrin Hatch was instrumental in its passage, debating other Republican senators on the Senate floor for seven days. However, on the House side of the U.S. Congress, ABC has been attached to another bill, HR3. About one-half of HR3 is composed of a modified ABC. One of the modifications is a strong antisectarian provision, disallowing religious instruction in any day care programs that receive federal funds under this act. This contrasts with the Senate's acceptance of what is being called "parental choice" in cases where child care certificates or vouchers are to be used. Parental choice regarding religious instruction in a day care setting is not an option under the provisions of HR3 because HR3 does not include a day care voucher component.

Although not greatly apparent in the halls of Congress, another critical issue in the passing of HR3 is "flow" of the funding. Most proponents of comprehensive day care legislation argued that ABC–HR3 funding should not be school-based. That is, day care programs developed under HR3 should not be attached to the public school system because (1) the public schools are not prepared to take on such responsibility and (2) the funding will be too thinly spread if distributed in this manner.

While the issues of antisectarianism and distribution are being debated, President Bush is encouraging day care tax supplements rather than massive federal expenditures and is supporting parents' option for religious instruction at the preschool level.

It is evident that child day care has become an intensely political issue. Proponents of religious instruction in the schools, generally viewed as politically conservative, have flooded Congress with letters critizing the antisectarian element of HR3. It is also evident that the politics of child day care is neither static nor clear cut. When President Nixon vetoed the child care bill of 1971, the conservative viewpoint was that nationalized child care threatened to become an instrument of political indoctrination, namely socialistic or left wing indoctrination. Perhaps this sentiment stemmed from occasional news reports that Cuba was successfully using its day care "circulos" for such a purpose or perhaps it stemmed from a vague fear of anything "socialistic." Whatever the source of this viewpoint might have been, almost 20 years later, it is the conservative viewpoint that the inculcation of values— this time religious rather than political—should be an intrinsic part of day care, and that federal funds (via vouchers) can be used to support this inculcation.

At the same time, the right of all children to maximum educational development is potentially threatened by those reluctant to flow the ABC–HR3 funds through the public schools. It is ironic that this right, traditionally supported by political liberals, is being counteracted, albeit inadvertently, by some of these very liberals. Parents who can afford elite preschools with programs focused on intensive educational development may give their children a distinct advantage over those who must rely on federal funds for day care. Because the true effects of highly educational day care will remain unmeasured until large numbers of children are studied for several decades, politics is grappling with distinct unknowns. Right and wrong, and left, right, and center cannot maintain intelligent points of view without admitting these unknowns.

Whatever and whenever legislation is passed, the solutions will be a long time coming. Moreover, legislation, no matter how good its intentions, does not guarantee an intended result. We as a nation are still lacking enough data to clarify what our goals regarding children and families are. Until we achieve such clarity, or at least admit our lack of clarity, child care, like many other social issues, will remain an issue that "happens" to us: we will continue to be "reactive" in our policy instead of "proactive." We will continue to be caught in the trap of reacting to perceived social problems rather than averting them. We will continue to experiment on our children.

The evolution of a coherent and lasting government position on family and child care policy depends upon answers to the basic questions: Who should be served? What problems should be addressed? Who should benefit? Although these are moral, ethical, and philosophical questions, in our democratic and pluralistic system they are most likely to be resolved in the arena of political debate.

Public child care policy can be viewed as either government intrusion into family life or government buttressing of family life. However, the situation is not cut and dried. There are countless variations on this traditional political theme. Beyond the skewing of these conservative and liberal viewpoints is a mixed understanding of the new corporate involvement in the child care issues. Where child care policy is articulated by private-sector employers, it is also viewed either as corporate intrusion into family life or as corporate support for families and children. The public sector has called for private-sector employers to respond to the child care needs of employees. This concept brings us to the next chapter, which examines emerging child care arrangements in the market and some of the issues raised from this perspective. As we further examine child care in our society, we see that our children are caught adrift in an increasingly tangled sea of societal weeds.

Chapter 3

THE MARKET SPHERE

Where Child Day Care Is Bought and Sold

> *Hush, little baby, don't say a word,*
> *Mama's gonna buy you a mockingbird.*
>
> *If that mockingbird won't sing,*
> *Mama's gonna buy you a diamond ring.*
> >   —"Hush, Little Baby,"
> >   Folk Song

Money cannot buy love, but money can and does buy child care. Proprietary child care services have served and will continue to serve a large portion of America's families. Even if the public sector eventually chooses to provide extensive child care services to all citizens, there will be a continuing demand for private-sector child care programs. Why? Consider the experience that this nation has had with public education. Our public schools have not met the educational needs or desires of all families in this country. As a result, private schools at all grade levels are in demand and many have waiting lists. Public child care, even if made universally available, cannot expect to meet the individual needs and desires of all families. Private child care will experience a pattern of demand similar to that of private education. The resulting inequities will also be similar. These will stem from the fact

75

that the parents who will be most likely to select expensive private child care programs will be those who can afford to make such a selection.

There will of course be exceptions to this rule. A few parents of low and moderate income may decide to make major economic sacrifices so that their children can receive private child care and any educational advantages it may have to offer. I am often reminded of the way one single mother explained her interest in private care to me: "I make $18,000 a year. But I send my daughter to a private elementary school where the tuition is $6,000 a year. You think this is expensive? Before she [my daughter] started elementary school, she went to a child care program that was really a preschool. That cost me $6,600 a year. I don't get any support from her father. But I grew up poor and my daughter isn't gonna stay that way. I don't care what it costs me. She's gonna get the best schools."

This mother was willing to spend 30% of her income on elementary school tuition and more than that on child care and preschool. Again, money itself cannot buy love, but it can buy care and education. It can buy opportunity. And it can buy social advantages, such as a way out of poverty, a way into the middle class, and a ticket to the much idealized American dream. For this reason it is important to examine the market sphere, the realm of activity where money motivates the provision and the purchase of child care services.

PARENTS AS PARTICIPANTS IN THE MARKET

This chapter begins by examining the way the economics of time, money, and freedom of choice affect child care consumers. Individual child care consumers are usually parents. They are the central players in the child care market because they are the source of children and they are responsible for the direct and indirect care of their children. Following the section on parents as participants in the market, the discussion turns to other participants in the child care market. These participants are organizational. They include business-government agreements, employers as day care sponsors, private proprietary operations, and nonprofit care providers.

The market may be described as an investment realm. Participants in the child care market weigh the costs of their investments against the benefits of their investments. Unfortunately, the output measures are usually functional, even though the service being purchased is child care and even when the purchasers are parents. The thinking runs: Two hundred dollars a week buys X hours of care. X hours of care will enable the parent to work Y hours and earn Z dollars. Z dollars minus two hundred dollars a week is a positive sum large enough to make the purchase of child care functionally, and economically, beneficial.

Economies of time and money moderate the provision of all care. In the sphere of familial care, there is no rigid formula for the best mix of dollars, time, energy (function), and affection (feeling). Although the economy of informal care is one of indefinite proportions, it is definitely a composite of its direct and indirect functions (diagrammed in Figure 3.1).

Few if any families are able to provide the optimal amount of care in each dimension. When they can, they buy what they need in the

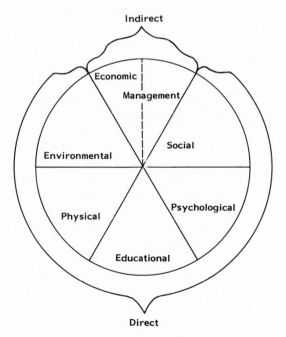

FIGURE 3.1. Primary dimensions of care.

market. For example, most families meet the nurturing requirement of physical care by purchasing food rather than by growing it. The market economy responds to consumer demands for food; it is available for a price, and this price is mediated by consumer demand. When a family cannot afford to buy what it needs, or when the market does not offer the goods or services it requires, the political economy may respond with food stamps or income support programs. These are taxpayer-supported social services as discussed in Chapter 2. Even with the assistance of friends, the market, or the polity, however, it is difficult for families to manage the delivery of all aspects of care within the home. A family must have both the fiscal and the organizational capacity to provide direct care and the stamina to maintain these capacities.

Parents are the primary sources of income and of management for their families. Thus it is parents who must have the stamina to maintain their families. They must also be prudent consumers of goods and services such as child care. Let us therefore briefly consider the problems of family economic capacity, family management, and family child-care consuming in terms of their role in the market sphere.

FAMILY ECONOMIC CAPACITY

A family's ability to provide the material aspects of care such as food, clothing, and shelter to its members is affected by its economic status. But parental care involves more than such economic provisions. It involves an instinctive, affective sense. Discipline, socialization, affection, and attention are not tangible goods. They have no dollar value. As I discussed in Chapter 1, they represent the aspects of care that consist of "feeling" more than of "function." However, "care, the feeling" is something which cannot be easily purchased, and there is no guarantee that an increase in economic status will make a family environment a more loving, caring home.

Unfortunately, the economic requisite of care, albeit indirect, determines a family's ability to (1) "buy time" for at least one of its members to stay out of the labor force in order to give direct care [1]; (2) purchase the services of a part- or full-time substitute for its own direct care, such as a live-in nanny, babysitter, or child care service; and (3) buy the material necessities, however defined by that family, for care.

Meeting the requirements for the material necessities of care is a relatively clear-cut task. There must be enough money available to purchase food at home, food away from home, clothing, housing, medical care, education, transportation, and other items such as personal care, recreation, reading material, and miscellaneous items. These eight budget categories have been identified by the U.S. Department of Agriculture and by the U.S. Department of Labor Bureau of Labor Statistics in their studies of family expenditure patterns [2]. According to averages reported by the USDA, families at different income levels spend accordingly. For example, the 1980 annual cost of raising a four-year-old child ranged from at least the "economy level" of $1,911 to the "moderate level" of $3,779 [3]. Doubtless, many families spend more than this in a year on one four-year-old.

The economic capacity to provide care is precariously balanced in single-parent families. Many low-income, single mothers can afford neither to stay home to provide direct care for their children, nor to pay for a high-quality substitute for their own direct child care. While single-parent families spend somewhat less for child care than husband-wife families, it comprises a higher percentage of their family spending. In 1985, the median expenditure on child care made by single women and married women without a husband present was $37 weekly, compared to $41 for husband-wife families. For a single-parent family, this comprised 7.3% of all family spending; the percentage was only 2.6% for husband-wife families. When these payments are considered in terms of employment status, the disparity is even greater. In families where the mother is employed part-time, the median weekly expenditure on child care is only $26. By contrast, mothers employed full-time spend $43 a week on child care [4]. As care providers and care consumers, employed single parents must trade off time in the home for time at work. They also have less money available to spend on tangible ingredients of care because of the significant percentage of their incomes that must be spent on child care.

However, the family economy of care includes more than the exchange of dollars for child care supplies and services. Many exchanges and trade-offs occur without the mediation of dollars. For example, services are traded informally between families and friends. Within families, time and energy are allocated according to ability and preference. Still, the economic requisite of care is a powerful determinant of the family's ability to provide for dependent members. It influences not only the ingredients of care that a family can purchase, but also the amount of time and energy available for family management.

FAMILY MANAGEMENT

The ability to participate in the market on behalf of the family is linked to the ability to manage family affairs and family time. The providing of care to children also requires numerous organizational and "coping" skills. Family management activities are both psychological and practical. The practical side of family management involves bill paying, time management, and meal planning. These activities, and all family management activities, are affected by the psychological state of the parents.

The role of the parent may be strained, distorted, or confused when he or she is both employed and involved in providing direct care. The Family Impact Seminar's "Job-Family Role-Strain Scale" identified five sources of psychological strain upon working parents [5]:

1. "Ambiguity about norms," manifested in parent's worries about the adequacy of their allocation of time to family and work, and concerns about what other people think of this allocation;
2. "Socially structured insufficiency of resources for role fulfillment," indicated by parents' difficulties in making satisfactory arrangements for the care of their children while they work;
3. "Low rewards for role conformity," providing little positive reinforcement for good parenting or good working or both;
4. "Conflict between normative phenomena," where social expectations of parents and employees conflict; and
5. "Overload of role obligations," causing parents to feel hurried, overworked, physically drained, emotionally drained, and overcommitted.

Practical problems in the provision of care include the organization of resources and activities. Although the economic status of a family determines its ability to choose from a wide range of consumer goods, its says little about the family's ability to organize its time and energy. Scheduling and transportation are problems for most families. The ability to arrange adequate commute time, time to shop for goods and services, time for community interaction, and, most important, time for family interaction is an essential product of family management. Without the time for it, there is no direct child care [6].

FAMILY CHILD-CARE CONSUMING

When day care is available for a price, it is a commodity. Theoretically, day care consumers may demand this service in sufficient quantity, with reasonable quality, at affordable prices, in convenient locations, and at the hours needed. Entrepreneurial care providers establish programs in response to these demands and lose money when their competitors offer better choices to their consumers. But how operative is the function of consumer choice, and how much choice do consumers actually have in the world of child care [7]?

Consumer choice may be limited by a number of factors. First, consumer choice may be influenced by financial considerations. Rather than choosing from among all options, consumers tend to buy the services they can afford. When consumers are fully or partially reimbursed for service costs or compensated by a public agency as is the case in voucher, sliding-scale-payment, and other publicly funded programs, they select only from among the options available under the funding program.

Second, consumer choice is susceptible to the influence of authority, or apparent authority. Consumers' preferences are sometimes "educated" by extrafamilial figures. These professionals dictate norms for good and innovative care. The aura of professional expertise is utilized in the marketing of many child care and parenting programs geared toward the rearing of "superbabies" and children prepared for the future. Those programs which advertise that they satisfy the presumed demands of modern technoscientific childrearing will sell to parents who do not want their children to be left behind.

Third, parents without adequate education either may not be susceptible to the guidance of professionals regarding the selection of child care or may be overly susceptible to the wrong or uninformed advice. Consumer choice thus may be influenced by educational background.

Fourth, cultural norms drive care consumers to make choices which are popular among their peers. This is true at all socioeconomic levels. Some parents join the run for intensive early childhood education, others for disciplinary care, other for care which offers sugar-free and vegetarian nutrition. Different dimensions of care are emphasized by different cultural groups.

Fifth, when confronted by the time pressures of modern life, choice is tainted, if not almost usurped, by matters of convenience. Is the location of the day care setting close enough to home or to work? Is the care service available during the hours when it is most needed?

Finally, day care choices are often limited. In the absence of alternatives, the consumer must take whatever is available—or nothing at all. The unavailability of child care is an obstacle to employment. Some .75 million mothers of low and moderate economic status do not work because they cannot find satisfactory child care. Many women who do use child care arrangements indicate that their "choice" of care does not reflect personal preference; instead it reflects a lack of choice. These women settle for child care programs with which they are dissatisfied and sometimes of which they disapprove [8]. A further variation of this phenomenon is contained in Chapter 7 and the "Conclusion," where I discuss my day care consumer study.

The ability of parents to choose appropriate child care is a critical factor in both the welfare of children and the quality of the child care market. With an abundance of factors inhibiting the strength of consumer choice, the parent is child-care consuming at a disadvantage. We now consider the auspices under which child care is available in the market.

WORK-RELATED CHILD CARE

In the market sphere, much of the significance attached to child care is related to employment. What is work-related child care? For employed persons who are responsible for dependents (children, severely handicapped or seriously ill persons, or frail elderly), there is a fundamental relationship between work and day care. The sharing of responsibility for a day care program enables an employed person to have the basic ingredients of shared care, i.e., the time to work and earn money. Work-related day care includes child day care provided by the government for workfare participants by government agencies and/or potential employers for participants in job-training programs by employers for employees, and by unions for their members. Most often, it includes private profit and nonprofit agencies, which working persons select and pay for on their own, independently of any government agency, employer, union, or other employees' organization [9].

These categories tend to overlap. For example, when unions and employers cosponsor a program, the role of the primary sponsor becomes vague. It is further obscured when a government agency and an employer subsidize a day care program together. The Integrated Community and Employer Sponsored Child Care Center at Pioneers Memorial Hospital in Brawley, California, provided just this form of cosubsidy. Hospital employees' children were enrolled with a "tuition subsidy" of $5 per child per day. The hospital paid this subsidy as an employee benefit. Low-income families living in the surrounding community were eligible to enroll their children in the same program, because it was subsidized by the State Office of Child Development [10].

BUSINESS-GOVERNMENT PARTNERSHIPS

A strong faith in the market's ability to provide an opportunity for all willing individuals to earn an income—an opportunity for every primary caregiver to acquire the economic requisites for the direct care of dependents—has inspired a number of partnerships between business and government. Descending from and looking beyond the tradition of the old Comprehensive Employment and Training Act, the federal Job Training Partnership Act (JTPA) of 1983 underscored this continuing belief that the solutions to the social problem of unemployment and those related to it are to be found in the marketplace. The JTPA's perspective upon its job trainees' needs for child care revealed that both the polity and the market consider the role of child care in work life as significant, but neither is anxious to assume responsibility for its provision. The JTPA descended from a series of government job-creation and job-training programs; it was not a form of day care program or policy.

In 1934, President Franklin D. Roosevelt created the Civil Works

Administration in the face of a 20% unemployment rate. This program lasted only two and a half months because of its high cost. It was succeeded by the Works Progress Administration (WPA), which aimed to hire as many people as rapidly as was possible but was unable to lift the depressed economy. Later, in 1961, the Area Redevelopment Act sent federal money to depressed geographical areas to create jobs and training opportunities. In the same year the Youth Employment Opportunities Act provided jobs for thousands of otherwise unemployed teenage youths.

Following this effort, the Manpower Development and Training Act of 1962 (MDTA) offered training to workers who were automated out of their jobs. The 1964 Jobs Corp Program was designed to train youths from low-income families. In 1965, the Neighborhood Youth Corps aimed to encourage low-income youths to stay in school while providing them with work experience. Again facing an increase in unemployment the Emergency Employment Act (EEA) of 1971 focused upon increasing the number of government jobs available in state and local agencies. Finally, Congress passed the Comprehensive Employment and Training Act (CETA) in 1973, continuing governmental training and employment. In the following years, government paid employing companies to provide on-the-job training (OJT), another approach to the alleviation of unemployment and the lack of job skills among low-income and unemployed individuals [11].

The Job Training Partnership Act thus evolved from a half-century tradition of state-initiated programs linking business and government. JTPA allocated $3 billion to the "partnership" between employers and government in the training and employment of teens and adults. Title 1 of this act established a "structure for the delivery of job training services and outlined the functions and responsibilities of state and local government and the private sector" in its implementation. Under this program state governments had the authority to oversee and monitor local-level compliance. Governors designated local service delivery areas, in which the chief elected officials selected persons to serve on local private industry councils (PICs). While the majority of a PIC's membership were to be representatives of business, the remaining seats were to be filled by other representatives of the community.

In the implementation of JTPA, PICs played a crucial role in deciding how to spend the funds allocated to their community [12].

One of the choices state governments and the employer- and business-dominated PICs faced was the extent to which funds should be spent on work-related child care programs. In California, for example, state legislation in Section 15073 of AB3424 (Lockyer, 1982) indicated that:

> To assure compliance with legislative intent regarding the availability of subsidized child care services provided through programs administered by the Superintendent of Public Instruction, each county's private industry council shall review and comment on proposals for expansion of child care services within the county submitted to the council by the Superintendent of Public Instruction pursuant to Section 8285.5 of the Education Code. The council's comments shall include a description of ways whereby child care services can be expanded to assure that such services are directed to participants of services under this division with the greatest need for child care. [13]

The role of county private industry councils in implementing this section of AB3424 was not without problems. Some of these problems can be attributed to the absence of a clear social philosophy regarding the importance of child care in facilitating improved labor force participation. As they prepared for compliance with the JTPA, many PICs decided that child care was not a necessary supportive service. For example, in California, one Bay Area county pinpointed youth unemployment as its target. Consequently, services other than child care, such as counseling and outreach, were developed. A PIC in Southern California found transportation to be the most needed supportive service and directed its share of JTPA funds in line with this priority [14].

The JTPA is but one example of how the polity has shifted responsibility for day care policy development over to local-level business interests. Yet this was actually a business-government partnership in the realms of labor and economic policy. Day care development was, if anything, only a side effect of the JTPA's implementation, and the incentives for day care development within the JTPA were weak.

EMPLOYER-SPONSORED CARE

When employers find themselves in need of remedies for parenting-related absenteeism and falling productivity within their organizations, their interests in child care take on a greater priority, as seen in emerging trends in employer-sponsored care. Employer-sponsored child care is not an entirely new concept. In the early 1900s, for example, some factories were known to sponsor child care in working-class neighborhoods, often in unsanitary facilities [15]. The motivation for employers to meet employees' child care needs has increased tremendously in recent years. However, the Council on Economic Priorities reported that 2,500 companies offered day care or day-care-related services to employees in 1985, up from 110 companies in 1978, but that out of 25,000 companies with over 100 employees, this was a very small number [16].

EMPLOYER INTERESTS IN CHILD CARE: THE TREND

In 1976, 5.6 million women with children under age six were labor force participants. This represented a tripling of the size of the group since 1970, and a major social and economic change [17]. Wives with "dependent children" have increased their labor force participation more rapidly than wives without dependent children. The dramatic increase in the number of working mothers with children of preschool age is a trend which continues as a result of economic and social pressures [18]. Many two-parent families who had assumed that, according to tradition, one parent would perform the primary child-caring activities while the other earned the family income, are confronted with economic motivation to become dual-wage-earner families [19]. Concurrently, the number of single-parent families is increasing, leaving a segment of our parent population with no alternative other than to both work and parent [20].

Over half of all women between the ages of twenty-five and thirty-four are employed. By modern standards, these women are in their primary childbearing and childrearing years. Women in this age cohort are exhibiting changes in their career patterns. They are marrying later, having fewer children, returning to the labor force sooner after childbirth, and remaining employed longer [21].

Business and industry, employing large numbers of women of childbearing and childrearing age, are developing increased awareness of the interrelationships between work and family life [22]. During the

1970s, women were more likely than men to report absences from work as sick days when they were actually caring for their children. By the end of the 1980s, men began to report that they were taking almost as much time away from work because of children's needs as were their wives [23]. Nevertheless, female employees continue to have a higher rate of absenteeism during prime childbearing and childrearing years than men of the same age [24]. Turnover and absenteeism rates of this age group can affect productivity. A desire to counterbalance detrimental affects of childrearing demands upon workplace productivity draws some employers into a search to define the specific needs of their particular labor forces. Employers are realizing that parents' strain of dual responsibility is most accentuated during children's preschool years, when children are most dependent, when their development is most rapid, and when there is no public school setting in which to enroll them.

During 1981, interest in employee child care needs continued to grow, evidenced by the convening of conferences such as the Aspen Institute "Corporation and Family" seminar held in August 1981 and the "Parents at Work" conference convened in San Francisco in November 1981. Employers who participated in these and other conferences expressed concern over child care and working-parent problems. Further evidence of momentum in the private sector is found in the proliferation of child care businesses and in the diverse attempts on the part of employers, service providers, communities, and families to cope with the increasing demands for work-related child care. Employers' motivations have also been encouraged by provisions in the Economic Recovery Act of 1981, which include tax incentives for employers to respond to the child care needs of their employees.

Much attention has been given to the needs for child care in other modern industrialized nations [25], where solutions range from state-supported preschool programs to encouragement of the private sector to develop its own responses to the diverse needs of labor force participants. In this country, several worthwhile programs and services are evolving in the child day care domain. Some employers have been involved in needs assessment and even program development activities [26]. Other employers have at least expressed recognition of the issues at hand. Overall, however, steps taken to respond to child care needs have been somewhat sporadic and not always methodical. No formal mechanism exists to aid employers in reviewing the experiences of others to gain insight into alternative day care possibilities and outcomes.

Although day care is so vital that it has been described as "the key job benefit of the 1990s" [27], employers are virtually on their own as they experiment with the array of possibilities for the provision of child care to their employees. These possibilities include private voucher programs; support of, or contribution to, existing community programs; development of new programs at the work site, between work sites, between employers, and between employers and other private agencies; and, of course, nonintervention in the area of child care.

There are several options open to employers in their administration of day care programs. Programs may be owned entirely by the corporation; the program may be affiliated with the company but remain a legally separate entity; or programs may be externally owned. Program management may be either internal (company-managed) or external. If the management is external, it may be done by either a for-profit or a nonprofit organization. Together and separately, management and ownership of employer-related care have been found in the hands of unions, health care organizations, government agencies, and proprietary day care providers [28].

EVALUATING AN INVESTMENT IN CARE

From an employer's perspective, the evaluation of employer-sponsored dependent care, or any form of employee benefit, is framed by market-oriented economic values and is based upon the logic of profit maximization. In the worst case, an employer's investment in an employee service is expected to have a neutral effect upon productivity (although child care benefits have brought out new concerns in a few employers who fear that on-site child care will distract parents and result in lower productivity). In the best case, child care or any employee service should enhance productivity, especially in labor-intensive industries.

Employers' investments in employee services have not always been applauded. In the United States, employee benefits were first earned during the rise of labor unrest, which began in the 1890s, almost half a century later than it did in Europe. Benefits were offered to mitigate worker antipathy toward the authority of management, which thereby sidestepped more central grievances. During these years, corporations such as General Electric, U.S. Steel, and International Harvester attempted to placate their employees with flush toilets, pure drinking water, health programs, and suggestion boxes. However, these efforts backfired as many of the corporations providing benefits were later to be hardest hit by worker unrest [29]. But views and interests have changed. Some eighty years later, in the early 1970s, corporate day care was considered a "fashionable" employee benefit or "perk" for a new breed of female managers and administrators of childbearing age. This "perk" was inspired by the large number of vocal and educated women entering middle management. However, several of the programs which started in those years were closed due to high operating costs and employee apathy. But these efforts were only the beginning of contemporary employer-sponsored child care.

By the end of the 1970s, offices, laboratories, and assembly plants were confronted with mounting shortages of skilled workers and declining productivity of all types of workers; amidst these problems family-oriented, employer-sponsored programs, including day care, were rediscovered as ameliorative devices. During the past ten years, big corporate names such as Xerox, Stride Rite, Measurex, Hewlett-Packard, and Polaroid have led the way in experimenting with employer-sponsored day care alternative [30].

Some of the nation's employers have sponsored unusual child care programs to meet unusual employee needs. The demands of rotating, night, swing, split, and on-call shifts have inspired American West Airlines to open a twenty-four-hour-a-day, seven-day-a-week child care program in Phoenix, Arizona. The Los Angeles Department of Water and Power has decided to sponsor a day care center which opens at 6:30 A.M. A new twenty-four-hour center opened near the San Francisco airport [31]. Governmental agencies, as employers, have also joined in the provision of employer-sponsored day care—a move encouraged by the complaints of government employees during the Carter administration's White House Conference on Families, when government made efforts to encourage private-sector employers to recognize the child care needs of private-sector employees, while apparently neglecting the same needs of its own employees.

However, the influx and visibility of female employees with children into the civilian and military ranks of the armed forces has generated significant governmental interest in day care services. As of the early 1980s, the Air Force operated 123 child care centers serving some 18,000 children and 101 preschool programs serving 11,000 children at its installations. The Army served approximately 23,000 children in 281 child care programs; the Marine Corps, 4,000 children in 33 programs; and the Navy, 12,000 children in 78 child care centers, throughout the world. Indeed, the U.S. Department of Defense itself operated more child care services than any other employer (public or private) in the United States [32].

EMPLOYEES' PERSPECTIVE

The working parent evaluates child care on many levels. Employers' focus on function spills over to employees' views regarding child care. The actual value of employee services has been described and measured in both qualitative and quantitative terms. The most commonly reported qualitative effects of employee benefits are improvements in public image and employee morale, as well as easier recruitment of new employees. Some qualitative effects have been calibrated, such as the relationship between stress due to employees' child care problems and workplace accidents.

How would the value of child care as an employee benefit be ascertained? The benefits accrued by the day-care-consuming employee can be compared to those of other employee services. One way to value an employee benefit is in terms of its utility to the employee. If the benefit takes the form of direct compensation, the utility to the employee is described in terms of the amount paid, or the outlay cost to the company. Another form of benefit is a company payment to a child care provider on behalf of its employees. In this case, the total outlay cost to the company is not the exact value of the benefit to the employee. Some employees might have thought the benefit was not worth the price and would not have been willing to pay for it at full cost. In the calculation of its value, the benefit is discounted by the estimated difference between its actual cost to the employer and the amount that employees would have paid on their own for the same benefit. (Job training and company-provided vacation retreats are examples of benefits which must be discounted for their actual value to employees and adjusted for cost to employees when otherwise not provided by their employer.) When there is a definite saving to the employee (the cost of employee-sponsored child care may be less than comparable care purchased by the employee outside of the corporation), the benefit may be valued in terms of actual dollar savings.

Another approach to evaluating benefits involves the estimation of the present value of future earnings or savings. For example, the value of a benefit, such as training, which will increase the income of the employee in future years, is estimated by the total expected increase in yearly income, which is discounted to its present value, based upon a statistical prediction of the turnover rate, the retirement age, and so forth of the employee [33]. Employer-sponsored child care may be viewed as an investment in the development of an employee's experience and skills. This evaluative perspective allows the present cost of the child care service to be weighed against the benefit of keeping the parent of a young child attached to the labor force during the child's preschool years. If the employee's skills and pay are higher in the future as a result of having remained on the job during child-bearing years, the value of child care as an employee benefit is enhanced.

The psychological effects of employee benefits are more difficult to measure. Some valuations of "psychic benefits" are made by estimating the difference in income which an employee is willing to accept in order to gain a psychic benefit. For example, some employees choose to earn less so that they can live in a preferred environment, others select lower paying jobs which offer better employee benefits, and some parents seek part-time work in order to have more time to spend with their children. Of all the recognized "psychic benefits" (including power, public respect, and self-realization) and the interrelated practical benefits (such as the convenience of work-site health services), the psychic benefit of an employee service to his or her family life is one of the most difficult to measure [34]. The day care consumer study results that I report in Chapter 7 and discuss there and in the "Conclusion" shed some light on this difficult matter.

EMPLOYER'S PERSPECTIVE

Although employers consider these services in terms of their value to employees, most corporate investments in employee benefits are ultimately evaluated for their direct impact upon labor productivity. Productivity, or the ratio of output to input, may be measured in various ways, e.g., output (numbers of units produced) per worker hour, or amount of sales in dollars per hours of work or dollars of capital investment. Measures of labor productivity focus, naturally, upon the output of the employees themselves. The term "productivity" is often used to refer loosely to production and performance. "Production" is a qualitative or quantitative measure of goods and services, of output. "Performance" refers to the behavior of workers and is operationalized in terms of rates of tardiness, absenteeism, turnover, and other typical employee behaviors [35].

Employer-sponsored day care is increasingly evaluated for its impact on production and performance. An investment in care should yield an increase in production. Because production is influenced by multiple factors, a day care program is frequently considered in terms of its cost to the sponsoring employer versus changes in employee performance and the dollar value (positive or negative) of these changes.

For example, in 1979, Intermedics (a manufacturer of pacemakers and other medical devices in Texas) opened a day care center which served 191 of its employees' children, for which they were charged $15 per week per child. An evaluation of this investment in child care indicated that job turnover decreased 60% during the first two years of its operation, and that reduced absenteeism saved 15,000 work hours. These two changes alone save the company over $2 million in two years [36].

Company research on the decrease in productivity due to absenteeism, tardiness, and turnover prompted Nyloncraft in Indiana to spend $150,000 on its new Nyloncraft Learning and Day Care Center for its employees' children aged six weeks to thirteen years. In that year, 1982, 85% of Nyloncraft's workforce was female; the average female employee was a single mother supporting two or more children by working as a press operator for $5.13 an hour and was limited in her employment options by an education that had not gone beyond the twelfth grade. For these women, the facility was open twenty-four hours a day. Employees paid $25 a week for the first child and $23 a week for each additional child. Night-shift workers paid a lower fee for night care of their children. Employees of other companies paid somewhat more ($45 to $52 a week) for the use of the Nyloncraft Center child care. Nyloncraft found it worthwhile to subsidize this program at a cost of $2,000 a week. It even offered care for handicapped children [37].

Perhaps the most touted corporate child care facility has been the one developed by a team of businesses, the Hacienda Business Park Child Care Center in Pleasanton, California, opened in 1986. This center features the newest types of toys and innovative design and teaching philosophies. It serves 200 babies and preschoolers of working parents. The facility is within a few minutes of participating workplaces. It cost $3 million and covers 17,000 square feet [38].

Some interesting variations upon family-oriented workplace policies emerged among European corporations during the 1970s. Volvo, the largest manufacturer in Sweden, asked men applying for jobs if they were married and whether they had children [39]. Chances for advancement in their corporation were threatened by competition from other men without commitments to parenting as a result of "profamily" company policies.

In France, with a predominantly (60%) female workforce at the beginning of the 1980s and a shortage of women in its higher corporate levels, Banque National de Paris (BNP) discovered in a survey of its female employees that child care responsibilities kept most of them from progressing upward in the organization. Among the administrative women, 60% of whom had at least one child, "a significant proportion expressed a disinclination to 'move up' due to parental responsibilities." Following the institution of flexible work hours and increased part-time work schedules, the absenteeism rate at BNP dropped and women began climbing the corporate ladder. Mutuelles Uniés, a French insurance company, also had a workplace which was 60% female. The backbone of its operation, contract preparation, was primarily in the hands of women with children. It had, since 1975, allowed over 90% of its employees flextime, offered generous maternity leave policies (twenty weeks with pay), and allowed mothers three years of leave without pay for childrearing without losing their jobs [40].

The policies of Western European corporations which affect families and children are shaped by two forces: government requirements and what the company needs to do to "get and keep productive workers at least cost" [41]. The factors that influence Western European corporations are to some extent found in the United States. However, private employment policies in most Western European countries differ from those in the United States mainly because their governments provide more incentives and pressures to respond to family needs. Despite these incentives and pressures, public administrative mechanisms for the enforcement of equal pay and equal opportunity are weak. To wit, European women are more underrepresented in the upper income and occupational brackets than are American women.

There are other public policies in European countries which have no American parallels. These European policies serve two explicitly stated goals: to raise birth rates and to encourage labor force participation. These policies are being implemented in part by government subsidization of child care and of lengthy paid maternity leaves. In the United States, the government has exerted less influence upon workplace policies.

Where public policy does not intervene, the economy of employer-sponsored care is expressed in the economic language of employer investment and employee performance. This is not to say that the quality of the care provided is entirely disregarded in employer-sponsored day care, but that the formal evaluation of such care looks more for efficient employee behaviors and increases in productivity than at quality of day care services.

PROPRIETARY AND NOT-FOR-PROFIT DAY CARE

Estimates are that from 40% to 70% of families needing child care services cannot find services that meet their needs [42]. This intense demand is bound to be heard by both for-profit and nonprofit corporations. How do these organizations differ? Social services provided under private for-profit auspices are characterized by their motivation to operate at an economy of firm optimum. By contrast, services provided under voluntary or nonprofit auspices are believed to operate in the absence of the profit motive, striving to contribute to the general social welfare. In reality, the operations of social service providers under either of these auspices are influenced by a mix of economic and moral incentives. Voluntary organizations experience economic pressures and compete for public funding and clients. Proprietary firms, in addition to their marketplace activities, have moved into the purchase-of-service domain (in which public agencies purchase services from voluntary agencies) once reserved for nonprofit organizations and branches of government [43].

Regardless of its auspices, the competition for and receipt of public funding influences an organization's behavior. In a review of the behavior of voluntary agencies, Gordon Manser suggests, "An agency's freedom and effectiveness in social action or advocacy may be in inverse proportion to the amount of public money it receives" [44]. The needs of an agency's clients may differ or be incompletely defined by the sources of its funding. Or economic pressures may force nonprofit service providers to deliver only those services for which public funds are available. For-profit providers, encroaching upon this domain, increase competition for funds and drive their companion nonprofit providers to temper their altruistic goals with greater concerns for economic efficiency. This trend affects the field of child welfare, where for-profit organizations have started to become a permanent part of the service delivery network, as is apparent in the delivery of child day care services, where for-profit organizations are the single largest source (31%) of publicly funded programs [45].

With and without public funding, for-profit day care centers provide a large and growing portion of the body of day care services in the United States today. At the end of the 1970s, there were close to 19,000 day care centers in the United States. While the majority were nonprofit organizations, 41%, or 7,500, of these were for-profit day care centers [46]. Child care chains are springing up everywhere. As a writer for the *San Francisco Chronicle* predicted, "Chances are there is a Kinder-Care (child care) Learning Center near you." Kinder-Care has grown so rapidly that in 1987 it offered its employees a $75 bonus for bringing in new employees [47].

Although ownership of proprietary day care may be in the form of a chain, a franchise operation, or an independent center, 86% of all for-profit day care operations are independently owned and managed centers (outnumbering all other types of for-profit day care operations)

[48]. This independent mode of day care service delivery contributes largely to the diversity present in the mixed economy of day care; the program quality and philosophy, as well as adherence to regulation among independent providers, varies widely. Free of the confines of stipulations attached to public funding and the bureaucratic reliability established by profit-making chains, independent owners (often husband-and-wife teams) have the greatest latitude in program development of all day care providers. Despite their advantage in the market, independent day care centers may wane in numbers as tougher regulations, such as minimum wage requirements, and competition from large day care chains develop [49].

Among the factors contributing to the diversification of child care services is the marked difference in economic status between consumers of nonprofit and of for-profit day care services. During the early 1980s, over 80% of the recipients of care in nonprofit centers came from families with annual incomes of $6,000 or less, while about half of those in proprietary day care were from families with annual incomes over $15,000 [50].

Public regulation overlays and further complicates disparities. For example, in 1985, San Francisco became the first major U.S. city to require office developers to plan for and provide child care services. The law required developers of more than 50,000 square feet to provide on-site child care for employees' children or to pay $1 per square foot into a fund that developed child care elsewhere in the city. This fund required that all of its money be used solely for families with low and moderate incomes as defined by the state. On the other hand, child care centers within a developer's building could be used by employees at any income level [51]. While it is innovative and commendable, this type of legislation creates a situation in which some employees acquire on-site child care in well-appointed and new buildings, while others acquire off-site child care in whatever setting it is placed. Although a disparity in quality does not necessarily result from this arrangement, a disparity in convenience, in proximity to children during working hours, and in opportunities for parents to provide immediate feedback regarding quality of care does result.

Among the factors inhibiting more rapid development of child care services is the problem of insurance. Most states continue to struggle with the questions of how much and what level of insurance to require of child care providers. California offers an example of this struggle. In the summer of 1985, the child care industry in that state was hit with doubling and tripling insurance premiums. These threatened to put and did put many providers out of business. Legislation was and continues to be written that will better regulate rising premiums and shrinking coverage. However, the California bill enacted in 1984 to do just this set liability limits that were interpreted to be $300,000 per child. Insurers considered this excessive, and a chain reaction of debate and proposed legislation continues [52]. In my work with corporations, I have witnessed employers' concerns that they will be liable for injuries to children that occur in employer-referred and employer-sponsored child care programs. These controversial and costly issues of liability and insurance coverage are perhaps a convoluted expression of concern for children. Whatever their source, they will linger as long as child care is bought, sold, and sponsored in the American market.

TIME, MONEY, AND CARE AS COMMODITIES

The examination of the market sphere of care presented in this chapter began with the child care consumer. Let us now return to that consumer, because it is in the consumer of child care that we find all of the dynamics and trade-offs among time, money, and care. I have discussed briefly the problems and psychology of family management. Family management is difficult for working parents of preschool-age children and especially difficult for female parents. Employed married female parents spend an average of 40 hours each week on their employment or "work," 20 hours each week on home chores, and 25 hours each week on child care. Employed married male parents with employed wives spend an average of 44 hours each week on their employment, 11 hours each week on home chores, and 14 hours each week on child care [53]. Compare the totals: these women spend 85 hours a week on a combination of employment, home chores, and child care, while their husbands' total of the same is 69 hours each week. If, on the average, an individual has 16 waking hours seven days a week, or 112 waking hours a week, these working women have 27 hours left after these responsibilities, while their husbands have 43 hours left.

We have heard it said that time is money. Time is also health, rest,

FIGURE 3.2. Money cannot buy love?

exercise, and attention to one's children. There will always be trade-offs between work life and home life and between personal time and time with one's children. These are inevitable products of our modern world as well as of our traditional and biological heritages. Whether or not the disparity between the sexes in the level of trade-offs is inevitable remains to be answered. While we seek to balance time, money, and caring for children among the sexes and between families and outside organizations, we must also develop a deep appreciation of direct care, the type of care that is being increasingly delegated and traded away.

Chapter 4

THE PRIMARY SPHERE

Dimensions of Care

Rock-a-bye, baby, in the treetop,
When the wind blows, the cradle will rock;
When the bough breaks, the cradle will fall,
And down will come baby, cradle and all.

Rock-a-bye, baby, way up on high,
Never mind, baby, mother is nigh;
Up to the ceiling, down to the ground,
Rock-a-bye, baby, up hill and down.

—"Rock-a-Bye Baby,"
Old Lullaby

At the heart of all care is the direct act of caring, the "hands-on" "taking care of" a human being who benefits from that care. As a parent, I am deeply aware that much of the caring I provide my child is instinctual. I do not think about each and every caring gesture. I often do what seems to come naturally. Many times I surprise myself by responding out of instinct so quickly that I later wonder how I was able to do so. For example, when my daughter was five months old, a friend who had never been around children set her on the edge of a table. I did not see my friend do this. The baby rolled and was in the process of falling off of the table when I automatically turned and caught her. I was shocked. I had not consciously known that the baby was on the edge of the table or that she was falling. This type of intuitive, instinctual behavior is common among parents, especially new mothers. It appears that we have some deep resources available to us in taking care of our babies. If we make a conscious effort to attune ourselves to them, will they become more accessible?

Despite my faith in instinct, I find myself looking very closely at what I and others around me are doing with our children. In researching and writing this book about child care, I seemed to see the process of caring for a child in minute detail. Even the most subtle nuances did not escape my eye. I am grateful for the opportunity to bring so much detailed research to my own parenting process. I am also saddened to realize that most parents and their children do not have the benefit of the time to research that I have had. I see this when I watch parents attempting to determine which, if any, babysitters and child care programs they should select for their children. And I see this when I watch parents feeling overwhelmed by the process of combining their economic and practical responsibilities with their basic parenting responsibilities. Parents struggle to find time for love—for feeling—in a world of function.

All of these responsibilities are affecting the quality of care provided in the primary sphere, the most basic level of social organization in which children exist. The primary sphere is, or at least used to be, the family. However, as more children spend increasing portions of their waking hours in child care settings, these settings become substitutes for, or even extensions of, the primary family environment. It is in this transition that the pivotal tradeoff between functional care and feeling care is occurring. When we cross the line, placing many young children in long hours of group care, are we creating a generation of children who know function well and feeling less well? The answer to this critical question regarding the evolution of human care is unclear. However, the question is all important.

The family setting is regarded by many observers as the optimal environment for the development of children. Still, as several studies have shown, poor child care offered by some familial environments may result in "developmental impairment" [1]. And even when the child care within a family setting is adequate or more than adequate, an out-of-family setting can serve as a beneficial supplement. For example, many two- and three-year-olds benefit from the stimulation they receive in a part-time group setting.

The basic dimensions of caregiving are similar, regardless of the auspices under which child care is delivered. Families, proprietary child care programs, and public care providers serve similar "functions" as far as the individuals being served are concerned. However, most parents experience and express a more genuine long-term commitment and form a more concrete attachment to children than do professional or occupational caregivers. People who are paid to care for children, no matter how much they like their work, are more prone to forced, deliberate interactions rather than spontaneous ones. Children feel the difference [2].

Wherever they provide care, good caregivers are more than custodians. The function of a good caregiver is to encourage mastery or competence. Parenting is the model of caregiving upon which all other models of child care are based. As natural caregivers, parents naturally encourage their children to develop masteries in several dimensions in four basic ways by providing: (1) a *setting* in which this development can take place; (2) *protection* from conditions which hinder or block this development; (3) *nurturing* attention, creating a general atmosphere in which this development can occur; and (4) specific instruments and activities which directly promote the *development* of specific masteries. These four interrelated components are present in every dimension of direct care, whether that direct care occurs at home or in a group setting.

In this chapter, I have categorized the interrelated functions of caregivers into five dimensions of direct care: social, psychological, educational, physical, and environmental. I have also specified one dimension of indirect care, economic and administrative, which is in essence the requisite for direct care. Because the environment has a direct impact upon its inhabitants, the environmental dimension has been included among the dimensions of direct care [3].

THE SPECIAL ISSUE OF RATIO IN CARE

The ratio of caregivers to children affects the characteristics of direct care in group settings as well as in family settings. Two parents who have one child under six may differ in the way they organize and provide child care from a single parent with four children under six. Older children, relatives, grandparents, and friends, when they are present, can increase the ratio of caregivers to children, depending upon the level of their own needs for care. (Adolescents and grand-parents tend to fluctuate between dependence and independence, often offering inconsistent contributions to the ratio of independents to de-pendents.) Generally speaking, "old-fashioned" large families with older children, extended families, multigenerational families, and fam-ilies who live collectively have the human resources to share the re-sponsibility of caring for their dependents in such a way that the num-ber of caregivers is increased.

If it is true that responsiveness to individual needs is enhanced as the amount of one-to-one attention per dependent increases, then it is true that the more caregivers present, the better. A high ratio of regular caregivers to dependents strengthens the flow of energy into the caregiving enterprise. When these caregivers are not regular but are, instead, an ever-changing succession of people, the child or dependent in care experiences the lack of attachment experienced by institutional-ized children [4]. However, to understand the actual character of the care provided, one must go beyond the sheer strength of numbers and consider the qualitative dimensions of social, psychological, education-al, physical, and environmental care. We must ask not only how many caregivers are present but what is the quality of the care they provide.

The dimensions of care are highly interrelated. The social dimen-sion focuses upon the development of social competencies, such as getting along well in a group with other children. The psychological dimension encourages the development of a psychological balance and of what is termed "individuation," the process of identifying oneself as an individual with individual characteristics. The educational dimen-sion provides impetus for the attainment of cognitive competencies. The physical dimension builds physical competence, in the form of health, growth, and physical ability. The environmental dimension is discussed here in order to emphasize the view that a caregiver has an impact upon the development of a dependent's relationship to his or her environment, and that this is a direct and developmentally oriented form of care. This perspective will be further addressed in the discus-sion of environmental factors.

There is no broad consensus concerning all the elements necessary to constitute "high-quality" child care. Moreover, the same elements of quality care are viewed differently, depending on whether the caregiver is the child's parent or a paid child care worker. So many of the essentials of care are defined differently by those who provide and procure it. Some have argued that "good caring" enables children and other dependents to "function" at least minimally above their current level and that the provision of this good care is "moderated by benevolence" [5]. Moderation of efficiency by benevolence does not, however, guarantee the presence of the feeling, or affective qualities, of care. Benevolence, at times, is an insidious mask for the purely functional elements of organized care.

THE SPECIAL ISSUE OF GROWTH AND DEVELOPMENT

Because developmental changes are most dynamic, rapid, and crucial during childhood, considerable research on growth and development has focused on children under six, or "preschool-age" children. The units of time allotted in the conceptualization of particular developmental periods are shortest for the earliest years of life as in the following calendar of early childhood development [6]:

Infancy
    Newborn (birth through 28 days)
    Early infancy (1 through 6 months)
    Late infancy (7 through 12 months)

Toddlerhood (1 through 3 years)
    The "terrible two's" ($1\frac{1}{2}$ to $2\frac{1}{2}$ years)
    The "trusting three's" ($2\frac{1}{2}$ to $3\frac{1}{2}$ years)

Preschool (4 through 5 years)

The ability to predict landmarks of normal growth and development has limited utility in that every individual develops at his or her own rate. Any form of care, especially group care, that fails to take into account an individual's unique characteristics of development risks the omission of crucial responses to that individual's needs. Familial care, and care provided by friends and relatives, is less apt to overgeneralize from one child to the next, primarily because there are fewer children and the caregivers, especially the parents, have a greater stake in their development.

Overgeneralization, typical in formal care settings, can have detrimental effects upon children. For example, a physically handicapped child of "normal" intelligence may be hindered in his or her development of normal competencies by his or her own social or psychological problems, or even by environmental inadequacies, such as the lack of wheelchair access to a playroom or library. When behavior deemed "normal" for that child's age cannot be developed, alternative behaviors emerge, sometimes more precocious or more backward than expected. The danger is that essential steps in that child's development may go unrecognized or will be labeled as deviant, when the child is actually progressing normally for his or her special condition [7].

Moreover, the comparison of any individual's development, whether he or she is considered to be "handicapped" or not, to one normal curve can lead to a serious misdiagnosis of intellectual ability. For a mildly retarded child, or one who is not retarded but fails to test well because of physical disability, emotional problems, or bilingual difficulties, IQ tests can lead educators to the wrong conclusions [8]. Other problematic applications of the notion of normal growth and development stem from a limited understanding of its concepts. The principles of growth and development are built upon the concepts of *growth*, which refers to any change in physical size; of *maturation*, which refers to the natural capacity of any individual to progress over time; of *learning*, which refers to the process of acquiring new skills and knowledge; and of *development*, which refers to any increase in competency due to maturation or learning [9]. Growth and development are thus the product of at least these four processes, but these processes do not always occur together. Someone who is growing may not be learning. Someone who is growing old may be developing but will not be recognized as doing so because his or her physical changes are not interpreted as "growth." The effects of simple maturation or the passage of time may be interpreted as development when they are not.

It is evident that there is no single pattern of growth and development which we can use to compare all individuals to each other. Similarly, if the caregiver's purpose is to encourage the development of competence among dependents, no single pattern of care can be recommended for all caregivers and all dependents in all care settings.

Still, many of the fundamental issues of care can be applied across settings, ages, and ability levels. Although the following dimensions of care are described primarily in terms of child care, most of the components of care are transferable to any group of dependents, even though the end results or expected developmental effects of this care would not be the same for all care receivers. It is perhaps safest to say that most components of care should be provided to most dependents, but geared always toward individual needs. This form of attention to individual needs is characteristic of the informal, interpersonal nature of primary care. Indeed, the informal economy of primary care (in which there are always exchanges and trade-offs within and among the dimensions of care) is the "core" of all care, out of which the following dimensions have been conceptually drawn [10].

WHAT IS DIRECT CARE? [11]

We see that care has many levels of organization: philosophical, political, and economic, and that amidst all of these levels, the day-in and day-out details of human care manifest themselves. Let us now examine care with a close-up lens. This scrutiny is essential. Note that the following examination tends toward the functional. As you read, ask yourself what form these details of care might take in a parent-child setting, and whether they are present there at all.

SOCIAL DIMENSION

Care is a social activity, because it is something which is shared between people. At the same time, the social dimension of care both reflects and has an impact upon the psychological, cognitive, and physical development of its recipients as well as upon the characteristics of its environment. This is especially apparent in early childhood, usually the second year, when the emergence of a sense of self is reflected in an expansion of other types of awareness. The toddler adopts a new physical posture: he or she stands and moves vertically, exploring the immediate physical environment. Toddlers begin to share the physical spaces filled by adults and older children. They also become more aware of

FIGURE 4.1. The social dimension of care.

symbolic systems, discovering that every object has a word or label. In this early period of development a marked change occurs in the child's pattern of social response: he or she now begins to respond more to words than to nonverbal expressions [12]. Interactions with the people around him or her expand along with this vocabulary. Whatever the individual's stage of development, it is within the social setting that cognitive, physical, and environmental masteries are born.

Setting. The social characteristics of the persons (both the caregivers and the care receivers) who inhabit the care environment mesh to form the social setting. The demographics of this meshed population determine its relationship to the world outside of the care setting and prescribe many of the interactions occurring within the setting. In child care, age and sex are naturally distributed differently among caregivers and care receivers. In the home, much of the direct care provided for children comes from a female, usually the mother, and frequently it comes from siblings as well. Other social characteristics such as race and religion are usually more consistent across the caregiver–care-receiver division, especially in the home.

When caregivers are paid staff members, the demographics of the caregiving population (e.g., the racial composition and the age range of staff) are artificially determined by hiring policies, wages, and program goals. Few shared-care settings succeed in matching the racial and sexual ratios of dependents to staff. Yet there is a great deal of debate about the importance of role models for young children, and the notion that cultural and racial identity enhance the effectiveness of role models, especially for minority children, is a popular one [13].

This argument is joined by claims that continuity between home and the extrafamilial care setting is desirable. Many proponents of shared care agree that, especially for very young children, there should be a proximate confluence with the home environment. This position would advocate racial and cultural similarities between caregivers and children, as well as environmental similarities between care settings and children's homes. On the other hand, an argument against social identity and continuity suggests that the socialization of children may actually be encouraged by an interracial, multigenerational caregiving staff of both sexes. This is seen as preparation for future interactions within society as a whole.

From a more practical standpoint, the age range of staff may determine its responsiveness to a broad range of needs. While some of the demands of caregiving require the physical vigor of youth, such as lifting, carrying, and physical recreation, others require emotional maturity and experience, which usually increases with age.

The age range of care receivers is also a characteristic of the social setting. Children who are segregated by age may receive care more directly responsive to their developmental stages and more efficient in its responsiveness. However, a care setting which segregates children by age places them in a contrived environment and denies them the developmental stimuli afforded by other individuals who are older or younger [14]. Any estimate of the quality of a given social setting will reflect underlying theoretical positions regarding similarity of racial and sexual representation (as well as other social characteristics) among caregivers and care receivers, as well as the appropriateness of caregiver and care-receiver age ranges.

Protection. Just as it seeks to provide role models and continuity, the social setting is also the source of protection. In the home, social protection entails an atmosphere of cooperation, the maintenance of a reasonable tension level, and effective management of interpersonal problems. Without these controls, home life can become so unpredictable and uncomfortable as to stifle development or, in some instances, to encourage inappropriate social development [15].

Paralleling the family, most organizations and their members benefit from cooperation. Cooperation involves the maintenance of a reasonable tension level and the effective management of interpersonal differences. In child care organizations, the mechanisms of social protection are often explicitly formulated. Many of these settings institutionalize a process for airing complaints, settling disagreements, encouraging cooperation, and involving parents in the agency's affairs.

Nurturing. The act of nurturing contributes to the general atmosphere in which development can occur. In the home, social nurturing is related to the sympathetic involvement of family members in the socialization of dependents. This entails a continuous series of interactions between children and parents, as well as interactions between children and friends and community members, arranged and facilitated by parents. These interactions are the medium for the development of social competency. In a shared-care environment, caregivers assume much of the parental responsibility for social interactions of a nurturing quality. They also facilitate a dependent's successful transition to and from the settings of home and out-of-home care.

Development. In addition to the staff's characteristics and their efforts at nurturing and protection, there are a variety of activities that induce social development. These activities include unstructured group play and recreation, structured group play and recreation, the observation of rituals (ranging from meals to holidays), and the recognition of rules and behavior codes (such as a posted list).

The role of play in development was the subject of heated controversy during the 1960s [16]. Although the controversy has lost some of its sizzle, the argument remains unsolved. Does play serve an assimilative function in development, and what is the ontogenetic history of play from infancy to adulthood? As an assimilative function, play is a social activity which helps an individual integrate into the social network. It encourages individuals to develop toward group uniformity or consistency, socializing them. As an ontogenetic function, play is a personal activity which is associated more with individual needs than with those of a social group or society. Its influence upon individual development is one of differentiation rather than integration [17].

These forms of play need not be mutually exclusive. If play serves both a public and a personal purpose, developmentally oriented care will encourage both. Because individual differentiation is as much a part of acquiring a social identity as is socialization, play which addresses either of them is a social activity. A caregiver can encourage both lines of development by providing opportunities for both structured and unstructured play and recreation.

Ritual is a special type of structured activity which often incorporates recreation; however, it involves much more than play. Rituals include daily patterns such as meals and bedtimes, arrivals and departures, as well as special celebrations such as birthdays and holidays. The importance of ritual in development is twofold. First, it provides the individual with a sense of social patterns—meals occur regularly, naptime is at the same time each day; these are activities which people have in common. Second, rituals, when they are observations of special holidays, serve to familiarize the developing individual with his or her culture, encouraging identification and thus assimilation-socialization.

Rules and codes of behavior are explicit guidelines for the development of moral judgment. Accompanying these guidelines is the motivation for staying with them, for acquiring socially acceptable patterns of behavior. Motivation itself is usually a product of enforcement (negative sanctions in the form of disciplinary action), reinforcement (positive rewards in the form of approval, affection, and increased responsibility), and reasoning skill. It has been suggested that moral reasoning grows through a developmental sequence of moral judgment stages, the earliest of which respond to traditional authoritarian control and the more mature of which depend on an ability to comprehend the reasons behind the rules. In this sense, the "reasoning" parent is thought to help foster the cognitive skills and the perceptual abilities which are considered necessary for the attainment of a "mature" moral outlook [18]. The same can be said for the "reasoning" caregiver. Assuming that mature moral judgment is preferred to its preceding developmental stages, one of the criteria for the provision of developmentally oriented social care should be that caregivers encourage the expression of mature moral judgment rather than impose unexplained and arbitrary rules.

When a caregiver or parent encourages mature moral judgment over blind obedience to arbitrary rules, he or she demonstrates a philosophical preference for individuation over assimilation. The juxtaposition of these basic developmental processes, individuation and assimilation, encapsulates one of the major dilemmas presented by out-of-home child care. Critics of child care argue that pressure to assimilate is inherent in any form of group care. This may threaten the development of independent thinking and independent moral judgment. Moreover, given this tendency, early child care is viewed as a potential vehicle for various forms of sociopolitical indoctrination against which children have little defense. While this accusation is not empirically grounded in the United States, child care program designers elsewhere not only report the presence of early childhood indoctrination but claim that it benefits children and society [19].

In light of the above discussion, some of the basic criteria for evaluating the social dimension of care include:

1. The relative mix of demographic characteristics between caregivers and receivers.
2. The effectiveness of organizational mechanisms for resolving differences among day care staff and for hearing childrens' or their parents' complaints.
3. The degree of cooperation among caregivers.
4. The positive involvement of parents, family members, and extrafamilial caregivers in the caregiving process. (Shared-care settings may regard a high level of staff involvement as a replacement for familial-parental involvement in the caregiving process. Yet, unless the extrafamilial setting is a total

institution, as defined in Chapter 1, in which the family is purposively omitted from the social setting, it must recognize the importance of familial involvement in the caregiving process.)

5. The planned design of unstructured and structured play, recreation, and ritual.
6. The attention to discipline, limits, and rules.

PSYCHOLOGICAL DIMENSION

As the *public* person grows before us, displaying "abilities" and "behaviors" and "cognitive development" and "social competence," a *private* person grows up in a running counterpoint. [20]

Psychological development, if at all separable from its social and cognitive parallels, is the most elusive and immeasurable aspect of development. Especially during early childhood, when the individual is

FIGURE 4.2. The psychological dimension of care.

least capable of verbally expressing his or her inner life, psychological development is a virtually invisible process. As soon as its effects are manifest in social and intellectual behavior, psychological development merges with social and cognitive development.

Setting. Contrasted with an adequately peopled social setting, the psychological setting must provide adequate psychological space. In both familial and group care, a child needs quiet time in order to discover him- or herself. Advocates of early child care argue that its benefits include a healthy dose of social interaction for young children in an era of decreasing family size. Opponents of early child care claim that if a child does not get enough quiet time or space, his or her process of individuation is threatened by the socialization process. In other words, following the discussion of play in the social dimension of care, the assimilative function of play may supersede its ontogenetic function when the social group is ever-present and engulfs the individual.

The psychological dimension of care structurally accommodates developing individuals' psychological needs along with their social needs. Some child care settings attempt to exert control over their relatively contrived psychological settings by a preenrollment screening of their wards' psychological readiness for extrafamilial care. Frequently, this screening is an informal evaluation of the child's readiness to leave his or her familial environment. Can he or she adapt to group care without being a disruptive influence? Do his or her level of individuation and needs for quiet time correspond with those of the others in the program? Whether at home or in group care, the quality of psychological space is reflected in the amount of privacy provided. A good psychological setting arranges its schedule in such a way that its members feel that time is well organized, i.e., that there is enough time for them to individuate as well as to participate in social activities.

Protection. Psychological protection is an even more abstract quality to define. When caregivers are unresponsive to the individual temperaments of children, they threaten to negate the value of the psychological setting. Individuation and individual well-being may be obstructed or inhibited by insensitive, impersonal caregiving. Critics of institutional care settings which maintain a poor ratio of caregivers to care receivers speak to the importance of psychological protection. They argue that with too many children to supervise, caregivers are simply unable to maintain an adequate degree of personal involvement in their caregiving activities, many of which occur on a one-to-one basis. From this perspective, good psychological care is probably maximized where the ratio of caregivers to care receivers is highest, such as small, well-staffed group care settings and attentive parent care in family environments. Of course, there is always the possibility of too much protection; individuation and privacy may be hampered by over-attentive caregivers and smothering parents.

Nurturing. Much of the literature on development contains references to the physical environment as one which can stimulate security, exploration, autonomy, and individuation. The subject-object distinction, which is viewed as the core of individuation, is accomplished largely through physical acts in the environment. Sibylle Escalona describes the process as follows:

> The heightened sense of kinesis and body boundary that always goes with intense physical effort makes vivid and affirms the sense of "me"—the one who pushes, pulls and heaves—as distinct from "it"—the thing that is acted upon and that resists one's muscular exertion, an exertion which is indistinguishable from the awareness of desire and of goal. [21]

The physical environment has an effect upon care which is psychologically nurturing in that it is an "input," an element of care. However, because I have organized the elements of care in terms of their inputs rather than outputs or effects, the developmental inputs of the physical environment are dealt with as a separate dimension of care.

Still, the physical props of psychological nurturing demand some acknowledgment here. For example, in both familial and group care settings, children should feel that they have a place in which to keep their own possessions. Again, individuation is effected through identification with a particular corner of physical space. This is especially important in shared-care settings and is usually provided in the form of large boxes or open closets along a wall, each one labeled with a particular child's name. The reason that this element of care is included here is that psychological nurturing stems not from physical arrangements, but from the caregiver's insistence that each child respect the property and space of the other children, and that each child learn to identify that which is her or his own.

Development. Apart from its more tangible elements, the nurturing aspect of psychological care is built upon the relationship between caregiver and child. This goes beyond the quantitative issues of ratios to the qualitative requirement of at least one significant and developmental relationship that the child experiences as personal, reciprocal, affectionate, and consistent. One of the bases of individual development is feedback, which is an important part of any caregiving process. Planned opportunities for personal feedback from caregiver to care receiver are valuable elements in the psychological dimension of care. Other bases for individual development are the providing of security and the management of childhood fears in a positive manner [22].

In summary, the quality of developmental activities in the psychological dimension of care may be assessed in reference to:

1. Efforts to provide appropriate amounts of structured quiet time and privacy for the children.
2. Appropriate use of protective and developmentally oriented psychological screening and evaluation.
3. The caregivers' responsiveness to individual needs and their respect for individual temperaments.
4. Sufficient personal involvement on the part of caregivers in their caregiving activities, including an adequate amount of one-to-one, personal attention delivered with appropriate affection, warmth, and physical contact.
5. The extent to which caregivers effectively manage psychological upsets and traumas.
6. The degree to which transition times (such as arrivals and departures of caregivers and care receivers) are smoothly planned and executed.
7. The encouragement of development by carefully generated frustration levels.

EDUCATIONAL DIMENSION

Both individuation and socialization are processes which demand numerous cognitive and physical competencies. The development of specific competencies can be encouraged by purposive educational care. In contrast to custodial care, which is not developmentally oriented, educational care addresses the potential for cognitive development. This dimension of care is unique in its intentional stimulation of specific types of learning.

Setting. There is no ideal setting for the education of children; they will learn in any stimulating environment that generally feels safe. For an environment to be stimulating, it must offer a variety of challenges. One source of challenges comes from interactions with other children. The screening of children, based upon mental aptitude or educational achievement, both positively and negatively influences the level of stimulation in shared-care settings.

Protection. Protective elements in the educational dimension of care aim to encourage survival competencies. These competencies in-

FIGURE 4.3. The educational dimension of care.

volve decision-making and problem-solving skills, along with practical mental abilities, such as adding up a bill, reading a sign, operating an appliance or writing a letter. In shared-care settings, other forms of protection may include testing for learning disabilities such as dyslexia and hearing problems.

Nurturing. A nurturing educational environment is one in which verbal interaction, personal relationships, and mental and sensory stimulation encourage cognitive development. The importance of educational "care" for preschool children is an especially sensitive issue. In the preschool years, social, psychological, and physical developments are least tractable. While cognitive development is rapid in early childhood, it is viewed as being dependent upon or secondary to other levels of development. In fact, there is disagreement over the actual learning potential of young children and the worth of early learning experiences. On the one hand, academic education for very young children is considered overinvestment. Long-term gains in academic achievement do not appear great enough to justify investments in early childhood education which attempt to teach specific skills. On the other hand, any assistance in cognitive development may be viewed as valuable, especially to underprivileged children.

This controversy was exacerbated in the 1980s when psychologists Carl Bereiter and Siegfried Engelmann devised a nursery school curriculum geared to enhanced achievement in later school years. They attempted to demonstrate that children from disadvantaged homes could benefit from purposively developmental nursery school curricula which were designed to replicate the diverse stimulation of middle-class familial environments [23]. As in other similar research efforts, Bereiter and Engelmann were successful, but not entirely.

Development. Numerous criticisms have been voiced against an early childhood academic curriculum. This form of developmentally oriented education is often highly structured, with an emphasis placed upon achievement and measurable, "linear" progress at a time in a child's life when his or her development is naturally most "global." Moreover, because children at early stages of individuation and assimilation may not have internalized discipline, the enforcement and reinforcement applied in these educational programs is explicit and appears more behavioristic than its implicit parallels in the education of older children and adults.

In many ways, the debate over the impact of Head Start reflects this controversy. Disagreements regarding the utility of teaching aimed to enhance specific academic skills in young children were thrown into bold relief in the debates over the Head Start program. Based upon alternative definitions of the goals, different methods of analyzing the data, and various characteristics of the sites and populations selected for study, researchers have obtained a wide variety of findings. In general, participation in Head Start appears to have at least a temporary impact upon the cognitive development of young children, and a possibility of valuable long-term effects. But, what of these long-range effects? Studies conducted by Martin Deutsch, Herbert Sprigle, and Susan Grey showed a positive impact on school performance in the form of a significant IQ gain over the control group. David Weikart found a significant difference which "continued through three years of schooling" [24]. In contrast, the Westinghouse Learning Corporation report on its study of the national impact of Head Start found summer Head Start programs to be "ineffective in producing any persisting gains in cognitive or affective development that can be detected by tests used in grades 1, 2 and 3." Full-year Head Start Programs were found to be only "marginally effective in terms of producing noticeable gains in cognitive development" (detectable in Grades 1, 2 and 3) and entirely "ineffective in promoting detectable, durable gains in affective development" [25].

Other studies confirmed that site-specific local implementation of Head Start goals, the nature of post–Head Start primary school follow-through efforts, the socioeconomic statuses of the children's families, and even the type and longitude of outcome measures selected by researchers influence the subsequent perceived intellectual performance of Head Start children [26].

What do these various findings indicate about the educational dimension of care? One thing is clear: while educational activities do have some influence, other dimensions of care can encourage or obstruct cognitive development [27]. The elements of social, psychological, physical, and environmental care continually interact with educational care. As Gray concluded:

> An effective early intervention program for a preschool child, be it
> ever so good, cannot possibly be viewed as a form of inoculation
> whereby the child is immunized forever afterward to the effects of
> an inadequate home and a school inappropriate to his needs. [28]

It is possible to encourage cognitive development in both a familial and
a shared-care environment. Activities specifically geared to promoting
educational development emphasize the exploration of the environment, creativity, the development of practical skills which may be
essential in meeting future needs, and academic instruction. In summary, qualities of developmental care in the educational dimension can
be assessed in terms of:

1. The clarity of educational philosophy and program design.
2. The effects of any preenrollment screening for mental or education level, and the procuring of treatment for those identified
   as learning disabled individuals.
3. The degree of sensory and mental stimulation.
4. Relationships between caregivers and care receivers which
   help care receivers to learn.
5. The presence of opportunities for the child to explore, experiment, and act upon his or her environment.
6. The adequacy of academic instruction, opportunities for creative expression, and practical skills training.
7. The effects of other dimensions of care on academic instruction
   and learning in the care setting.

PHYSICAL DIMENSION

All psychological, social, and cognitive developments are facilitated or impaired by the physical condition of the individual. Especially
during early childhood, the stage of life when physical growth is most
accelerated, the elements of physical care are essential. Because environmental care (the provision of objects and spaces) will be treated
separately, this section deals only with the elements of care directly
related to physical growth and development.

FIGURE 4.4. The physical dimension of care.

Setting. In most instances, the family assumes primary responsibility for the physical care of its members. However concerned for the physical health and development of their dependents, shared-care providers usually view themselves as secondary sources of care in the physical dimension. When physical care beyond the scope of normal public health functions is provided, it is usually considered to be compensatory physical care, compensating for the inability of a family to provide it. Whatever its motivation, the provision of physical care in a shared-care setting is often simplified by obtaining uniformity (age, health, ability-disability levels) among participants. One way to ensure such uniformity is through screening child care applicants by health and general physical condition.

Protection. Protection against impediments to physical development necessitates an awareness of health requirements and efforts to detect disabilities and ailments. Physical protection also requires that caregivers be aware of the degree of contagion associated with a particular illness. As the number of children in out-of-home group child care grow, this becomes an increasingly critical issue. The likelihood of contagion among large groups of unrelated children who spend long hours together in relatively small spaces is exacerbated in crowded and understaffed settings. (Ratio and group size, two elements of the social dimension of care, are therefore clearly related to the physical dimension of care.) General upkeep, cleanliness, and sanitation are more difficult to sustain in overpopulated environments. Time-pressed caregivers may fail to separate infected children from the group and may skip procedures such as hand washing and regular diaper-changing. Among the diseases frequently transmitted in settings which care for young children are measles, mumps, and chicken pox (childhood diseases); respiratory syncytial virus, to which infants are especially susceptible (while RSV produces colds in adults, it may lead to the development of bronchitis and pneumonia in infants); infectious diarrhea; and hepatitis. Recent studies indicate that about half of the adult cases of hepatitis A (infectious hepatitis) which occur in the United States can be traced to outbreaks in child care centers. There is also growing concern regarding the spread of bacterial meningitis, which has a high fatality rate and can cause permanent neurological complications in survivors. Ninety-five percent of all cases occur in children under five. Day care centers with large populations and many drop-in attendees pose the greatest threat. And concern regarding AIDS contagion is also mounting [29].

Nurturing. All physical development is dependent upon nutritional intake. To satisfy the nutritional element of physical care, providers must not only understand the dietary requirements of young children and the developmental processes which depend upon nutrition but be certain children get enough to eat. Toddlers from one to three years old need between 900 and 1,800 calories daily. Children from four to six need between 1,300 and 2,300 calories daily [30].

Development. Physical development is often regarded as something which is visibly apparent through changes in the form of either bodily or motor developments. However, beneath the surface many internal developments are taking place. Changes in the brain and nervous system are important indicators of maturation. Myelinization, the process of coating or sheathing particular nerve fibers in a fatty substance called myelin, is incomplete in infancy. During early infancy and early childhood, myelinization proceeds most rapidly. According to many sources, some myelinization continues in certain parts of the brain until at least the age of thirty. Significant myelinization is also believed to occur between the ages of six and ten, when the corpus callosum (connecting the nerve fibers of the right and left hemispheres) is completed, as are the parietal and frontal areas of the cortex, the outer layer of the brain.

Neurologists suggest that the myelinization process, which occurs only in the higher regions of the brain, affects learning, the development of language and memory, and the control of impulses. Analytic and spatial abilities may be connected where the hemispheres of specialized regions of the brain are linked by myelinized nerves [31]. Where myelinization fails to occur, learning and physical disabilities may ensue. Other nervous system changes include the speeding up of brain waves and the changing of sleep patterns during childhood. Fine motor and hormonal developments also occur during infancy. All of these less visible physical developments accompany the development of gross motor skills (including walking and running) during childhood.

The physical dimension of care thus addresses subtle and complex forms of development. Consequently, the quality of developmentally oriented physical care is dependent upon many factors, including:

1. The general range of physical capabilities or disabilities of children in a child care setting.
2. Systematic efforts at early diagnosis and evaluation (detection and screening) of illness, physical development disabilities, and other health problems.
3. Adequate sick care for children when they are ill.
4. Adequate attention to cleanliness, hygiene, and health education.
5. Adequate supervision to safeguard against accidents.
6. The provision of balanced meals on the site and information to parents regarding nutrition.
7. The degree to which age-appropriate developmentally oriented physical education is included.

ENVIRONMENTAL DIMENSION

The environmental dimension encompasses the more tangible physical properties of the caregiving milieu, such as physical size, buildings, facilities, playgrounds, special areas, equipment, and toys [32]. As child psychiatrist Lois Murphy notes, "Environment contains space, time patterns, things, and people" and it offers such "important qualities [as] . . . attractiveness or unpleasantness, order or confusion . . ." [33]. Alone, the tangible elements of environment are inanimate.

FIGURE 4.5. The environmental dimension of care.

Only an interaction between the setting and its occupants creates a caregiving atmosphere.

Setting. An environment exerts influence over the activities which take place within it. This is the work of spatial forces, as they are called in the terminology of ekistics. All spatial forces are either directional or nondirectional. Directional forces attract or repel, by establishing either a positively or a negatively working focal point, surface, volume, or boundary. For example, the front of a classroom, a family dinner table, a large tree, or a playground fence attracts or constrains the physical activity of children. Nondirectional forces, including physical dimensions, proportions, and textures, are also determinants of behavior within physical spaces [34]. The physical spaces (or ekistic units) pertinent to this discussion are "minor shells or elementary units," including persons, rooms, houses, and buildings. The caring environment shares with all other ekistic units the fact that "human settlements consist of and require four dimensions (height, width, length and time) in order to be understood" [35].

Protection. Never enough concern can be directed at the safety of a child care environment. Toys, equipment, building designs, and nearby streets or parking lots all represent potential dangers to young children. The physical environment must be regulated for safety.

Nurturing. The nurturing elements in the environmental dimension of care involve the physical structuring of private spaces. These may include study corners and special places for each individual's possessions. And from an ekistic perspective, the environment will have special areas for which particular activities are designated, such as a dining area, a sleeping area, a work table, and a dressing room.

Development. What exactly is it about a physical environment that directly gives impetus to individual development? There are several examples of environmental characteristics which affect development. For example, experiments have demonstrated that the "blink response" (normally beginning early in infancy) develops an average of three weeks earlier in young infants who have been regularly provided with a stable visual pattern over their cribs to focus upon (for at least one-half hour a day) [36]. There are also numerous reports of the negative effects of environment, or of a deprived, unstimulating environment, upon development [37].

In summary, in assessing the environmental dimension of care, the following factors should be considered:

1. The condition of the surrounding neighborhood, its amenities and safety, the level of noise and pollution.
2. The square footage of indoor and outdoor areas.
3. The presence and condition of a kitchen, a toilet, bathing facilities, equipment, and supplies.
4. The organization of space in terms of its influence upon the group inhabiting it.
5. The safety of the grounds, accesses, and equipment.
6. The means of controlling indoor air quality, such as heating, cooling, and ventilation.
7. The aesthetics and comfort of the physical surroundings.
8. The extent to which physical surroundings provide an opportunity for privacy, a sense of order, and a stimulating experience.

PRIMARY CARE IN TRANSITION

The increased acceptability and efficiency of contraception have allowed more adults to make rational choices regarding parental investment, an investment of emotion, energy, time, and money in bearing and raising children. Nevertheless, a good many decisions to form families are made on the spur of the moment, without considering the relative costs and benefits. Parents' evaluations of their investments in care are thus frequently inexplicit, intuitive, and irrational. Unlike public investments in the provision of care, where program funding is often justified according to the political criterion of voter appeal, or marketplace exchanges, in which money is traded for child care services, parental caregiving is not offered in exchange for power or profits. The motives for parental provision of care are deeper and more complex, and in recent decades they have undergone subtle changes.

Until the turn of the century, physical survival was the dominant objective of childrearing. For most parents, the question was not one of how to rear a child, but whether or not the child would survive to be reared at all [38]. In England, during the mid-1700s, the mortality rate for children under five was close to 75%, declining to about 15% a century later, and to under 2.2% by the 1960s [39]. The trend was similar in the United States. This trend has been paralleled by significant decreases in maternal, infant, and fetal mortality [40]. However, even today, in most underdeveloped countries one in three or four children die before reaching the age of five. Infant mortality during the first year is five times higher and child mortality between the ages of one and four (after weaning) is forty times higher than in the United States [41]. When survival is at stake, the physical dimension of care dominates parental energies. Only when a child's survival is taken for granted does a parent have the liberty to focus attention on other aspects of childrearing.

There are other explanations for the nineteenth-century change in the perceptions of childhood. Historian Carl Degler argues that recorded shifts in child mortality do not correspond closely enough to the increased interest in childhood. He suggests that encompassing social changes in the family and in the status of women gave impetus to a redefinition of childhood [42]. Whatever the origins are of such a redefinition, childhood has come to be regarded as "prime time" in human development. It is in this phase that a human being's development can be most enhanced or curtailed [43]. It is in these early years that many modern parents see themselves as having the opportunity to produce and rear a "superbaby" into a "superkid," a person who will later excel in adulthood [44].

Yet, even this vision of the "superchild," reared for success in a culture characterized by competitive individualism, does not blind parents to the almost mythical innocence of their children. Children's complete dependence and naivete evoke sympathy and affection from onlookers. Their energy, purity, and sheer youthful vibrancy are qualities which are rare in our contemporary world. And just the speed with which a child changes holds many a parent riveted upon its monthly, daily, and even hourly development. The parental investment in care is one which accrues short-term existential, as well as long-term, rewards. The value of these rewards is being challenged by modern egalitarian views of family life.

Nowadays, we hear women say, "I'm *just* a housewife," or "I'm *just* a mother." The egalitarian ideology of family organization contends that much of the maternal energy invested within the family can be transferred to extrafamilial work. With a reduction of maternal activities, women can increase their psychic investment in extrafamilial work, in labor force participation. Add to this a reciprocal increase in paternal investment, and women can finally advance toward sexual parity. Reorganization of the family then reorganizes society. This ideology also advocates an overall reduction in parental investment, to be replaced with a greater social investment in childrearing. For it is only with the social provision of supplemental institutional care that men and women can invest equally in family and work.

This modern egalitarian view of the family overlooks the central biological fact that the care function of any family system is human continuity through reproduction and childrearing. As a biosocial perspective on parenting would argue, the inherent conflict between the demands imposed upon us by a complex technological society and the physiological equipment we have inherited from our "long mammalian past" is aggravated as we progress far beyond our survival-oriented family and kinship systems. The "parenting script" composed of "social rules and norms governing the birth and rearing of children" is being rewritten [45]. Responsibility for care is being redirected, the dimensions of familial care are being reconceptualized, and the meaning of care is being redefined. But do the basic parenting instincts change? Mothers are still instinctually engaged in *en face* contact (full, direct eye contact) with their infants. The sound of her infant's cry still triggers physiological reactions (such as the secretion of oxytocin) in the mother [46]. Despite their changing social status and their increased participation in the labor market, women continue to conceive and bear children, and because their biological role has remained constant, they are differentiated from men socially and by their children. From a purely physiological standpoint, sex differences continue to influence parental investment in care.

As discussed in Chapter 3, a parental investment in child care can assume several forms. Emotions, hours, and dollars are all allocated to the provision of care in every dimension. In recent years the range of investments has come to include the increased purchase of substitutes for parental care.

As the family has been socialized and many of its duties and decisions have been relinquished to extrafamilial bodies, parental wisdom regarding what is best for one's child is also bowing to the evaluative perspective of professionals. But on the issues of child care, professionals often disagree. In trying to assess the value and quality of substitute care, parents are caught in the crossfire between child care advocates and opponents. Should parents relinquish direct and intensive care which can be provided in the home to an institutional experience which may be counterdevelopmental or, at least, less than optimal for a young child? Should parents keep their children at home, causing them to miss out on the heightened developmental (especially social and cognitive) stimulation which may enable them to succeed decades later in their adulthood [47]? On these questions the jury is still out, and it may remain so for at least another generation. Yet then, as now, it is true that:

> the burden of proof rests on all proposals to deprive children of the intensive interaction with their mothers that, for good reason, has been the norm throughout history. [48]

In the meantime, however, many parents have either been persuaded by child care advocates or driven, out of economic necessity, to place their children in child care settings. Function is triumphing over feeling in the realm of child care. Numerous child care arrangements have evolved in recent years under several auspices outside that of the natural family. These various arrangements serve different population groups and perform a range of child care services. Together, these arrangements constitute a mixed economy of child care. This is an economic system that provokes new trade-offs and generates new conflicts over very important but mostly functional issues of purpose and social change. Somehow, the emerging conflicts seem dangerously unconcerned with the march of child care into the realm of the purely functional. Let us now look closely at the specific characteristics of six child care programs and the revealing perceptions of the parents who use them in our mixed economy of care as I detail them in Chapters 5, 6, and 7.

Chapter 5

ORGANIZATIONAL VARIATIONS AMONG DAY CARE PROGRAMS

Six Programs in California

> *Hush, your mother's gone to the marketplace,*
> *Hush, mama will soon be back.*
>
> *Long may you live for I wish it to be true,*
> *Mama's gone to provide for you.*
>
> —"Babysitter's Song"
> Yiddish Folksong

Child care is an organized extension of babysitting. A babysitter comes into the home and cares for one or more children while the parents are out. A child care worker goes to a child care center or opens the doors of her own home, where parents drop off their children for some or all of the day. As the demand for child care services has grown, the variation among these services has grown as well. Organized babysitting is now serving parents from all socioeconomic brackets and all walks of life. Many parents now expect more out of child care than just babysitting; they expect that their children will receive educational experience and developmental stimulation.

What parents want and what they get from child care programs vary tremendously, largely because the mixed economy of day care in the United States utilizes services delivered under a variety of financial and administrative arrangements. To capture the character of these diverse arrangements we must leave the realm of theory and carefully analyze specific cases. I selected six day care sites in California, each operating under a different auspice, for this kind of analysis. This chapter examines the varied organizational and fiscal characteristics of these sites.

The information in this chapter is organized in such a way that readers interested in specific details about programs can locate them under specific subheadings.

Each site is discussed in terms of its (1) history and current issues; (2) program components and licensing; and (3) costs, credentials, and ratios. This information was obtained through interviews with program directors and staff, reviews of program documents and budget statements, and lengthy observations of administrative and organizational behaviors.

In this chapter I consider each of the six sites separately and then summarize selected characteristics of these day care programs. Table 5.1 provides an overview of the variations in the day care sponsors, providers, and consumers by auspices for the six sites studied. For dollar fiscal years see Table 5.2.

SITE 1: A STATE-SUBSIDIZED SCHOOL DISTRICT PROGRAM FOR LOW-INCOME FAMILIES

This day care service is provided by a public school district under contract with the state department of education. It is subsidized entirely by state and federal funds through the statewide child development program. This is one of six local programs (the others are not included in this study) where the county office of education offers a child development service under the aforementioned contract. Altogether, the county serves a total of 250 children between the ages of 2.5 and 14. Eighty percent of these children are between the ages of 2.5 and 5. All children served are from low-income families, and over three-quarters are from single-parent families.

This center is in an older urban residential area. It operates out of a building which used to house an elementary school program. Two separate day care providers share this now otherwise vacant school building. The other provider, not under state contract, is Site 2 in this study.

HISTORY AND CURRENT ISSUES

The history of this program can be traced back to the mid-1960s, just prior to the appearance of the Head Start programs. At that time, there was a city-run day care program, left over from the Lanham Act era, which was poorly funded and haphazardly administered. The teachers in this struggling program banded together and went over the city fathers' heads to the county board of supervisors to request financial support and sponsorship. Their request was denied. However, the county superintendent of schools overrode this decision. To this day, the lingering conflict over this decision continues to influence intergovernmental relations within the county. While the county agreed to support the program, it has not borne the entire cost of its development. Federal and state funds eventually became available and encouraged the growth of county-sponsored child care for low-income families.

The program now housed at Site 1 started in a church building, which it rented in 1967. After expanding and moving twice, in 1979 federal and state cutbacks in social services caused this program to be combined with another state-subsidized program and to be moved into the school building in which it is now located.

In July 1982, there was a severe reduction in force at all state-subsidized child development programs in the county. At this site, one full-time, fully credentialed teacher was lost; three instead of four teachers were left, without a reduction in the number of children served. As a result, the curriculum and program goals of this day care service shifted, moving away from compensatory and developmental functions and toward less expensive custodial care.

PROGRAM COMPONENTS AND LICENSING

In this county, child development programs which are operated by the County Office of Education fall into two categories: full-year children's centers and state comprehensive preschool education programs.

TABLE 5.1
CHARACTERISTICS OF DAY CARE PROGRAMS: SPONSORS, PROVIDERS, CONSUMERS, AND ELIGIBILITY OF CARE RECIPIENTS

Characteristic	Site 1	Site 2	Site 3	Site 4	Site 5	Site 6
Auspice	Public (state-subsidized)	Public (municipal)	Quasi public (military)	Quasi private (employer sponsored)	Private non-profit (preschool)	Proprietary (family day care)
Public support (direct)	State subsidized	Building rental only subsidized by city	Entire program Navy subsidized	No	No	Meals only subsidized by state
Public support (indirect)	—	—	—	Tax incentives for sponsoring employer	Tax breaks for non-profit organizations	None reported by proprietor[a]

Sponsor	State dept. of education	City dept. of recreation	Navy dept. of recreation	Employer	Self-sponsoring	Self-sponsoring
Provider	County school district	City employees	On-base Navy office of recreation	A contracted for-profit provider	Self-providing	Self-providing
Consumers pay full cost	No	Yes	No	No	Yes	Yes
Eligibility of care recipients is restricted to:	Low-income families	City residents who can pay fees	Navy enlistees' and Navy employees' families	Employees' families	Families who can pay and who meet behavioral requirements	Families who can pay

[a]Proprietor has not paid taxes on his or her income and has taken no tax deductions or credits.

Five full-year children's centers serve 200 children between the ages of 2.5 and 14 years for 250 days a year, up to 10.5 hours a day. According to the county department of education:

> The full-year Children's Centers often provide the bridge for a single parent head of household to quit receiving public assistance and be able to become self-supporting, as they can enter the labor market while their child is receiving full-year quality care. [1]

In the second category, state comprehensive preschool education programs, funded through the state department of education, "provide a preschool program to compensate for early deprivation" [2]. The comprehensive preschool programs serve a total of 40 children, ages three through five, during the school year. Both of the county child development programs emphasize prevention and provide social services, parental involvement in activities, education, health care, nutrition, and, in general, an environment in which day care can be provided [3].

At Site 1, both of the above-described child development programs are offered. These programs cannot be distinguished by an outside observer, except in the afternoon, when the state-subsidized preschool program is not in session. Sixty-two children are served at this site. Some spend half the day in preschool and half the day in center care. A few spend all day in center care. Older children spend their after-school hours in center care (a number of these are school-age special education children). Although these programs are officially described as being separate, the children are not segregated by age or the number of hours they are cared for. All children receive a hot breakfast, a mid-morning snack, and a lunch and afternoon snack if they are present at the time the meals are served.

Two out of the ten caregiving staff are credentialed teachers. Of the remaining eight, four have had some college coursework in child development, and two are parents of children who are now or were recently enrolled in the program.

COST, CREDENTIALS, AND RATIOS

The program is expected to meet state guidelines for a 1 : 8 adult-child ratio, which is usually accomplished by combining teachers and aides. However, since 1982 cutbacks, at certain times of the day, the center does not comply with the guideline of one credentialed teacher to twenty-four children, substituting aides for teachers. Moreover, numerous periods of time were observed when the number of adults present (teaching credentials or no credentials) dropped far below the mandated ratio. At times the actual ratio went as low as 1 : 18 [4].

SITE 2: A CITY-SPONSORED, SELF-SUPPORTING PROGRAM FOR RESIDENTS

Although this program is located in the same physical setting as that of Site 1, it has a different sponsor. This sponsor is a municipal public agency, the City Department of Recreation, rather than the County Office of Education. Unlike that at Site 1, the program at Site 2 has no contract with the state or any form of state subsidization. In fact, the only public funding or subsidy comes from the city, which does very little, other than discount the rent of the otherwise vacant school building and provide some administrative and accounting services. The program is open to any family who can afford to pay for the service. The income from parent payments constitutes the program's sole source of revenue.

HISTORY AND CURRENT ISSUES

This program began in 1963, when the city department of recreation founded the Tiny Tot program, operating initially from 9 to 11 A.M. and 12:30 to 2:30 P.M. Given these operating hours, the program generally was not viewed as an employment-related service. Most participants enrolled their children in only one of the two-hour sessions and remained during the sessions or returned within two hours.

During its first ten years, the age range of the children served and the operating hours of the program expanded very little. In 1976, however, child care was added to the Tiny Tot program, along with after-school care for elementary-school-age children. The director of the program explains that this transition was initiated when parents began removing their children from the part-day program, in favor of other child care programs with expanded hours. In fact, when the director looked at parent's options within the city limits and found few places to leave a child during a working day, she went to the city recreation department and requested that it extend the hours and age range of the existing program to meet parental needs.

This programmatic transition marked a sharp departure from the original recreational intent of the two-hour Tiny Tot program toward a full-day care program designed to meet parental need for a "good place" to "leave" their children. Today, there is a sizable waiting list. Despite its expanded functions, this day care program has remained under the jurisdiction of the city recreation department. The city reluctantly continues to oversee the program, but not without balking. The city fathers are still "wondering what the city is doing in the day care business."

While the city may be a reluctant sponsor, the program is not funded by the city, except on paper. Instead, it is "self-supporting." Its revenue covers the cost of all but one salary, purchasing all supplies and determining, to some degree, the rate at which the program expands. The city, however, exerts a degree of formal control and retains the final say in the development of new program components. Thus, while the director would like to begin a new infant care component, the city has yet to be convinced that it will be self-supporting.

The relationship between the municipal (city) sponsor and the nonprofit organization which delivers day care at Site 2 has only begun to be formalized. Previously, there was no legal contract between the city and the providing organization. The director of this program has been on the city payroll for years, but she collects none of the employee benefits or scheduled increases in pay given to other city employees. Nor do any of her staff. The only exception to this situation is the case of one employee of the city recreation department who directs the after-school program component and is paid twice as much ($25,000 a year) as the director of the preschool-age program. The disparity between the recreation department pay scale and that scale designed by the city for day care workers recently led the non-recreation-department director and her staff to affiliate with a union. This resulted in a sudden 3.5% pay increase.

But the child care educators and workers continue to earn less than either the city recreation workers or the elementary school teachers in the local public schools. At this child care site, a head teacher's beginning pay is $5.74 an hour. An assistant teacher earns $4.15 an hour and a child care aide earns $3.74 an hour. As stated earlier, these notably low wages are not buttressed by a benefit package comparable to that enjoyed by other city employees.

PROGRAM COMPONENTS AND LICENSING

The city day care program is now in operation at five locations. The largest of these is Site 2. Its program components are toddler care (one program for ten children, 1.5 to 3 years of age), preschool classes (one program for forty 3-year-olds and another for forty 4-year-olds), all-day care for all of these children, and after-school care (for ninety 5- to 10-year-olds). These school-age children are eligible for school bus transportation between school and day care settings. During the summer months, an on- and off-site day camp is added to the roster of program activities.

Because the program operates under the city's auspices, the city assumes responsibility for meeting state and local health and fire department requirements, rather than leaving this to the nonprofit agency which delivers the day care service. The city also provides accident insurance, relieving the nonprofit provider of another administrative cost.

Every year, when the budget is established, the city conducts an evaluation of the program and its staff's performance. According to the director, there is little interest on the part of city evaluators in how the parents view the program or how well the children are actually being served. This apparent disregard for the parents (the day care consumers) and the children (the day care recipients) may reflect the fact that the program remains under the control of the recreation department rather than the office of education.

In this city environment, child care is viewed as "merely babysitting." It may also reflect the fiscal and organizational limbo in which this program is suspended. The program provides the city with no revenues, and yet it pays for itself. It is not a profit-making institution, and although it is affiliated with the city in the consumer's eye, in reality it is almost an independent body. Understandably, the program makes its number one goal that of achieving a balanced budget.

COST, CREDENTIALS, AND RATIOS

At Site 2, the annual budget for preschool-age care and school-age care combined is $251,571, serving an average daily attendance of 115. The average annual cost to the provider per child is therefore $2,188. As noted earlier, the enrollment fees are paid entirely by the parents, at an average of $46 a week. These program fees are geared toward the low middle-income family budget.

For their fees, which are considered comparable to those of other programs in the area, parents purchase a child care service that offers an average ratio of one caregiver for every six children. Three of the caregivers have teaching credentials, two in elementary and secondary education and the third in early childhood education. Three other caregivers have earned "regular children center instruction permits." All of the staff are provided opportunities for on-the-job training, although much of it is informal.

SITE 3: A MILITARY BASE PROGRAM FOR ENLISTEES

This day care program is located on a naval base. It serves children of enlistees and employees of the Navy and is now controlled and funded by the Navy department of recreational service. The director is a civilian hired by Navy recreational services. She considers this child care program to be an employer-sponsored child care program. However, she points out that enlistees do not view themselves as employees. "Employee" implies civilian status. In the eye of the enlistees, the Navy is not their employer and its services are not "employer-sponsored." The Navy itself categorizes child care as one of its several "family services" [5].

HISTORY AND CURRENT ISSUES

This child care program evolved from one which has been sponsored by an on-base retailer since the early 1960s. The program was first devised to serve parents of young children while they were shopping. As Navy families' needs for child care increased during the

1970s, the sponsorship of Navy child care shifted from that of the base's retail store to the Navy department of recreation in early 1979.

In its early years, Navy child care had acquired the poor reputation of being a low-cost, low-quality, and sometimes even undesirable service. That this stigma lingers today is evident in the reportedly negative attitudes of "officers and their wives" toward the program. And it is manifested in the low proportion of officers' children to enlisted men's and women's children in the program. In recent years, naval child care service has undergone considerable change and now advertises itself as offering "top quality developmental care" at prices "one-third to one-half lower than in the civilian community." On-base child care is convenient for a middle-income naval family because of its proximity to both their place of employment and their residence. Navy families share with civilian families two major problems: managing the family budget and locating child care in the community. For these parents, cut-rate, on-base child care speaks to the cost, access, and quality dilemmas confronting families everywhere.

PROGRAM COMPONENTS AND LICENSING

This child care program offers all-day care to children between the ages of six months and five years, after-school care for children enrolled in kindergarten through third grade, and daytime and evening drop-in care for infants and children. The total number of children served is 265. At any one time, there is an average of 7 babies at the drop-in center and 20 in infant day care.

Unlike other public child care programs, fire and sanitation licensing is done by the Navy. No outside city, state, or federal public agency has jurisdiction. The premises are inspected monthly, which is more frequently than in many nonmilitary day care centers.

As with fire and sanitation, the Navy determines its own day care standards and goals. The primary "mission" is "to improve the quality of Navy family life by providing quality child care." A commissioned officer evaluates the program regularly. Child care staff performance is evaluated biennially by the personnel department of recreational services.

Despite the military-style evaluative structure, the civilian program director reports that she has "a lot of latitude" because she is the "only expert in child care and child development" on the base and because there are, to date, few centrally mandated program specifications. This may be because family-oriented and developmental child care in the Navy is a relatively recent phenomenon. The director pointed out that by contrast the Air Force is "further along toward the elaboration of program characteristics."

The director has established her own in-house program guidelines and staff evaluations. However, she states that her views do not always coincide with the Navy's philosophy or style of organizational management. For example, in hiring staff she emphasizes the qualities of personal initiative and involvement, rather than strict adherence to hierarchical status and rules. She expects staff to create an atmosphere which permits the "management of children with few negative sanctions," and which is a less authoritarian stance than that of the surrounding military environment. On the other hand, the director is quick to point out that she does not operate a "normal liberal open classroom" which "breeds behavior problems," especially among children with family backgrounds "common to those of enlistees."

COST, CREDENTIALS, AND RATIOS

The director has worked toward building a developmentally oriented program. She has encouraged recreational services to hire a developmentally oriented rather than custodial staff whenever possible. There is one caregiver with at least twelve college credits in early childhood education in every room. The Navy does not, as yet, specify education and licensing requirements for child care staff. It also has not specified group size but has instituted ratio requirements [6]. The director points out that in large groups such as those at her child care center, density can affect the quality of care even more than the staff-child ratio. For example, she explains that a ratio of one adult to five infants may be manageable, but four adults with twenty infants would be chaotic. The ratios now specified by the Navy are not ideal and their shortcomings are magnified by the large group sizes at this site. The adult-child ratio for infants is 1 : 5, with an average group size of 20. For toddlers (twelve to eighteen months), it is 1 : 8; group size, 34. For two- to three-year-olds, it is 1 : 8; group size, 33. For three- to four-year-olds, it is 1 : 12; group size, 36. And for four- to five-year-olds, it is 1 : 15; group size, 45.

SITE 4: AN EMPLOYER-SPONSORED PROGRAM FOR HOSPITAL EMPLOYEES

The child care program at Site 4 is sponsored by an employer, who has contracted with a for-profit child care provider. The employer is an 850-bed hospital with a staff of 3,000. The child care setting is located on the hospital grounds.

HISTORY AND CURRENT ISSUES

The Site 4 child care center was opened in 1981, as part of the hospital's effort to attract nurses during a nursing shortage and to fight job turnover and absenteeism. The program is operated by a child-care-providing subsidiary of a large corporation, which produces baby food and related products. The subsidiary was organized in 1970, placing its first center in the Midwest. It now operates fifty-six centers in several states, serving thousands of children with a staff of almost 1,000. Five of these centers are employer-sponsored. Site 4 is one of these [7].

The program director and the managerial representative of the providing corporation describe the program's philosophy as one which "emphasizes childhood" and "the consistency of caring." When asked about interests in early childhood education, the director explained that she believes in providing a close approximation of the familial environment rather than a structured, high-pressured educational milieu. Regarding the importance of early childhood education, she stated that "the job of preschool is to give firsthand experiences to children." These should be "successful experiences" because "if children like preschool, they will like school." However, only the "appropriate skills" and experiences should be provided, such as touching, tasting, smelling, playing games, and some exposure to the alphabet, so as not to "cheat the children out of childhood experiences." The director hopes to educate the parents of the children she serves about the meaning of care. Ultimately, she says, the program's priority is "to meet children's basic needs."

The corporate manager noted that parents had voiced some dissatisfaction with the educational dimension of the program at this site, but he viewed these complaints as uninformed criticism, typical of the site's clientele. For example, in a previous study, when parents were asked whether or not they were satisfied with the program's hours, the majority expressed dissatisfaction. This was a curious criticism, since the program at this site was then, as it is now, open twenty-four hours a day, seven days a week. For the provider, who views herself as working for her employer rather than the parents, this is one more example of the unsoundness of parents' judgment as consumers of child care.

PROGRAM COMPONENTS AND LICENSING

This program is licensed to accommodate seventy-six children (all age groups combined) during the day and more than that during sleeping hours. Formal program components include care for toddlers, young 2-year-olds, 2.5- to 3-year-olds, 3.5- to 4-year-olds, and 4.5- to 5-year-olds. Although children are generally segregated by age, the informal rationale for group assignments is based upon behavioral rather than chronological criteria. For example, children are grouped according to their stage in the process of toilet training, their degree of mobility (crawling, walking), and their readiness to adapt to a group setting. Occasionally parents enroll a physically handicapped child, who may be unable to walk or who may wear diapers. This child, regardless of age, may be grouped with younger children who are not toilet-trained. This was recently the case when a five-year-old girl with spina bifida (paralyzed from the waist down) was placed in the toddler's program, where the staff-child ratio is 1 : 4, as opposed to the 1 : 12 ratio for five-year-olds.

Some school-age children are enrolled in the evening and all-night-care programs, but there are not specific program components designed for children over five. The oldest child in all-night care is eleven years old. Because night care is primarily custodial, involving merely the supervising of sleeping children, the age range can be expanded beyond that of daytime care, and staff-child ratios can be relaxed.

The regulation of night care is an issue on the horizon of child care licensing. Currently, children who nap in day care centers are usually provided with foam pads or cots. However, as the business of nighttime child care expands, concerns about the care of sleeping children are likely to emerge around standards for size of sleeping rooms, ventilation, and bedding equipment.

COST, CREDENTIALS, AND RATIOS

Parents have the option of enrolling their children and paying their tuition by the hour, the day, or the week. The average full-time (forty hours per week) cost of child care per child is $80 a week for infants and toddlers and $50 a week for preschool and "extended" day care. Parents receive a 20% discount for the second child they enroll in the program. Parents pay 100% of the $80 fee for daytime care. The employer pays 50% of the fee for evening care and 100% of the cost of all-night care.

Even when parents pay the full tuition, they are receiving what the contracted provider and employer describe as quality child care in the workplace at about $2 an hour, which is less than the going market rate for comparable care in that geographical area. The building, utility bills, and maintenance costs are covered by the employer, who is thus both sponsoring and subsidizing this child care program. The program is open only to employees of the sponsoring employer. Even though it appears to be an employee benefit, this service is not formally labeled as such. The employer takes no deduction from participating employees' paychecks or from their other benefits. Employees who do not utilize the workplace child care program do not receive substitute benefits or larger paychecks than employees who do use the program. The employer does not consider its workplace child care program an employee benefit, because it is not an "ongoing" or permanent benefit; employees use the service only as long as their children are young.

The total annual budget for the child care program offered at this site is $390,420. Of this total, $193,050, or almost 50%, is allocated to teachers' and caregivers' salaries, and $57,381 (approximately 15%)

covers administrative costs. Employer and employee payments provide for all of these costs as well as an additional sum which allows the provider to operate at a profit.

The budget of $390,420 is expected to serve an average of 135 preschool children a week, with the staff-child ratios being 1 : 4, with a group size of 12 for infants; 1 : 4 with a group size of 16 for toddlers; and 1 : 12 with a group size of 12 for 2.5- to 5-year-olds.

If one divides the overall budget by the average attendance, the average per capita budget is approximately $2,892 a year, or $55.62 a week. Parents pay $80 a week. At this price, children who are not yet toilet-trained enjoy a relatively good staff-child ratio of 1 :4 . However, few of the staff are trained professionals, though several of the pre-school teachers are working toward their early childhood education credentials. In fact, many of the staff have been recruited among the students in the child development program at the local university.

SITE 5: A PRIVATE, NONPROFIT PRESCHOOL FOR FAMILIES WHO CAN PAY AND WHO MEET "BEHAVIORAL" REQUIREMENTS

This program is located in a small, quiet community just ten minutes outside of a large city. The neighborhood is primarily popu-lated by middle- and lower-middle-income black families who reside in apartment buildings. However, the majority of students enrolled in the program are white. The program director and founder reports that the school is a self-supporting, nonprofit operation. The program has never received outside support but currently considers applying for grant money. The criteria for admission to the program are that a parent can pay the tuition (or, in some cases, is willing to provide a service in exchange for a reduction in fees), that a child is able to fit into the program's special learning environment, and that the parents are in agreement with the program's philosophy. A recently added stipulation is that the program will admit no child whose parents spank him or her. The director would like to add a dietary requirement of no sugar at home to the admission criteria. Such considerations are unusual "be-havioral" requirements for admission into a day care or preschool pro-gram.

HISTORY AND CURRENT ISSUES

This program was founded in 1972 in another location as a Montessori School. In 1977 the program moved to its current site and dropped Montessori from its name. The program offers a strong educational base, which has expanded upon the Montessori method by incorporating a version of the Doman early reading and math methods, an amended version of the Suzuki method of teaching music, and computer and other innovative activities. For all of its children, the program aims to stimulate development, especially of cognitive and related abilities, and to prepare students for the competitive school years ahead of them.

PROGRAM COMPONENTS AND LICENSING

Children from the age of fourteen months to six years old are enrolled in this preschool (the program is licensed to accept children from birth). Although day care is available, it is generally offered in conjunction with the preschool program, in the hours before and after "school" (from 7 to 9 A.M. and from 2 to 6:15 P.M.). Parents have the option of enrolling their children in full-time (9 A.M. to 2 P.M.) preschool or part-time preschool (9 A.M. to 12 noon) three or five days a week. For these parents, drop-in and other day care is available at the site.

As noted above, the program is licensed to enroll children from birth through age six. The director hopes to incorporate infants into the program on the basis of the theory that the educational process will be most effective for children who have been enrolled longest, preferably since their birth.

Like most day care and school programs, this one must be licensed by the board of health and the fire department and must meet the guidelines set forth by the California Health and Safety Code.

COST, CREDENTIALS, AND RATIOS

The director of this program does not keep a formal budget. Several times, the program has operated in the red for months, and on at least one occasion, the director had to take out a personal bank loan to pay the staff. The director reports that she spends a lot of her own income on this program, that it is a "labor of love" for her. Nonprofit status has not made a marked difference in fiscal matters. The director applied for this status in order to rent a building from a church in the early years of the program. Despite budgetary constraints and ambiguities, the average staff-child ratio is consistent with the program's philosophy of providing an enriched environment. There is at least one adult, who has been specially trained to administer the preschool's educational program, to every six children at all times.

SITE 6: A FAMILY DAY CARE PROGRAM

This family day care program is owned and operated by a woman in her early twenties. The program is based in a small, old home, owned by the director's mother and located in a low-income residential neighborhood. During one of my interviews with the director, a man came to the front door, which had been left wide open. He attempted to sell a handful of rings which he wanted to "get rid of right away." When the director informed him that she was not buying, he proceeded to ramble on about children and asked whether she took care of children and what her family day care sign (posted outside the house) meant. Finally, she said goodbye and closed and locked the door. Returning to her seat, she said, "That was a weirdo selling rings. There're so many weirdos around here. But I wasn't worried, because if he tried to do anything to me I'd of screamed and my mama's upstairs and she'd a given him hell."

HISTORY AND CURRENT ISSUES

The twenty-one-year-old director and sole employee of this family day care program began working in day care at the age of fourteen. After high school she went to work at a bank, but in her words, "I had to quit my job, didn't want to go to school, and so got back into day care." That was one year ago, at which time she went to the county welfare office and was directed to meet with a child care caseworker. This caseworker helped her fill out the necessary forms and had them sent to the state licensing office in Sacramento. Within two weeks, the application was approved, and the director was informed that she could begin her family day care business, because she had been officially licensed.

The family living in the house (the director's mother and brother), as well as the director, were required to have fingerprints and TB tests taken. The caseworker also instructed her to register with the city children's services office in order to receive the state child care food subsidy. Although a children's services representative visited this day care site to certify that it had a suitable kitchen, there was no visit from the state day care funding and licensing authorities. The caseworker explained to the director that only 10% of all family day care homes were visited by licensing authorities, but that she should always be ready for an inspection. After one-and-a-half years in operation, licensing authorities had not visited this site.

The director also noted that, to the best of her knowledge, none of the several family day care homes in her neighborhood had been visited by licensing authorities during the past two years.

PROGRAM COMPONENTS AND LICENSING

At the beginning of 1983, four children were enrolled at Site 6, ranging in age from seven months to twenty-two months. One-half year later, four more in that age range and one five-year-old had joined the program. All children in this program follow the same feeding, playing, and sleeping schedule, regardless of age. This consists of breakfast, followed by a playtime, a nap time, lunchtime, another playtime, a second nap time, and a late afternoon snack time. All meals are prepared by the director. Day care is provided eleven hours a day, from 7 A.M. to 6 P.M. The parents usually leave their children for the full eleven-hour day and, much to the director's displeasure, often fail to return by 6 P.M. to take their children home. The director reported to me that she asked one parent who was consistently hours late not to come back. The only other instance of rejection from this day care program occurred when another parent failed to pay the fees.

As noted, within a six-month period this program's enrollment jumped from four to nine children [8]. The director attributes this increase to a combination of word-of-mouth advertisement, the increased demand for day care during the summertime, and her lower than usual rates. Moreover, neighboring family day care homes are full; they have long-term customers and turn away new customers. According to the director, the neighboring family day care programs are run by older women, and many parents prefer a young woman to care for their children.

The increased enrollment at Site 6 has diminished the staff-child ratio from the original 1 : 4 to the present 1 : 9. Although only licensed to care for six children, the director claims that "the parents don't seem to mind the number of kids. I guess they think it's good for them—or cheap, anyway." Because she has a waiting list, the director plans to apply for a family day care "center" license to replace her present family day care "home" license. This will allow her to care for twelve children in her home with the half-time help of an assistant of at least fourteen years of age. In order for her to qualify for this license, the director's mother and brother are moving out of the home and taking away most of the large furniture. The director expects this to increase the cubic feet per person and total square footage to approximate state licensing requirements. If she follows through with her plan, the director expects that her application for a second licensure will bring a visit from the authorities.

Cost, Credentials, and Ratios

Regardless of the hours per day a child spends at this site, there is an enrollment fee of $10 a day, or $50 per child per week. Because the children usually attend this program for eleven hours a day, the parents are paying approximately $1 an hour for their child care. According to the director, this rate is considerably below neighborhood competitors, who charge an average of $2 an hour per child.

The director notes that the low price of her program includes meals. She is reimbursed by the state for these food costs but does not appear to have an exact understanding of the formula for reimbursement. She sends the state officials a menu (which must provide a nutritionally balanced diet) and a food bill, and she receives a check for the amount requested.

Bookkeeping for this program is informal. The director deposits fees and state food reimbursement checks into her personal checking account. She does not keep an account of expenditures and pays no taxes on her income. She is not certain, but she believes that the children are costing her "a lot of money, because they have broken all of the toys." It appears, however, that the program costs at this site are low and have remained fairly constant with the public reimbursement for food, a small house rental fee of $200 a month (paid to the director's mother), and minimal equipment costs. At the same time, with increased enrollment, program income has more than doubled in five months from approximately $800 to $1,800 per month. While official state requirements concerning staff-child and per capita square footage ratios have been exceeded, the child care at this site is inexpensive and, despite the shortcomings of this program, parents are apparently, "happy to buy it."

SUMMARY: THE DIVERSE STRUCTURAL CHARACTERISTICS OF DAY CARE SERVICES

An examination of the six study sites reveals a wide variation in the programs' fiscal and organizational characteristics. As noted in Table 5.2, the average daily enrollments among the centers ranges from 9 (or 4 at the inception of this study) to 265 children, with the average number of children at all sites at 110. The annual average per-child costs of day care to these providers varies between $2,188 and $5,150. The mean cost for all the programs is $3,030. With the exception of Site 1, the most expensive and heavily subsidized program, consumers pay most of the cost of care. For all sites, the average annual cost to consumers amounts to $2,282. The program at Site 1 offers state-subsidized care on a sliding fee scale to low-income families at an annual cost to the provider of $5,150. This cost is about twice that of the same cost in other programs. The cost to the provider at Sites 2, 4, 5, and 6 ranges from $2,188 to $2,892. Site 1 is the only program where the provider pays more than the consumer. At Sites 5 and 6, according to information provided by the program directors, the consumer charges are equal to provider costs, while at Sites 2 and 4 consumers pay almost $20 per week more than program costs per child.

TABLE 5.2
FISCAL AND ORGANIZATIONAL CHARACTERISTICS OF DAY CARE PROGRAMS

Characteristic	Avg. all Sites	Site 1	Site 2	Site 3[d]	Site 4	Site 5	Site 6
Fiscal characteristics							
Overall budget[a] for fiscal year	$211,827	$195,715[d]	$251,571	NA	$390,420	NA[f]	$9,600[g]
	FY '83 or '84	FY 1983	FY 1983	NA	FY 1984	NA	FY 1984
Average daily enrollment[b]	110	38	115	265	135	100	9[j]
Average cost to provider per child							
Annual	$3,030	$5,150	$2,188	NA	$2,892	$2,520+	$2,400
Monthly	$252	$429	$182	NA	$241	$210+	$200
Weekly	$58	$99	$42	NA	$56	$48+	$46
Average charge to consumer per child[b]							
Annual	$2,282	$180	$3,168	$1,584	$3,840	$2,520[h]	$2,400
Monthly	$190	$15	$264	$132	$320	$210	$200
Weekly	$44	$4	$61	$31	$74	$48	$46
Organizational characteristics							
Average staff-child ratio[c]	1:7	1:8	1:6	1:10	1:8	1:6	1:4
Number of caregiving staff	26	10	25	56	40	25	1

Staff credentials[c]							
Number of:							
Teaching credentials	2	2	2	1	0	5[i]	0
Early childhood ed. credentials	1	0	1	1	0	2	0
Children's center permits	1	0	3	2	0	0	0
College coursework in child development	3	4	0	4	8	4	0
Operating hours[d]							
Hours per day	14	10	11	18+	24	11	11+
Days per week	5	5	5	5	7	5	5

[a] Budget for all program components combined.

[b] All program components combined.

[c] Averages for all program components combined. For example, where staff-child ratios differ for different age groups at the same site, they have been averaged.

[d] Information labeled "NA" in this column was not made available by program administrators.

[e] Because the budget for this site is incorporated into that for six cofunded programs, the budget is computed based upon the percentage of ADA (average daily attendance) for all sites which this site comprises.

[f] Director of this site states that she does not keep a formal budget and runs in the red for several months at a time.

[g] Estimated.

[h] For one child, full-time preschool (9 A.M. to 2 P.M.) five days a week plus day care from 7 to 9 A.M. and 2 A.M. to 6 P.M. at $1.75 per hour costs $210 per month, or $2,520 per year.

[i] Montessori credentials.

[j] Average daily enrollment at site 6 increased from 4 to 9 during this study.

As with size and cost, there are wide differences among programs regarding the employment of professional staff. Overall, only 25% of the 157 staff working at the six sites have some formal training relevant to early childhood education. Fourteen of these staff (9% of the total) have teaching or early childhood credentials. The remaining 25 (16% of the total) have either children's center permits or some college courses in child development. The degree of staff professionalism is not distributed proportionately among the centers. The highest levels of professionalism are at Sites 1 and 5, where caretakers with some relevant training account for 60% and 44% of the program staffs, respectively. Sites 3 and 6 have the lowest level of professionalism, with as little as 14% to 0% of the respective staffs having any formal training.

While children in these programs may be receiving a small portion of their care from professionals, overall they are receiving a remarkably high quantity of care. The average program operates fourteen hours per day, five days a week. However, there is considerable variation in program hours. For example, actual operating hours range from the continuous twenty-four hours per day, seven days a week at Site 4, down to ten hours per day, five days a week at Site 1. This difference in schedule reflects the difference in purpose served by these two programs. Continuous care is provided by the employer-sponsored program at Site 4, where a round-the-clock nursing staff is required by the employer, a hospital, which, of course, operates twenty-four hours a day. In contrast, Site 1 offers day care only ten hours a day, five days a week to children from low-income families. Many of these children's parents are required to work or train for employment in order to reduce their dependence upon public welfare.

Finally, staff-child ratio is one more characteristic of care that varies among programs, ranging from what began as 1 : 4 at Site 6 and what remains 1 : 6 at Sites 2 and 3 to 1 : 10 and sometimes 1 : 18 at Site 3. Looked at together, Site 3 and Site 6 contrast an institutional setting with a family setting. Site 3 is located in a naval barracks and its program is designed to serve 265 children at the least possible cost to parent and provider. Site 6, a family day care program, is located in a small house in a residential neighborhood and its program is designed to serve as many children as legally and practically possible at the least possible cost to the parent and the provider. Site 6 serves about one-thirtieth the number of children served by Site 3.

The six sites examined in this study clearly illustrate the high-degree of structural diversity in the mixed economy of day care. However, it is one thing to describe such structural diversity and quite another to draw meaningful conclusions about it. The important question is: How do these diverse arrangements affect the quality of day care that children receive? For instance, the cost of care at Site 1, a heavily subsidized day care program, is twice as much as the cost of care at Site 6, a family day care program. Is Site 1 providing care which is *double* the quality of the care provided at Site 6? Are these programs merely different structural designs for providing equally beneficial services? To answer these questions we must go beyond the structural arrangements and attempt to analyze the substantive provisions of care. This is done in the following chapter.

Chapter 6

COMPARING THE QUALITY OF CARE

Mister sun, sun, mister golden sun,
Please shine down on me.
These little children are asking you
To please come out so we can play with you. . .
—"Mr. Sun,"
Traditional Song

It is all too easy to forget that our children are the ones who are most affected by our choices of child care. They do not vote, they do not pay taxes, they do not hold jobs. When young children speak up, it is easy to assume that they are simply trying out their vocal cords, learning new words, testing their parents' limits, vying for attention, or complaining about hunger, thirst, or dirty diapers. Still, children have a lot to tell us about our child care choices. Their words and cries, their gestures, the looks in their faces, their interactions with others, their attention spans, the flush of their skins, and many other details are speaking to us. It is up to those of us who design child care programs, who choose child care for our children, who have children (whether in or out of child care programs), and who vote for politicians that have particular opinions about child care, to listen to and look at our children. They will tell us a great deal about the tangled problems of child care.

It is the children who really are the ultimate concern of this study. Regardless of the extent to which day care programs seek to serve parents, the government, or employers, it is the children who are most directly affected by the quality and philosophy of their day care programs. Child care is, and must always be, ultimately, care for children. The overriding issue in the discussion which follows is whether or not the diversity inherent in the mixed economy of child care benefits children.

The question of who should be the primary beneficiaries of care influences the orientation of child care programs. When children are truly the primary beneficiaries, the care provided them will lean more in a developmental direction than when working parents, the state, an employer, or an entrepreneur is the primary beneficiary. However, most, if not all, programs serve a combination of children and other interested parties and tend to provide care that ranges from merely custodial care to genuine developmental care. In assessing child care, the measurement of quality is confounded by conflicting philosophies of what is important for young children. One program may emphasize social development, while another emphasizes cognitive development. Yet another may give primary emphasis to the religious development of its children. And still another program may openly market itself as an aid to working parents, claiming that the best thing to do for children is to care for them while their parents work.

The mixed economy of child care offers the opportunity for variety and experimentation in child care. This opportunity derives from the broad disagreement regarding quality in care and from the presence of diverse motivations for providing care. But what does the mixed economy do for the children? What level of quality does it provide them? To answer this question, I analyzed both quantitative and qualitative characteristics of the care provided in the six day care programs studied.

In order to conduct such an analysis, I have organized the characteristics of the child care into the five dimensions of direct care. These dimensions were delineated in Chapter 4. Again, these five dimensions are social, psychological, educational, physical, and environmental. I have organized selected data in Table 6.1 to illustrate the five-dimensional framework that I have developed for comparing the quality of child care programs. In this chapter, I examine the care provided at each of the six day care sites, first presented in Chapter 5, along each of the five study dimensions.

The following analysis seeks to gain an understanding of the diversity of quality in child care. Most of my observations are presented in narrative form with accompanying photographs. I have, however, given a score to the quality of care in each of the five dimensions at each site, based upon my observations comparing four elements of each dimension of care across the six sites.

My analysis is undertaken with the understanding that the five dimensions of care are highly interrelated and that they are influenced by fiscal, administrative, and organizational variables. The method used to obtain these scores is described in Appendix A. The actual scores and their implications are discussed in the final section of this chapter. Readers concerned with particular characteristics of care will do well to select the subheadings in this chapter which refer to those particular characteristics. For a reminder regarding the organizational characteristics of each site, consult Table 5.1.

FIRST IMPRESSIONS

Site 1, a state-subsidized day care program for low-income families, and Site 2, a municipal program for paying city residents, shared a common facility in an old, otherwise vacant public school building. As I walked into the different areas of the building, separately claimed by the two programs, I was impressed by the differences in the arrangement of furniture, the noise level, the cleanliness, and the general sense of organization. Although the facilities were the same, Site 2 presented a more inviting and organized environment.

Site 3, a program for Navy enlistees' families, was, at first glance, very spacious, both indoors and outdoors. However, a large number of children attended this program. I was visually struck by the population density there. Rarely did I find so many diapered babies in one room (see Figure 6.1), and rarely did I see so many babies with so few adults in the vicinity. The site was clean in some areas, but it smelled unsani-

TABLE 6.1
DIMENSIONS OF CARE IN DAY CARE CENTERS: SELECTED OBJECTIVE INDICATORS

Dimension	Site 1	Site 2	Site 3	Site 4	Site 5	Site 6
Social dimension						
Average staff-child ratio	1:8	1:6	1:10	1:8	1:6	1:4
Age range of children	2½ to 5 yrs.	18 mo. to 12 yrs.	2 mo. to 12 yrs.	Birth to 10 yrs.	14 mo. to 6 yrs.	4 mo. to 5 yrs.
% of children who are white	80%	90%	60%	90%	90%	50%
Age range of caregiving staff	18 to 48	14 to 60	18 to 40	20 to 36	22 to 42	21
% of staff who are white	66%	90%	60%	75%	80%	0%
Parental participation	Some	Some	Little	Some	Some	None
Psychological dimension						
Each child has a space of his or her own	Yes, but not in use	Yes	No	Yes	Yes	No
Programmatic emphasis upon key staff person for each child	No	Yes	No	Yes	No	No

Educational dimension						
Educational philosophy	Nonexplicit	Nonexplicit	Nonexplicit	Nonexplicit	Explicit	None
Formal structured learning sessions	Few	Some	Few	Few	Many	None
Physical dimension						
Provisions for sick care	No	No	No	Yes	No	No
Cooked meals served	Yes	No	Yes	No	No	Yes
Cold meals served	Yes	No	Yes	No	No	Yes
Snacks served	Yes	Yes	Yes	Yes	Yes	Yes
Children bring meals from home	No	Yes	No	Yes	Yes	Yes
Environmental dimension						
Location	School	School	Workplace	Workplace	School	Family residence
Has kitchen	Yes	Yes	Yes	Yes	No	Yes
Has separate sleeping quarters	No	No	No	Yes	No	No
Has outdoor playground	Yes	Yes	Yes	Yes	Yes	Yes
Sq. footage (estimated):						
Indoor area	1,200	3,000	3,500	1,500	1,800	180
Outdoor area	2,000	2,000	1,500	380	600	300

tary and unventilated in others. With its low staff-child ratio it was especially difficult to keep an area occupied by many small infants clean.

In contrast, Site 4, an employer-sponsored day care program for children of hospital employees, was sparkling clean. I was immediately struck by the hygienic atmosphere. In fact, everything appeared so sterile that the children looked somewhat out of place in this environment.

The first impression I had at Site 5, a private nonprofit preschool, was that the place was clean, thoughtfully decorated, and well organized. All of the furniture, its arrangement, and even the rooms themselves seemed to be geared toward child-size perceptions. Everything was colorful and fascinating. The child care center captured my attention and was clearly educationally oriented. There were lots of colorful flowers in the outdoor play yard, and flowers and murals adorned the outdoor walls of the buildings. Overall, Site 5 was the most inviting atmosphere (see Figure 6.15).

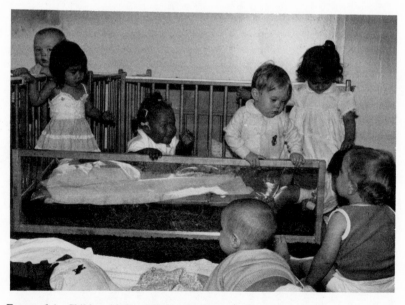

FIGURE 6.1. Child packing at Site 3. Infants and toddlers are crowded together in order to compensate for inadequate staff-child ratios.

On the other hand, the family day care home at Site 6 was uninviting. It was located in an old ramshackle house in a low-income neighborhood. The first things I noticed when I approached this home were a broken sign and a torn screen door on its front lawn. Indoors it was dark. The windows were generally kept closed and the shades were drawn. The children slept a lot and did a lot of their playing in the basement, which was also dark and cluttered. A spacious backyard was available for play, but there was no lawn in it, and when the day care home did use it, the children played in the dirt, among wood scraps and rusty nails.

To summarize my first impressions on the quality of care at each site, I placed Site 5 highest, as most developmental, and Site 6 lowest, as most custodial and leaning toward detrimental. But initial impressions can be deceptive. A closer examination of these sites and how they function, from the perspective of the five dimensions of direct care, was necessary before any conclusions, however tentative, could be drawn about the overall quality of care.

THE SOCIAL DIMENSION OF CARE

In Chapter 4 I reviewed various elements of the social dimension of care. Among the most important of these elements are (1) size/ratio, (2) organizational cooperation and tension management, (3) family involvement, and (4) planned group playtime. These four basic elements were selected for analysis in my qualitative assessment of the social dimension of care in the six study sites. Refer to Chapter 4 for further explanation of these basic elements.

SIZE/RATIO

One of the most essential characteristics of direct care is the caregiver–care-receiver ratio. Where the ratio of adults to children is inadequate, day care staff are engaged in *child packing,* herding children together into small, contained, and easily supervised spaces. As I noted in the previous chapter, the formally prescribed ratio at Site 1 was one adult to eight children. But from my observations, which were made over a period of five months, I saw that practice did not always follow policy. On frequent occasions the 1 : 8 staff-child ratio dropped to one staff member to fifteen children, if not lower than that. In fact, on two occasions I was asked by a member of the staff to sit in a room in order to satisfy the law's requirement for the staff-child ratio, because there were not enough staff for the children. One time I found myself sitting in the room alone for forty-five minutes and counted eighteen children playing in the room under my sole "supervision."

Site 2 adhered more strictly to its formal staff-child ratio of 1 : 6. During my three visits to this site I did not observe the ratio drop below 1 : 8, and even then, this less desirable ratio did not continue for more than fifteen minutes at a time. When the ratio dropped because of staff illness or tardiness, the director and her secretary substituted for missing staff.

At Site 3, where the ratio was formally 1 : 10, I noticed several times a 1 : 15 ratio. And at one time, for a period of a least a quarter of an hour, there was one adult to twenty infants in the infant room. The other adult was reportedly "getting lunch." I saw a ratio of two adults to twenty toddlers several times, and in the play yard I saw the same ratio of adults to preschool or three- to five-year-olds quite often. And for a period of at least forty-five minutes, I observed one elderly woman, the cook, making pizza for lunch with a group of fourteen seated children, and three or four other children wandering in and out. The caregiving ratio at Site 3 was unstable and unsatisfactory.

At Site 4 the staff-child ratio of 1 : 8 was highly regulated. During my visit the ratio did not drop below that figure. In the infant room I twice observed a ratio of one adult to one infant for at least fifteen minutes each, and one adult to two or three small infants during feeding time for several half-hour periods. And the staff-child ratio was also enhanced by parents who visited their children. Because the day care site was in their workplace (on the hospital grounds), parents frequently dropped by the center.

At Site 5 the staff had been hired primarily to serve an educational purpose. The number of teachers and teaching assistants per child is very high. The staff-child ratio never dropped below a 1 : 6 ratio and was often above that. Parents visited, but not as frequently as at Site 4.

TABLE 6.2

ASSESSMENT OF RATIOS AND AVERAGE GROUP SIZES IN SIX DAY CARE PROGRAMS[a]

	Site 1	Site 2	Site 3	Site 4	Site 5	Site 6 Early	Site 6 Late[b]
Average staff-child ratio	1:8	1:6	1:10	1:8	1:6	1:4	1:9
Average group size	32	13	28	14	16	4	9
Ratio–group-size assessment[c]	Fair ratio, poor group size	Optimal ratio, good group size	Fair ratio, poor group size	Fair ratio, Fair group size	Optimal ratio, fair group size	Optimal ratio fair group size	Fair ratio, good group size

[a]These averages are calculated based upon each site's officially stated average ratios and average group sizes for all program components together (group sizes and ratios for infant care are averaged in with those provided older children).
[b]Site 6, five months after the study began.
[c]Includes consideration of staff competence and stability of group sizes and ratios in practice.

At the beginning of the study Site 6 had a staff-child ratio of one adult to four children. (This is the ratio indicated in Table 6.1.) Over a five-month period the number of children cared for by the one adult at this site increased to nine. This 1 : 9 ratio was excessively low in light of the children's needs and in light of the fact that the adult caretaker appeared to be immature and naive.

Any discussion of staff-child ratios in a care setting must consider group size, because a ratio manageable at one group size may not be at another. If the quality of care were simply a product of group size and the staff-child ratio, then we could conclude that Site 6 in its early stages offered the highest quality care. It had a staff-child ratio of 1 : 4 and the smallest group size: four children. And five months into the study Site 6 continued to offer the smallest group size: nine children total. Staff-child ratios and groups size are important indicators of the social dimension of care, but they cannot be fully assessed without reference to the skill and competence of the caretakers, as well as the *regularity* with which they adhere to the program size and ratio standards.

Observing the interaction of these variables, my assessment of the ratio–group-size relationships at the six sites is reported in Table 6.2. Optimum group-size–ratio relationships were observed at Sites 2 and 5. Both had a ratio of 1 : 6. Site 2 had an average group size of 13, and Site 5 had an average of 16. The group size and staff-child ratios at Sites 2 and 5 were not only very manageable, they were also well managed by an enthusiastic staff. In contrast, the official program standards for size and staff-child ratio were often exceeded at Sites 1 and 3.

ORGANIZATIONAL COOPERATION AND TENSION MANAGEMENT

Another element in the social dimension of care involves the degree of cooperation and effective management of interpersonal differences among staff. Site 1 made a strong effort to have staff members communicate with one another while on the job. Nevertheless, there was a clear hierarchy of staff at Site 1, with little democracy in the decision-making process. The clear line of authority seemed to contain potential interpersonal disagreements that might have been expressed in a looser, more democratic setting such as at Site 2.

The social atmosphere at Site 2 was warm and friendly, but one could detect some staff conflict. The director worked at resolving these conflicts informally by calling staff members who were involved in a conflict to a meeting and allowing them to air their feelings. At these meetings the director acted as a mediator and came up with suggestions to resolve the conflict. She also held meetings with the staff after hours.

At Site 3, I detected little conflict, but also little communication among the staff. All of the staff members seemed to report to the director, whose administrative authority was pronounced. This may have been reflective of the military environment in which Site 3 was located.

At Site 4, there were growing tensions between staff and the administration. Staff members wanted to be unionized. They felt they were being underpaid and wanted more fringe benefits and greater support from the management in dealing with unhappy parents. On the other hand, at Site 5, there were no apparent conflicts among staff members. Regular meetings were held before and after hours. All of the staff were required to attend these meetings and were paid for their time. The staff also appeared to be in agreement with the philosophy of the school. Because Site 6 had only one staff member there was no issue of conflict resolution among staff.

FAMILY INVOLVEMENT

At Site 1, family involvement was required of the parents. Each child had to have three hours of parent participation per week. At Site 2, frequent family involvement was invited, especially on certain holidays and on children's birthdays. There was no formal arrangement for family involvement at Site 3. At Site 4, family involvement was informal but substantial, in that parents came to the center and visited their children during their lunch hours or breaks. Site 5 encouraged family involvement on birthdays, for picnics, and by inviting parents to sit in on classes. This enabled parents to learn teaching methods which they could apply at home. Site 5 also offered camp-outs, sleep-outs, and meetings in the evenings, and it encouraged parents to attend lectures with staff members on early childhood education. At Site 6, I saw no parental involvement and none was indicated by the director.

TABLE 6.3
ASSESSMENTS OF SOCIAL DIMENSION OF CARE

Elements of social dimension	Site 1	Site 2	Site 3	Site 4	Site 5	Site 6
Size/ratio	3	5	3	3	5	2
Organizational cooperation and tension management	2	5	4	2	4	3[a]
Family involvement	3	4	2	4	4	1
Group playtime	4	4	3	4	5	2
Total	12	18	12	13	18	8

[a]With only one staff member at this site this variable is a middle-range (neutral) score.

GROUP PLAYTIME

Playtime in groups is perhaps the most significant contribution a child care program can make to the social development of its children.This element of care should include both unstructured and structured playtime. Attention was paid to both of these types of play at Sites 1 and 2. At Site 3, some attention was paid to both of these, but not as much as at Sites 1 and 2. At Site 4, there was visible but limited attention given to both types of play. Site 6 seemed to pay no attention to either of these, except that the children, in the absence of any program objectives, took part in unstructured play together.

OVERALL ASSESSMENT OF THE SOCIAL DIMENSION OF CARE

Based on my observations at these six study sites, the four elements of social care I describe above were rated on a scale of 1 to 5, indicating lowest to highest quality. These ratings and an overall assessment score for each site are reported here in Table 6.3.

THE PSYCHOLOGICAL DIMENSION OF CARE

The psychological dimension of care interacts closely with the social dimension of care. For analytic purposes these dimensions are treated separately. Among the elements of the psychological dimension of care are (1) privacy, (2) responsiveness to individual needs, (3) identity enhancement, and (4) planned transitions. These four elements were examined at each of the study sites. Further explanation of these elements is provided in Chapter 4.

PRIVACY

The opportunity and respect for privacy is one of the most important elements in the psychological setting of child care programs. Privacy is more than a product of physical space. It involves a conscious effort to use space in ways that allow solitude (see Figures 6.3 and 6.4). To illustrate, let us examine the situation in which two of the sites split a school building between themselves. One of the programs was willing to provide its children with more privacy than the other. Site 2 made a special effort to create opportunities for privacy. Sites 1 and 3, despite the utilization of similar rooms and large spaces, tended to herd

FIGURE 6.2. Frustrations mount when children intimidate each other at Site 3.

FIGURE 6.3. Figure painting at Site 1. This easel is set off from the center of activity. This child can paint quietly, without losing interest, for thirty-five minutes.

children into the same areas in order to compensate for the small number of staff. (See Figure 6.2. Also note that an exception to Site 1's child-packing tendencies is pictured in Figure 6.3.)

Despite its less than optimal staff-child ratio, Site 4 allowed children ample opportunity for privacy. However, this allowance seemed to stem from a laissez-faire attitude on the part of the staff. At Site 5, however, it was the program's policy to encourage privacy and autonomy. As part of their educational experience, its children were taught to

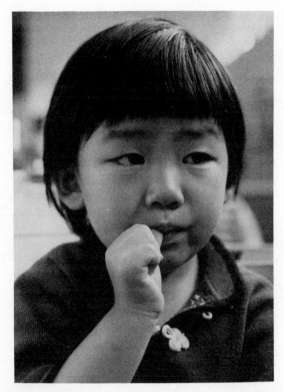

FIGURE 6.4. A child takes the time to reflect. Privacy is an important element of the psychological setting.

be independent in their use of learning materials and to request assistance only when necessary. In contrast to the arrangements at Sites 4 and 5, the children at Site 6 had relatively little privacy, except when they slept at naptime. Even then they were crowded together, because there were only a few cribs and only one adult was available to watch the entire group. Here, the poor adult-child ratio and the cramped quarters contributed to a general sense of crowding and of insecurity on the part of the children. The outcome of crowding and peer supervision can be aggression and violence (see Figure 6.2 and 6.5). Whether or not crowding and insecurity are clearly related, these psychological conditions appeared together at Site 6.

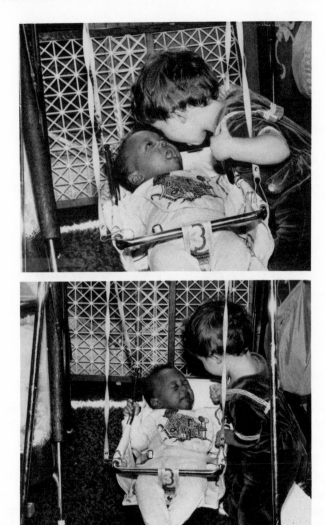

FIGURE 6.5. One child intimidating another at Site 6. Because supervision is poor and children are crowded and understimulated, the older children "bully" the infants, as seen here. In the lower photo, the older boy threatens to hit the infant.

RESPONSIVENESS TO INDIVIDUAL NEEDS

The responsiveness of program and staff to individual needs other than privacy is another element in the quality of psychological care. When the individual's needs were learning needs, Site 5 was especially responsive, given its high educational orientation. Responding to learning needs is currently considered an important part of psychological as well as educational care, because young children are believed to hunger for mental stimulation. At Site 4, the individuals' most important needs were considered to be a combination of physical maintenance and creature comforts (needs for diaper changes, feeding, and physical comforts are viewed as related). Among the six sites studied, staff members tended to be most personally involved with the children where the operation's staff-child ratio was favorable and where the program goals specified this type of interaction. This was true at Sites 2 and 5. Nevertheless, it was difficult to evaluate the emotional responsiveness of the staff. Staff members' and children's feelings were difficult to observe.

The degree of programmatic responsiveness to individual needs is, in part, a function of the opportunity for one-to-one attention. Programmatic recognition of children's need for consistent relationships with their caregivers is also reflected in the level of one-to-one attention that is made available. Sites 1, 2, and 4 claimed to recognize this need and to build it into their program designs. Yet one-to-one care appeared mechanized at Site 4 and inconvenient for the staff at Site 1. By contrast, staff at Site 2 seemed genuinely affectionate and expressive of this attention on a one-to-one basis. At Site 5, staff members were not overtly affectionate, but there was an obvious amount of caring. I sensed the presence of much more structure and discipline at Site 5. The director there noted that her children were in a school environment (for the most part), an environment that should, in her opinion, "be clearly distinguished from the familial environment."

Finally, staff members at Site 3 made little effort to provide individual attention to the children. And Site 6 did little more than provide the one-to-one custodial care associated with specific tasks such as feeding and diaper changing.

IDENTITY ENHANCEMENT

One way to enhance identity is to provide children with special spaces, usually called "cubbyholes," labeled with their names. This was done at Sites 2 and 5, where children kept their drawings and personal possessions apart from the communal property. It is quite common for day care programs to have a box, closet, or drawer for each child. Site 5 provided personal boxes for the older children. These were not labeled with the children's names, but each child selected a special box for him- or herself each day. Although Site 1 had boxes for children's belongings, they were not in use. Both Site 3 and Site 6— the former, the most institutional, and the latter, the most familial of the six programs—had no special places for children to store their private possessions.

PLANNED TRANSITIONS

Planned or well-managed transition times (arrivals and departures) are a critical element of psychological care. For example, at Site 2, parents talked with staff members and staff members with the children during arrivals and departures. There was an explicit programmatic concern for these transition times. By contrast, at Site 1 children were simply "dropped off" with limited communication between parents and staff. There was also very little formal emphasis on transitions at Site 3, except when a parent took the initiative.

At Site 4, staff members were concerned about transitions because the parents made it important. The location of the day care setting was in the parents' workplace, allowing them to be very involved with their children. Site 5 structured the transition during arrival and departure every day. Site 6 had no explicitly stated objective regarding transitions, but communication did occur informally.

OVERALL ASSESSMENT OF THE PSYCHOLOGICAL DIMENSION OF CARE

These four elements of the psychological dimension were rated, again, on a scale of 1 to 5 (lowest to highest). The ratings

TABLE 6.4
ASSESSMENTS OF PSYCHOLOGICAL DIMENSION OF CARE

Elements of psychological dimension	Site 1	Site 2	Site 3	Site 4	Site 5	Site 6
Privacy	2	3	1	5	5	2
Responsiveness to individual needs	3	3	2	3	4	2
Identity enhancement	3	3	3	3	4	3
Planned transitions	2	3	2	5	5	3
Total	10	12	8	16	18	10

and an overall assessment score for each site are reported here in Table 6.4.

THE EDUCATIONAL DIMENSION OF CARE

A day care program's elaboration of the educational dimension of care indicates its interest in the cognitive development of its children. Programs which claim to be educational describe themselves as more developmentally oriented than other programs which may emphasize different qualities of care. I studied four different educational elements at the six day care programs: (1) explicit philosophy and goals, (2) time spent on educational activity, (3) verbal interaction, and (4) sensory stimulation. Further explanation of these elements can be found in Chapter 4.

EXPLICIT PHILOSOPHY AND GOALS

Day care programs vary most in the level of emphasis upon education. Of the six sites I studied, only Site 5 had an explicit educational philosophy. The others had implied philosophies, except for Site 6, which had none at all. Site 5 offered a comprehensive and structured educational program. Site 2 had a number of daily educational activities. Its staff members made a serious attempt to meet their stated learning goals, but it had fewer trained teachers per child than did Site 5. Site 1 sought to provide compensatory education, but its goals in that regard were vague and did not appear to be systematically pursued. According to the director, Site 4's program philosophy was against

FIGURE 6.6. Reading circle at Site 5. These children seat themselves at the reading circle and concentrate on their reading without adult direction. This is expected of children who enroll in this preschool program.

forcing young children to learn. It had no explicit educational goals, but it emphasized what it called "preconditions to learning," such as adequate perceptual stimuli and emotional security. Staff members at Site 3 had some learning goals, but they were severely hampered in meeting those objectives because of the unwieldy staff-child ratio and the large group size. Site 6 had no educational goals.

From an educational perspective, Site 5 clearly had the most thoughtful design and distinct philosophy. Based on the Doman and Montessori methods, it incorporated a computerized early learning program and a number of other activities. Children were screened for admission through interviews that attempted to ascertain whether they could cope with its educational environment and its demands for self-motivation (see Figure 6.6).

TIME SPENT ON EDUCATIONAL ACTIVITY

As might be expected, the amount of time spent on educational activities in the various study sites is closely related to their respective

FIGURE 6.7. Computer learning at Site 5. This four-year-old demonstrates the procedure for hooking up the computer, playing learning games, and writing simple programs. At Site 5, children begin "playing" with the computer as soon as they are interested, which, in some cases, is at two years.

emphasis on educational goals. Most of the children's time at Site 5 was focused on educational activity (see Figures 6.7 and 6.8). A moderate amount of time was spent on education at Site 2. I observed sporadic efforts at education at Sites 1, 3, and 4. At Site 6 virtually no time was invested in education.

FIGURE 6.8. Toddlers reading at Site 5. Children are encouraged to read as early as possible at Site 5. Flash card sessions (with pictures and words in English and Latin) are conducted daily, followed by the independent reading session pictured here.

VERBAL INTERACTION

The amount of time spent on educational activity can be allocated to different forms of instruction. For young children one of the important elements of instruction involves one-to-one verbal interaction with staff. At the six study sites the amount of educationally focused one-to-one interaction with staff varied along the same lines as did the pattern

FIGURE 6.9. A singing session at Site 3. This caregiver is responsible for more than the eight toddlers here. Several others have wandered away from the group.

of overall time spent on education. Site 4 was the exception. It had a relatively higher one-to-one level of educationally oriented interaction. The frequent presence of parents at this site improved the adult-child ratio, which allowed the staff more opportunity for one-to-one interaction with children.

SENSORY STIMULATION

Adequate sensory stimulation is another important element of the educational dimension of care. Here again, Site 5 ranked highest, with its games, learning equipment, geometrical shapes, and big letters and charts (see Figure 6.10). Children were attracted to these things because of their shapes and color and because of the sounds they made. Site 5 was a stimulating environment with a lot of light and variety. In comparison to Site 5, the environment at Site 2 was rather drab. While Site 4 was more stimulating than the dark and crowded Sites 1 and 3, it too lacked excitement. Sterile, spacious, and organized, Site 4 afforded a sort of book-learned, clinical stimulation. Site 6 seemed comfortable

FIGURE 6.10. Learning materials at Site 5. At this site, children are encouraged to select learning materials and "play" with them on their own. This four-year-old girl has just explained that "These are geometric solids."

for its children, insofar as it was similar to their own home environments. Yet there was no structured effort to stimulate the children's curiosity or imagination. Furthermore, the cluttered disorganization at Site 6 seemed to discourage exploration, as well as to promote the insecurity noted earlier.

TABLE 6.5
ASSESSMENTS OF EDUCATIONAL DIMENSION OF CARE

Elements of educational dimension	Site 1	Site 2	Site 3	Site 4	Site 5	Site 6
Explicit philosophy and goals	2	4	3	2	5	1
Time spent on educational activity	2	3	2	2	5	1
Verbal interaction	2	3	2	3	5	1
Sensory stimulation	2	2	2	3	5	1
Total	8	12	9	10	20	4

OVERALL ASSESSMENT OF THE EDUCATIONAL DIMENSION OF CARE

Ratings on each of the four elements in the educational dimension of care, as well as an overall assessment score for each site, are summarized in Table 6.5.

THE PHYSICAL DIMENSION OF CARE

Four elements of the physical dimension of care were selected for assessment at the study sites: (1) health protection and sick care, (2) cleanliness, (3) nutrition, and (4) hygiene and physical education. Chapter 4 further explains these elements.

HEALTH PROTECTION AND SICK CARE

The ability of a day care program to protect the health of its children is basic to the provision of physical care. This ability is in part related to how the decisions regarding sick children are handled. Most programs have rules stating whether or not children are allowed to attend when they are ill and how ill children are to be treated once they are present.

At Site 1 many children attended when ill and exposed the others to contagion. Site 2 preferred not to have ill children come to school. It also called parents immediately and asked them to take their children home when they became ill. If the parents could not be reached, the ill children were taken to the director's office or to rest on a cot in the staff lounge. Many children arrived at Site 3 with colds, despite program rules against this. Contagion was therefore high in this densely populated setting. Although Site 4, located on hospital grounds, had a special sick room, its parents were asked to remove children if they became ill during the day, and not to bring them in when they were ill. Because these parents worked in a health care environment, they were very responsive to this requirement. Site 4 was the only one of the six sites that had a sick room with a crib, a bed, blankets, and toys. Site 5 did not want sick children attending and made no provisions for sick care. Children who fell ill during the day were sent home. The director was strict about this policy. Site 6 preferred not to have sick children attend but was often (as the director stated) "stuck with them." The director complained about this but felt that she could not enforce a no-sick-children rule. She stated that she was willing to take children with colds, but not with the flu, and that in the end she "gets them all."

CLEANLINESS

Cleanliness is another important aspect of physical care. It reduces contagion and contributes to the general health of caregivers and care receivers. Of the six study sites, the most institutional (Site 3) and the most familial (Site 6) ranked lowest on cleanliness and contagion control. At Site 3 I was surprised at the number of children toddling around in dirty diapers. At Site 6 I was constantly aware of the dust, dirt, and debris on the floors and tables, chairs, and walls. By contrast, Site 4 seemed to maintain reasonable, if not high, hygienic standards. This may reflect its encompassing hospital setting. Site 5 was also very clean, but not as overwhelmingly sterile. Sites 1 and 2, located in the same setting and sharing the same custodial service, maintained an equally average level of cleanliness.

NUTRITION

The most concrete element of physical care is nutrition. There is wide variation in the frequency, quality, and method of the serving of meals and snacks in day care. In some cases, parents must send lunches and dinners from home; in others, fully prepared meals are provided on-site. The different nutritional procedures at Sites 1 and 2 caused awkwardness. The children from the low-income families enrolled in Site 1's state-subsidized day care program received a hot breakfast. The aroma of that breakfast wafted over to Site 2. Site 2's children did not get any hot meals. Site 1 provided all meals and snacks, while children at Site 2 had to have breakfast at home and had to bring their own

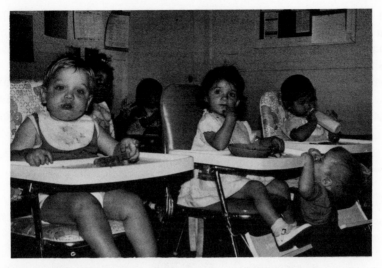

FIGURE 6.11. Mealtime at Site 3. Children are poorly supervised during meals and at other times at Site 3.

lunches. Both programs offered snacks. Of the remaining four sites, only Site 3 regularly provided cooked meals, with the children assisting in their preparation. Crowding and chaos accompanied mealtimes at this site, as indicated in Figure 6.11. When she had time, the director at Site 6 cooked for the children. At Site 4, staff members were willing to warm the meals cooked by parents at home and sent to the site with the children.

HYGIENE AND PHYSICAL EDUCATION

The final element in the physical dimension of care is the period of time devoted each day to both hygiene and physical education. None of the six study sites put a strong emphasis on either of these types of education. Apparently, this was viewed as the families' responsibility. While there was some attention to fine motor skill development, it was usually in conjunction with educational activities, especially at Site 5. At Site 2, there was some effort in motor skill development, but it was less formal (see Figure 6.12). The program description at Site 1 claimed to address this aspect of physical development in its care, but delivered little in the way of structured activity (see Figure 6.13). All of the programs provided opportunities for their children to get unstructured exercise in the form of outdoor play. But there is more

FIGURE 6.12. Group physical activity at Site 2. Four-year-olds prepare to start the day with sharing time, songs and stretching exercises.

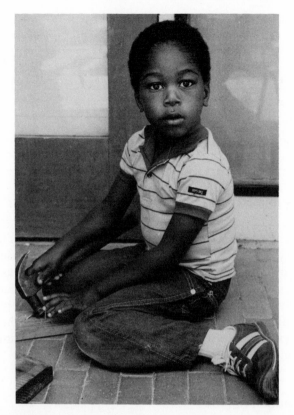

FIGURE 6.13. At Site 1, the children enjoy using saws, hammers, screwdrivers, and other tools. This boy is hammering nails into wood scraps, an activity which contributes to the development of his motor skills.

to physical education than simply turning children loose on a playground.

OVERALL ASSESSMENT OF THE PHYSICAL DIMENSION OF CARE

The study sites' ratings on each of the elements of physical care discussed above and an overall assessment score for each site are shown in Table 6.6.

TABLE 6.6
ASSESSMENTS OF PHYSICAL DIMENSION OF CARE

Elements of physical dimension	Site 1	Site 2	Site 3	Site 4	Site 5	Site 6
Health protection and sick care	2	3	3	5	4	1
Cleanliness	3	3	1	5	4	1
Nutrition	4	2	5	2	2	3
Hygiene and physical education	3	4	3	2	4	2
Total	12	12	12	14	14	7

THE ENVIRONMENTAL DIMENSION OF CARE

The environmental dimension of care is one of the first things that enters a day care observer's awareness. This awareness is accentuated when the observer is comparing several child care centers, as I was. In assessing the environmental dimension of care, four elements were selected for comparative analysis: (1) the impact of the neighborhood setting, (2) the amount of indoor space per child, (3) the physical organization of the space, and (4) the amount and condition of the equipment. These elements are discussed in Chapter 4.

NEIGHBORHOOD SETTING

Together, the building and the neighborhood in which a day care program is situated form the influence of the "setting" of a day care program upon its children. There is a wide variation in the types of buildings which house day care programs. For example, Sites 1 and 2 were located in an unoccupied school building. Site 3, on a naval base, was in a large building which was once a barracks and mess hall (see Figure 6.14). Site 4 was on the grounds of a large hospital in a building which was originally used for semi-outpatients and for families of patients. Site 5 was in a school building (see Figure 6.15). Site 6 was in a home (see Figures 6.16 and 6.17).

There was also definite variation in the neighborhoods surrounding the day care programs. Sites 1 and 2 were situated in an older residential neighborhood, which was quiet and safe, except for the

FIGURE 6.14. Day care in the workplace at Site 3. On this naval base, these children play close to a hangar where many of their parents work.

traffic around the school. The school yard was fenced in to keep children out of the street. Site 3, the child care program located on a naval base, kept its front exit secured so that its children could not walk out unnoticed. Its children had easy access to a large, fenced-in out-of-doors playground through two back exits. Just behind this center was a large aircraft hangar, and Navy jets were continuously flying overhead. The noise and the visual cues did not enhance this child care program's atmosphere.

Site 4 was located close to the hospital that it served. This proximity and the frequent visiting of parents, in their nurse's uniforms and custodial and other hospital garb, lent a distinctly clinical ambience to the Site 4 child care center. Site 5 was in a school with spacious surroundings, located in a lower-middle-income neighborhood that was undergoing rehabilitation. The school was surrounded by a fence and sat back from the road (see Figure 6.15). Site 6 was in a low-income neighborhood. Although the backyard was fenced in, the children were easily able to wander out through the screen door, either through the hole in it or by pushing the door open when it was not latched (see Figure 6.16).

FIGURE 6.15. The outdoor environment at Site 5. Every detail of the environment at Site 5 has been attended to with the aim of creating an inviting, child-oriented milieu.

INDOOR SPACE

Children respond to the character and amount of indoor space in their day care environments. A comparison of the amount of indoor space at each of the six sites revealed significant variation regarding this element of environmental quality. As shown in Table 6.7, the indoor space measured by square feet per child at each site ranged from a low of 11.1 square feet per child at Site 4 to a high of 31.6 feet at Site

FIGURE 6.16. The entrance at Site 6. Site 6 advertises its family day care services with a handpainted sign leaning against a bush.

TABLE 6.7
INDOOR SPACE PER CHILD

	Site 1	Site 2	Site 3	Site 4	Site 5	Site 6
Average daily enrollment	38	115	265	135	100	9
Square feet of indoor space	1,200	3,000	3,500	1,500	1,800	180
Average square feet per child	31.6	26.1	13.2	11.1[a]	18	20

[a]This average underestimates the actual square footage per child. Because the site is open twenty-four hours per day, there are additional children enrolled at night.

1. However, because of its poor staff-child ratio and its consequent need to pack children together in small, readily supervised spaces, Site 1 failed to utilize its ample indoor space.

PHYSICAL ORGANIZATION OF SPACE

With regard to the physical organization of space, an important consideration is the extent to which there is appropriate separation for

FIGURE 6.17. Child climbing stairs at Site 6. Family day care offers the comforts and familiarity as well as the hazards of a home.

FIGURE 6.18. The chaotic setting at Site 6. This disorganized and cramped sleeping and play room is in the basement.

different activities. For example, do children nap while others are roaming around in the same room? Only one of the sites in this study, Site 4, had a special sleeping room. Four sites—Sites 1, 2, 3, and 5—closed up one room for sleeping at particular times of the day. Children who were not sleeping, or who could not rest quietly, were moved to another room. Sites 2 and 5 administered this daily reorganization of space most effectively. Site 6 permitted playing and wandering children to disturb sleeping children, for the simple reason that there was but one caregiver who felt that she had to keep the children in close proximity to each other at all times in order to control them (see Figures 6.5, 6.17, and 6.18).

EQUIPMENT

Finally, there is the question of the adequacy and safety of equipment. A visual comparison of this characteristic of care at each of the

FIGURE 6.19. Exploring the environment at Site 3. The day care environment should be stimulating and challenging and should encourage exploration.

FIGURE 6.20. The infant care environment at Site 4.

TABLE 6.8
ASSESSMENTS OF ENVIRONMENTAL DIMENSION OF CARE

Elements of environmental dimension	Site 1	Site 2	Site 3	Site 4	Site 5	Site 6
Neighborhood setting	4	4	3	3	5	2
Indoor space per child	5	4	2	3	3	3
Physical organization of space	3	4	3	5	4	1
Equipment	3	3	3	4	5	1
Total	15	15	11	15	17	7

six sites revealed much variation. Toys and equipment that had been especially designed for children proved generally safer than a collection of household objects (including knives), such as that which Site 6 (with its low budget) offered its children. Of the remaining programs, Site 5 was the setting most sensitive to children's needs for special equipment. Site 4 was ranked second in this area, and Sites 1, 2, and 3 ranked third (see Figure 6.19). Figures 6.19 and 6.20 note that the equipment provided children should provide challenging, stimulating developmental activity.

OVERALL ASSESSMENT OF THE ENVIRONMENTAL DIMENSION OF CARE

The comparative ratings of the four elements of environmental care and overall assessment scores for each site are reported in Table 6.8.

AN OVERVIEW OF DIVERSITY IN CHILD CARE

Although quality of care is an elusive concept, it is possible to compare the quality of child day care programs. I have demonstrated this by comparing specific characteristics of care at each of the six study sites within social, psychological, educational, physical, and environmental dimensions. I have combined my ratings within

TABLE 6.9
ASSESSMENTS OF DIRECT CARE AT SIX DAY CARE SITES

Dimension	Site 1	Site 2	Site 3	Site 4	Site 5	Site 6
Social	12	18	12	13	18	8
Psychological	10	12	8	16	18	10
Educational	8	12	9	10	20	4
Physical	12	12	12	14	14	7
Environmental	15	15	11	15	17	7
Total direct care assessment	57	69	52	68	87	36

these dimensions of care to construct an overall assessment score for each site.

The sum of these overall assessments in each of the five dimensions of care ranges from 20 to 100. I have called this overall score the "total direct care assessment." As shown in Table 6.9, Site 6 received the lowest overall assessment of 36, and Site 5 received the highest overall assessment of 87. The scores for the remaining four sites fell in the middle range, from 52 to 69.

In interpreting these data it is important to note that the sites have been arranged in order of their relationships to the public and private sectors, with Site 1 operating under the most public auspices and Site 6 under the most private auspice (see Appendix A). Among the six sites included in this study, there is no direct relationship between quality of care and the degree of public or private sponsorship. This analysis of auspices and quality lends empirical weight to the normative proposition that the mixed-economy approach to the provision of child care generates a high degree of diversity. As seen in the overall assessment scores, the quality of care varies not only among different settings, but also among the several dimensions of quality measured within each setting.

The findings summarized in Table 6.9 suggest that the choices faced by child care consumers who seek to obtain the highest quality care for their children are indeed complex. The extent to which children will benefit from the diverse offerings in the mixed economy of child care is in large part a function of their parents' ability to discriminate among these choices. This critical issue is examined in the next chapter.

Chapter 7

CONSUMER RATINGS OF DAY CARE SERVICES

A Question of Looking Away

> *Hush a bye, don't you cry,*
> *Go to sleep little baby.*
> *And when you wake, you shall have*
> *All the pretty little horses.*
> —"All the Pretty Little Horses,"
> Traditional Song

The provision of child care or any social service in a mixed economy is believed to offer several advantages. Among these advantages are the freedom of consumer choice, the responsiveness of diversity to individual need, and the improved quality of service which derives from competition among providers. This view is often challenged by those who question the extent to which the market economy operates according to theory. In reality, consumers are not always free to choose, the range of program choices often does not meet their needs, and competition does not guarantee improved quality.

Social services such as child care are by nature difficult to evaluate. Even if these services were easy to evaluate, consumers of social services typically lack the financial resources and the information required to make good choices [1]. The consequences of poor choices are often more critical in the selection of care services than in the purchase of goods in the market economy. The purchase of an inferior television set is of much less consequence than the selection of an inferior nursing home. The purchase of a poorly made shirt is less painful to the consumer than the selection of a child care program which proves to have a negligent staff. While the advantages of competition may operate in certain parts of the market economy, social services frequently lack the geographical density of providers that is necessary for the positive effects of competition to occur.

Many of the general questions raised about the mixed economy of social services are particularly relevant to child care services. Informed consumer choice requires that the child care consumer, usually a parent, be highly knowledgeable about a complex service. Choices may be influenced by fads, misinformation, cultural norms, and matters of convenience and of cost. And poor choices can have detrimental consequences, as witnessed in recent cases of child abuse in child care centers [2]. Regulation of quality is always difficult in services where care is provided, and as we have seen, in the field of child care there are special problems with quality control. These stem from the diversity of program designs and philosophies which have evolved to meet the diversity of demand for child care in the mixed economy. Consumers of child care services come from a wide range of cultural, economic, and educational backgrounds. Given the complexity of choices, the difficulty of regulation, and the large variety of consumers, one of the central issues in assessing a mixed economy of child care is: How well is the diverse population of consumers able to judge the quality of these diverse offerings?

To explore this issue, I conducted a survey of 241 parents at the six different child care programs described in Chapters 5 and 6. The survey asked consumers to rank certain features of child care in order of importance and then to rate their children's child care programs along several dimensions of quality care. The following analysis examines child care consumer characteristics and preferences and then compares the consumers' ratings of their child care with the overall assessment scores for each child care study site computed in Chapter 6.

RESPONDENT CHARACTERISTICS

The 241 respondents returning questionnaires represent about 30% of the total number of parents to whom questionnaires were distributed. As reported in Table 7.1, 68% of the respondents represented two-parent households; however, 94% of the respondents were female. Of the questionnaire respondents, 81% were white, corresponding roughly to the proportion of white children (about 75%) in the six centers studied. Only 3% of the respondents had no high school diploma, and 46% had at least a college degree. Seventy-three percent of the respondents were employed full-time and worked a median distance of eight miles from home, with their child care programs located a median distance of four miles from their workplaces and three and a half miles from their homes. The average annual family income for all respondents was $27,670, and the average annual child care expenditure was $1,850, with the average percentage of family income spent on child care calculated to be 7%. But because some 18% of the respondents declined to state their incomes, the calculated average annual family income may not be entirely accurate. (For fiscal year notation, see Table 7.1.)

Also, 20 of the 241 respondents paid nothing for their child care services. Of these 20, 4 were employed as child care workers at the day care site where their children were enrolled; the other 16 were utilizing state-subsidized day care for low-income families. In total, 28 respondents were participating in the state-subsidized program at Site 1. Those who were not receiving the service free of charge were charged for the service on a sliding fee scale. They were not the only recipients of subsidized care. Although the fees charged were not means-tested, all respondents at Site 3 purchased Navy-subsidized child care at what was reportedly one-third of the going rate for that geographical area. Respondents at Site 4 purchased employer-subsidized day and night care at reduced rates.

CONSUMER PREFERENCES

As indicated in Table 7.1, the respondents represented a broad socioeconomic spectrum. These respondents were divided into six

TABLE 7.1

CHARACTERISTICS OF DAY CARE CONSUMER QUESTIONNAIRE RESPONDENTS[a]

Characteristic	Total	Site 1	Site 2	Site 3	Site 4	Site 5	Site 6
n =	241	28	110	44	28	27	4
Auspices	All	State-subsidized	Municipal	Military	Employer-sponsored	Private nonprofit	Proprietary family day care
Female	220 = 94%	28 = 100%	99 = 93%	38 = 86%	26 = 93%	25 = 93%	4 = 100%
Median age[b]	32	28	34	30	30	33	29
Single[b]	76 = 32%	22 = 79%	34 = 31%	8 = 18%	3 = 11%	6 = 22%	3 = 75%
White	196 = 81%	23 = 82%	95 = 86%	32 = 73%	25 = 89%	21 = 78%	2 = 50%
Education							
No high school diploma	6 = 3%	2 = 7%	15 = 14%	10 = 23%	1 = 2%	1 = 4%	0 = 0%
BA degree or higher	110 = 46%	4 = 14%	51 = 47%	15 = 34%	15 = 34%	17 = 63%	2 = 50%
Employment							
Employed (full or part time)	189 = 78%	19 = 68%	84 = 78%	37 = 84%	26 = 92%	19 = 70%	4 = 100%
Employed full time	146 = 73%	12 = 42%	65 = 59%	35 = 80%	21 = 75%	9 = 33%	4 = 100%

Distances (median)							
Home from workplace	8 mi.	7 mi.	6 mi.	8 mi.	15.5 mi.	8 mi.	11.5 mi.
Day care from home	3.5 mi.	3 mi.	2.5 mi.	5 mi.	15 mi.	4.5 mi.	7 mi.
Day care from workplace	4 mi.	4 mi.	6 mi.	2 mi.	0 mi.	7 mi.	12 mi.
Economic status[d]							
Annual average family income	$27,670[c]	$9,444	$30,076	$25,452	$26,576	$32,500	$21,500
Average annual day care expenditure	$1,850[c]	$231	$1,899	$1,718	$2,533	$2,589	$3,000
Number who pay $0 for day care	20	16	2	0	2	0	0
Average percentage of family income spent on day care	7%	2%	6%	7%	7%	8%	14%

[a] As reported by respondents themselves.
[b] Includes single, separated, widowed, divorced.
[c] Weighted average.
[d] Fiscal year 1984.

groups of parents, each group being parents whose children were enrolled in one of the six child care programs. There were statistically significant differences regarding three important consumer characteristics among these groups of parents: annual family income, monthly day care expenditure, and educational background. But despite these varying characteristics, there was a powerful consensus among the parents when they were asked to rank particular features of child care in order of their importance. As shown in Table 7.2, parents listed staff warmth as the most important characteristic of a child care program. Only respondents at Site 5, which offered a highly structured preschool program with a well-articulated educational philosophy, deviated from this

TABLE 7.2

WHAT DO DAY CARE CONSUMERS WANT? PREFERENCE RANKINGS ON CHARACTERISTICS OF CARE[a]

Characteristics of a day care program	All sites	Site 1	Site 2	Site 3	Site 4	Site 5	Site 6
Staff warmth	1	1	1	1	1	2	1
Educational program	2	2	3	2	2	1	3
Social activities	3	5	2	3	4	3	5
Program hours	4	3	4	5	3	5	4
Physical activities	5	6	5	4	5	4	2
Cost	6	4	6	6	7	6	6
Distance	7	7	6	7	6	6	7
Building	8	8	7	8	8	8	7

[a]Respondents were asked, "When choosing a day care program, what do you consider the most important features?" and were directed to rank the eight characteristics of care listed in this table in order of importance. (These characteristics were not listed in the order presented here.) This table shows the average overall ($n = 241$) preference ranking (in the column labeled "All sites") and the average rankings disaggregated by site. Note that the characteristics listed represent an aspect of each of the dimensions of direct and indirect care defined by this study:
Dimensions of direct care:
Social: social activities
Psychological: staff warmth
Educational: educational program
Physical: physical activities
Environmental: building
Indirect care:
Program hours
Cost
Distance
Consumer's mean preference rankings: 1 = most important; 8 = eighth in importance.

preference, listing the education program as most important and staff warmth as second. In general, respondents at all sites tended to agree upon the order of importance of the eight program characteristics listed in the questionnaire.

The findings in Table 7.2 are particularly interesting in light of the tension between function and feeling, which I discussed in Chapter 1. Policy discussions about the mixed economy of child care focus on questions of purpose such as developmental versus custodial purposes and regulatory standards. However, the survey results suggest that consumers place greater emphasis on the intimacy of child care than on the functional designs through which it is carried out. Concrete variables of convenience, such as cost and distance, are reported as among the least important elements in the personal equations of consumer choice.

Consumer Ratings of Program Quality

The above discussion focuses on consumers' preferences; now we turn to their evaluation of the child care they were actually using. To gather consumers' judgments about the quality of day care programs in which their own children were enrolled, my questionnaire contained a set of twenty-four special rating questions. This set included a subset of four questions in each of the five dimensions of direct care and four questions in the indirect or practical dimension. The responses to each set of questions were summed to provide an overall consumer rating in each dimension of care. The five direct care ratings were combined for a total direct care rating, and the indirect care rating was added to that for a total care rating (see Appendixes A, B, and C for further explanation).

The findings shown in Tables 7.3 and 7.4 reveal a very positive and tightly clustered set of ratings. The average score on each dimension of care varied just slightly between 14 and 15 on a scale of 4 to 20 points. For each site the total direct care ratings ranged from 71 to 79 points on a scale of 24 to 120. In general, for each site consumers rated each dimension of care as being close to what they would imagine as ideal conditions. In no case did the total care rating for each site represent less that two-thirds of what consumers thought were ideal conditions. What this means is that parents at each different site rated their programs similarly.

TABLE 7.3
OVERALL CONSUMER RATINGS OF DIMENSIONS OF CARE

Ratings by dimension of care	Rating range	Mean for all consumers	Standard deviation
Social dimension	4 to 20	16.25	± 2.57
Psychological dimension	4 to 20	15.48	± 2.82
Educational dimension	4 to 20	14.55	± 3.14
Physical dimension	4 to 20	14.25	± 2.59
Environmental dimension	4 to 20	15.05	± 2.98
Total direct care rating	20 to 100	75.44	±10.81
Indirect care rating	4 to 20	16.34	± 3.01
Total care rating	24 to 120	91.87	±11.61

How does one interpret these findings? There are at least three explanations for the consistently high ratings. First, it is theoretically conceivable that in every dimension of care each program actually provided a high quality of service. This is a dubious proposition, how-

TABLE 7.4
CONSUMER RATINGS OF DIMENSIONS OF CARE BY SITE[a]

Ratings by dimension of care	Rating range	All sites	Site 1	Site 2	Site 3	Site 4	Site 5	Site 6
Social	4 to 20	16	16	17	16	15	17	16
Psychological	4 to 20	15	14	16	15	15	16	18
Educational	4 to 20	15	13	15	15	13	17	11
Physical	4 to 20	14	14	14	15	13	13	16
Environmental	4 to 20	15	15	16	14	15	16	13
Total direct care rating	20 to 100	75	72	78	75	71	79	74
Indirect care rating	4 to 20	16	17	16	17	17	15	15
Total care rating	24 to 120	91	89	94	92	88	94	89

[a]Respondents were asked, "How does this day care program compare with what you would imagine to be your ideal day care program?" and were directed to rate four listed characteristics of care in each dimension from 1 (far from ideal) to 5 (the ideal). The responses were added together in groups of four in order to attain a consumer rating for each dimension of care which would fall between 4 and 20. The five direct care ratings were added together to produce a total direct care rating which would fall between 20 and 100. The indirect care rating (falling between 4 and 20) was added to the total direct care rating to produce a total care rating with a possible range of 24 to 120.

ever, in light of the evidence from the comparative observations of these programs discussed in Chapter 6.

The second explanation is that these ratings reflect a more general trend in consumer assessments of social services. A number of studies suggest that consumers are prone to assess social services favorably [3]. This tendency to report a high degree of satisfaction on social service consumer surveys has been subject to several interpretations. It can be seen as a reflection of consumer fear (especially among consumers of publicly subsidized programs) that poorly rated services might be discontinued. Whether made by a recipient of a state-supported service or by a full-paying consumer of a proprietary service, such a consumer evaluation is a forced expression of gratitude, politeness, or approval. It represents an inclination to rationalize program participation as a valid and satisfying activity. This is a sad adaptation of consumer expectations to the level of service actually available [4]. It is my concern that this type of adaptation is taking place all around us and among us. We are adapting to the increasingly functional and possibly deteriorating quality of care.

In designing this study, I made an effort to minimize the possible effects of these different motives to exaggerate consumer satisfaction with day care. The survey questions concerning quality of care were phrased to avoid a direct expression of the consumers' satisfaction and to tap the consumers' perception of the program relative to what they would consider an *ideal* service (see Questions 29 through 54 on the questionnaire in Appendix C).

Finally, the consistently high and very similar ratings of the six study sites may require a third explanation: Parents may not recognize the deficiencies of their child care programs. Child care programs are places where parents leave their children for periods of time which would otherwise be spent at home. The consumers' view that child care is a substitute for the home is implicit in their emphasis on staff warmth (Table 7.2) as the most important feature of these programs. Because child care is, in essence, so "close to home," it is possible that parents find it exceedingly difficult to report, or even to recognize, that they are leaving their children in a setting which may have deficiencies. And this may be the case whether consumer assessment questions are phrased in terms of either direct satisfaction or some imagined ideal conditions.

THE IMPACT OF EDUCATION, INCOME, AND COST ON CONSUMER RATINGS

Although the consumers' assessments are consistently high, there is some variation in their ratings. There are many factors that might account for this variance; education, income, and cost stand out as the most influential. Well-educated consumers are more likely to possess the knowledge and skills to make discerning judgments about the quality of their child care programs. Affluent consumers can exercise more choice, and thus they are less likely to feel constrained in making critical judgments for lack of alternatives. And consumers who pay high costs for day care services no doubt feel a greater entitlement to get their money's worth and cast a somewhat more critical eye upon services than those who pay little or nothing for day care.

In examining the impact of these three factors on consumer ratings, education appears to make the strongest and most consistent difference. A comparison of ratings by consumers with at least some college education to the ratings by those with no college education reveals a statistically significant difference on four on the five dimensions of care. The more educated the consumers, the less favorable their rating of care in terms of an imagined ideal. Similar patterns emerge for the factors of income and cost. Those with high incomes were more critical in their assessments of care than low-income consumers, and those who paid high fees for child care services tended to rate the dimensions of care *lower* than those who paid small fees or nothing for the service.

While education, income, and cost have a statistically significant impact on consumer ratings, the substantive significance of these findings is not terribly profound. In fact, it is minimal. The mean ratings for different education, income, and cost groups varied, at most, by little more than 1 point and were all quite favorable in their assessments of the quality of care. For a more detailed analysis of their substantive impact on consumer ratings, these independent variables were entered into two multiple-regression equations in which consumer ratings for direct care and the total of both direct and indirect care were the dependent variables. In neither case did the independent variables combined explain more than 6% of the variance in consumer ratings. Thus, while consumer ratings differed as anticipated by education, income, and cost, those differences were very small and of little predictive value.

IMPLICATIONS FOR THE MERITS OF CONSUMER CHOICE IN THE MIXED ECONOMY OF DAY CARE

We began this chapter with the question: How well are consumers able to judge the quality of the diverse offerings of day care? The findings of my survey do not offer a definitive answer, but they are suggestive. A few points stand out clearly: Consumer ratings on every dimension of quality were uniformly high regardless of the auspices under which their programs operated. When controlled for individual characteristics such as income, education, and cost, the consumer ratings showed small differences. But overall, the ratings remained very high for every group.

When we match consumer ratings by site with the ratings obtained from direct and systematic observations comparing these sites, there are large discrepancies, as noted in Table 7.5. The research assessments of the sites on each dimension of care produced a set of scores with a much wider range than the consumer ratings. More important, the research assessments of five of the six sites were considerably less favorable than consumer ratings in rating the dimensions of care (from 3 to 38 points lower).

The findings suggest that child care consumers do not exercise a high level of discrimination in assessing the quality of care delivered by the programs in which they participate. In part this may be because of the complexity of the phenomenon. As I discussed in Chapter 6, quality of care has many elements that are difficult to grasp. However, the general difficulty in assessing quality of care does not account for the uniformly high ratings, nor does it explain why the consumers' education made so little difference in the ratings. In addition to the complexity of child care as a service, there is also the tremendous sensitivity involved when parents leave their children in settings that substitute for home. This sensitivity may inhibit consumers from looking closely at something as difficult to examine as the quality of care [5]. A discussion of this point can be found in Chapter 3.

TABLE 7.5
RESEARCH ASSESSMENTS (RA) AND CONSUMER RATINGS (CR)[a]

Dimension of care	Site 1		Site 2		Site 3		Site 4		Site 5		Site 6	
	RA	CR	RA	CR	RA	CR	RA	CR	RA	CR	RA	CR
Social	12	16	18	17	12	16	13	15	18	17	8	16
Psychological	10	14	12	16	8	15	16	15	18	16	10	18
Educational	8	13	12	15	9	15	10	13	20	17	4	11
Physical	12	14	12	14	12	15	14	13	14	13	7	16
Environmental	15	15	15	16	11	14	15	15	17	16	7	13
Total direct care	57	72	69	78	52	75	68	71	87	79	36	74
CR − RA =		+15		+9		+23		+3		−8		+38

[a]This table compares research assessments (RA) of the care provided at each site with the mean consumer ratings (CR) of that care, by dimension and by total direct care. For each site, the total direct care consumer rating is compared to the total direct care research assessment, producing a figure which may be either positive or negative and indicating the direction and magnitude of difference between consumer ratings and research assessments. Note that consumers at five out of the six sites rate their care higher than the research assessment of their care.

Whatever the explanation, if these findings accurately reflect a broad tendency among child care consumers from varied backgrounds (1) to be inattentive regarding the basic elements of care and (2) to overestimate the quality of care, then the mixed economy of child care functions in the absence of informed consumer choice. As noted earlier, one of the theoretical advantages of the mixed economy of child care derives from competition among providers seeking to attract well-informed consumers. To the extent that consumers lack the knowledge, skill, and, perhaps, inclination to discriminate among day care provisions of different quality, the mixed economy operates with a low degree of internal regulation. Under these circumstances, the mixed economy of child care tends to benefit providers more than the children they serve. Child care providers continue to profit regardless of the quality of their product whenever consumers are unable or unwilling to "vote with their feet" by removing children from their programs.

Are parents settling for less, for lower quality care, because they are unable to envision anything better? Have we, as parents and as a society, become indifferent to the trade-off between function and feeling? Are we already so deeply committed to what is "functional" that we are denying our instincts and our feelings about what quality child care really is? Perhaps being comfortable about what we do with our children has become a question of denial. What we do not see will not hurt us; it may hurt our children, but at least we won't know it.

Conclusion

THE MIXED ECONOMY
OF CHILD CARE

Speaking Truth to Social Change

> *Sometimes I feel like a motherless child,*
> *A long, such a long way from home.*
> —"Sometimes I Feel like a Motherless Child,"
> Old Spiritual

> *It is 11 o'clock.*
> *Where are your children?*
> —Public Service Announcement

We have looked at the tangled problem of child day care from several perspectives. Chapter 1 began by placing child day care in the general context of human care. The function vs. feeling trade-off, which was presented in Chapter 1, must always be the basic philosophical question in our consideration of child care and of all other forms of human care. We must always weigh the level of function against the level of feeling provided by our care services. Each trade-off we make between function and feeling is complex and critical. Our humanity can be put in jeopardy whenever we choose a functional mode of care over the most humane mode of care. Although every rational decision can be argued for with logic, only the heart can feel the other side of the argument. Trade-offs are necessary compromises, yet each small step away from a humane approach to human care is a step that we must scrutinize.

What does this have to do with child day care? Everything. We are a large nation, grappling with a major sociological and economic transition. Mothers, the traditional providers of child care, have entered the work force in droves; their children are now in the care of someone other than their parents for all or part of each working day. We must keep a watchful eye on our response as a society to this development. Child day care is a major social experiment that we are conducting on our children and, therefore, on our future. Experimentation can lead to great discoveries, but it also can bring on undesigned and undesirable consequences. The truth is that no one, not even the "experts," can say for certain what is best for our children. No one can predict the outcome of our modern social experiment upon child care. But we must continue to ask who cares and why along the way.

Understanding the political, economic, and psychological motives behind the provision of child day care will allow us to better evaluate the quality of the care being provided. And an understanding of our motives when we evaluate our day care programs will allow us to penetrate our own barriers of denial and guilt. All too often, it is easier to look away from our innermost concerns about whom we leave our children with while we work, than to experience anxiety and guilt when we feel that we have no choice but to leave our children in the care of others while we work.

I concluded Chapter 1 by suggesting that we must keep an eye on what we do with the individuals who are cared for in institutional settings. Anytime it becomes economically or politically effective to warehouse human beings, the human soul is threatened. We then move into the advancing domain of material and mechanical values—the domain in which the human spirit is ignored, denied, depleted. No, we are not warehousing our children, at least not on a massive scale and not officially. But we are warehousing—storing at least cost, with little attention to anything but minimum function—some of our elderly, our mentally ill, and our prisoners. The questions I ask are: Are we alert enough to see even minor indications that we are doing a subtler version of this to our children? Are we looking away from minor indications that forecast a disastrous trend in human care? We are already choosing child care based upon economic incentives. And child care programs are frequently subject to functional economic limitations, limitations which diminish the quality and personal nature of the care provided our children. It is up to you, the reader, to look at the world we live in and answer these questions.

Chapter 2 focused on the realm of the polity, in which public policy grapples with child care issues from a perspective that is, by and large, politically motivated. The fact that child care emerged as a national political issue in the 1980s is both inspiring and discouraging. This development is inspiring because it signifies that child day care issues are moving toward center stage. This movement can attract a concentration of attention, research, and resources to the improvement of the child care scenario in the United States. This same development is discouraging in that child day care is becoming a political issue that ties into the important questions we must ask regarding relegating the best interests of children and their families to political opportunism and strife. The ethical clarity we need in order to see what we as a society are doing with our dependents becomes murky in the realm of politics. And politics is not the only realm of activity that clouds our vision.

Chapter 3 noted that the free market, trademark of the American dream, continues to answer many of our child care needs, offering a wide variety of programs provided by numerous organizations at a range of prices. Again, there are advantages and disadvantages attending these developments. Clearly, many parents are experiencing greater freedom of choice as a result of the private sector's involvement with child care.

Yet, however beneficial it is to have the participation of the market in meeting the demand for child care, the bottom line in the marketplace is economic gain. The function of business—in this case, the child care business—is to produce a profit. Without profit, child care businesses cannot remain in business. This means that feeling, the counterpart to function in care, is going to survive in the market to the degree that it is profitable. This renders the feeling side of care vulnerable to economic forces. Feeling is at a disadvantage because money cannot buy love.

Money can, however, buy child care, and parents work to earn money to pay for child care so that they can work to earn money to support themselves and their families. The child care market depends upon the existence of child care consumers. This places much of the responsibility for the behavior of the child care market on the consumer. As a participant in the market economy, the consumer, usually a parent, makes many decisions based upon the value of time and money. All too often, family economics and family management take the forefront over family feelings. Working parents with low- and middle-class incomes are discovering that although money cannot buy love, enough of it can buy time for love and caring, time for parents to spend with their children and time for the "hands on," direct caring native to the primary sphere, native to the family. This hands-on caring is the core of and model for the expressions of care that these children will later make as adults.

Chapter 4, therefore, focused on the primary or family sphere, the first home of direct care, detailing the basic needs of developing children. While each detail of development may seem insignificant in isolation, it is out of a combination of these ingredients that a whole and healthy child grows. An analysis of child care issues must tie the larger influences, composed of policy, politics, and economics, into the smaller picture of a young child's growth and development in order to show the whole picture. Every step in a young child's development is a precious step. Chapter 4 is located in the central part of this book for several reasons. First, it enables the reader to combine broader philosophical (Chapter 1), political (Chapter 2), and economic (Chapter 3) developments with a detailed understanding of the intimate world of the developing child. The child does not exist in isolation; he or she is affected by all of these overarching forces. Chapter 4 also suggested that there is a great deal to know about caring for children. This chapter categorized information about care in a way that child care programs can be analyzed, along five dimensions of direct care. This format was applied in the study presented in Chapters 6 and 7.

The discussion to this point sets the stage for a close look at six child care programs presented in Chapters 5, 6, and 7. My study revealed a great deal of organizational and programmatic variation among the six child care programs. As I recorded this broad variation, I observed that quality in child care may take many forms. I also observed that the absence of quality in child care is subtle and at the same time pervasive. This absence of quality is so common that it exists almost unrecognized. It is so prevalent that we allow ourselves all too often to call mediocrity "quality" and to accept the status quo in human care without asking why it is the way it is.

Toward answering this question, my study delineated three important characteristics of the care services that are distributed in our mixed economy. First, heterogeneity of services is inherent in the mixed economy of care, with the result that the quality is highly variable. In a mixed economy, public policy of care encourages diversification. This reduces the power of the polity to guarantee equity of care to all recipients of care. The power of the polity naturally diminishes by its intentional dispersion of responsibility for the distribution of that care.

Keep in mind, however, that this indictment of the mixed economy of care is equally applicable to its major theoretical alternative, the centrally planned socialized welfare state. Neither the diversity promoted by a mixed economy nor the uniformity of a centralized public program can ensure both quality and equity. Efforts to balance quality and equity often weigh in favor of the latter. A socialized day care program may improve equity of access. Access is more readily controlled than quality. When quality is not controlled, it is not evenly distributed. When quality is not evenly distributed, there is no equity of quality. If the quality of care is reduced to mere function, it remains difficult to control. If feeling is part of the quality of care, it is even more difficult to control. Again, money cannot buy love—not even public money.

The second characteristic of human services distributed by a mixed economy is limited options. There are not always as many choices as might be expected. Consumer choice plays an integral role in mediating between cost and quality in the for-profit sector. In the mixed economy of child care, choices may be constrained by income, geography, and employment. For example, employer-sponsored care in the workplace offers a convenience with which outside centers can rarely compete. Similarly, publicly sponsored child care programs, which are highly subsidized, offer the only choice available for many low-income participants. Where consumer choice is limited, its regulatory power is curtailed. Mixed-economy consumers, as a group, often lack the full measure of power exercised by consumers in a completely private sector.

Third, and most central to the question of choice, is the ability to make choices regarding child care services. That is, where choice is available, how well informed are consumers in exercising their options? The empirical study of consumer ratings of child care described in Chapter 7 strongly suggests that child care consumers are not highly adept at discriminating between optimal, mediocre, and suboptimal care, regardless of economic and educational status. The complex character of child care makes it difficult for consumers to understand and assess quality. Efficient consumer choice of child care services is further impeded by the fact that choosing a child care service is a sensitive issue which strikes close to home. Especially when it involves children and family responsibilities, many consumers find it difficult to be critical of an agency to whom they entrust their children. Thus, because of the complex nature of child care and its sensitive nature, consumer choice is often muddled. And the selection of care services may favor affordability and convenience over quality.

The three characteristics of the mixed economy of child care highlighted by the empirical study are:

1. The presence of structural and substantive variations in services available to consumers.
2. The diminished capacity of consumers as a group to exert a regulatory influence upon the quality of services.
3. The inability of consumers to evaluate the quality of their care services when their objectivity is obscured by both the complexity of care and the moral implications of their choices [1].

This view of child care consumers must be extended beyond parents to public agencies, as well as to employers, taxpayers, and every other individual and organizational member of our child-care-consuming society. As a society, we are no better prepared to evaluate quality in care than are individual parents. What is required is a major effort to learn about human care and the conditions that either enhance or jeopardize it.

QUESTION THE GOALS OF CARE

An ongoing examination of our goals as we develop child care (and any form of dependent care) policy is essential. Many of our existing goals are laudable; however, they may be goals for which caring for children is secondary. They may be goals which sound as if they seek the best interests of children but do not, in reality, address children's needs for care. Let us consider a few of these goals.

THE GOAL OF PROMOTING LABOR FORCE PARTICIPATION

Child care undoubtedly facilitates parents' participation in the labor force. Labor force participants and would-be participants report that the lack of adequate child care prevents them from seeking employment and from entering job training and even causes them to quit their jobs [2]. Despite these reports, as mentioned in other chapters, there has been no public policy response to the universal need for child care among working parents of young children. Instead, policies have selectively focused on the child care needs of low-income families or on the child care costs borne by middle-income families.

Child Care for Low-Income Families. The provision of child care to low-income and unemployed parents is designed to facilitate labor force participation as an alternative to welfare dependence. For example, the 1981 Community Work Experience Program (CWEP) allowed states to require all recipients of Aid to Families with Dependent Children (AFDC) to register under the Work Incentive Program (WIN) to work "up to a maximum number of hours equal to the amount of AFDC that the family is entitled to receive divided by the greater of the applicable federal or state minimum wage" [3]. A parent of a child between the ages of three and six was exempt from this requirement unless "child care is available for such child" [4]. According to this law no one was required to participate in CWEP if, as a result of such participation, children were left "unsupervised or improperly supervised." The quality of child care for CWEP participants was vaguely defined by statutory reference to "appropriate" and "adequate" care [5].

However, this was a very meager assurance. In the absence of federal funds under CWEP for setting uniform standards of adequacy and monitoring child care services, states were left to enforce their own health and safety standards for child care centers within their jurisdictions and, in most cases, to regulate family child care homes. Such regulatory functions were and continue to be tasks which the states have limited resources to perform. Also, because CWEP earnings were not legally considered to be earned income but were instead merely the equivalent of the recipient's AFDC grant, the CWEP participant was ineligible for any "child care expense disregard." Nothing like a child care tax credit was available for CWEP participants. CWEP parents, already strapped for funds, were therefore given little incentive to pay for quality child care.

Child Care for Working Parents. Other policies have been and continue to be designed to affect labor force participation among the nonpoor. While the CWEP participant who was merely "working off" his or her AFDC payment was ineligible for a child care income disregard or tax credit, his or her privately employed middle-class counterpart was and continues to be eligible for this type of tax assistance.

With the Economic Recovery Act of 1981, Congress increased incentives for the development of work-related child care, creating two important tax benefits for employees and improving the tax incentives for employers [6]. There were several conditions attached to these tax credits for care of dependents. Employed taxpayers who received welfare benefits in the form of child care were not eligible to claim the tax credit, as this was viewed as a double benefit to them. The definition of "dependents" covered more than just children. A working parent who maintained a household might claim child or dependent care credit for any child under age fifteen, and a dependent or spouse of any age "who is physically or mentally incapable of caring for himself or herself" [7]. Credit for the cost of enrolling a dependent in a "dependent care center" was only to be claimed if the center complied with "all applicable federal and local laws and regulations" [8]. This stipulation exerted some control over the taxpayer's choice of child care in the direction of centers that met quality requirements in the areas which regulations attempted to control.

While employers were not, as the law read, to design their day care programs to produce particular tax results, they were allowed to structure day care programs to "meet both their fiscal and physical needs."

THE GOAL OF PROMOTING THE WELFARE OF WOMEN

The women's movement, concerned in part with the liberation of women from the "subjugation" of motherhood, childrearing, and homemaking, has advocated a public child care policy as a step toward the equalization of the sexes. The argument is that universal child care (available to all citizens) will allow women to take their rightful place as gainfully employed members of society. A woman's employment provides independence, economic security, and an opportunity for fulfillment in the adult world of work. Single mothers depend upon employment, as do many married mothers, for basic economic survival. Moreover, employment "alters relationships of power and submission within marriage" and the family [9], and therefore in all of society.

One of the important questions raised by this approach is whether paid employment outside the home is worth more than the economic value of homemaking and childrearing activities [10]. Another question that warrants attention is whether working women actually do two jobs: full-time employment outside the home and full-time household management inside the home.

THE GOAL OF PROMOTING EARLY CHILDHOOD EDUCATION

When the primary goal of a child care program is to encourage the development of skills among its participants, the program is usually considered a nursery or preschool program—the term "day care" is replaced by "school." When the word "care" is dropped from the description of what programs children under six are enrolled in, we must ask whether care, itself, is also dropped in favor of education.

Discussions of preschool policies for early childhood education tend to emphasize either compensatory or developmental approaches. The compensatory approach argues for preschool education selectively aimed at disadvantaged children. The objective is not to accelerate the intellectual development of young children as much as it is to help some children to develop at the same rate as their peers from more advantaged homes. In contrast, the developmental approach argues for universal access to preschool education for the purpose of promoting early cognitive development in all children. This approach would require an expansion of the public education system to incorporate prekindergarten-age children.

Compensatory Coverage. The compensatory approach continues to be represented most vividly in the Head Start program, which promotes "an evolutionary approach to the problem of designing effective interventions for economically disadvantaged children and their families." Head Start has served as a "stable base from which to experiment" with a variety of methods [11]. One of many lessons learned from this program is that motivational and health factors, rather than cognitive inadequacy, may influence children's academic performance [12]. In the education of young, especially disadvantaged, children, building self-esteem and physical health as well as the provision of other components of care may be as essential as a well-designed academic curriculum. Although there is debate over their long-range effects, which are difficult to test, Head Start and other compensatory prekindergarten programs have been applauded for their favorable effects on the cognitive development of disadvantaged children. (This debate was further discussed in Chapter 4.)

Over the years of experimenting with compensatory preschool, it has become apparent that postpreschool continuity is important, but only worthwhile if it is a follow-up to a significant amount of time in preschool. One recent study demonstrated that the total number of hours children spent in prekindergarten influenced the effect of later educational continuity upon their verbal-conceptual abilities. Specifically, it concluded that: "For continuity to be effective in enhancing knowledge of verbal concepts at the end of second grade, the pre-Kindergarten experience apparently must be of sufficient duration, that is, something beyond 500 hours" [13]. These are only a few examples of what has been learned about educating young children since the inception of Head Start.

Developmental Coverage. The Head Start program has, along with other compensatory preschool experiences of recent decades, opened the minds of the public and the policymakers to the developmental potential of preschool education for both poor and nonpoor children. There is increasing support for early childhood education. With the advancement of scientific knowledge regarding cerebral physiology and educational psychology, popular as well as professional perceptions of learning potential in early childhood have been altered.

The rapid development of connections among brain cells and the consequent growth of brain capacity occurring between birth and age three suggests that these are the years in which the young mind is most receptive to learning. Research suggests that approximately 80% of these connections are formed by age three. Within the first six months of life, brain capacity reaches 50% of adult potential. By age three, this capacity reaches 80% of that potential. About the age of four, the developmental emphasis shifts from the formation of sensory pathways in the rear brain to the forming of auxiliary connections in the frontal lobes of the brain. However important the frontal lobe phase of cerebral development, the connections formed during it are dependent upon the quality of the cerebral "hardware" forged during the first years of life [14].

Arguments for the great cognitive potential of early childhood are supported by reports that young children can learn to operate and program computers [15]. This view is reinforced by claims from other learning theorists that young children can learn an astounding array of things: to play violin and piano through methods such as Suzuki's "talent education" or "Suzuki method," to solve mathematical problems, to speak foreign languages, and, even before they can talk, to read their own, foreign, and even ancient languages [16].

An increasing number of parents feel pressured to provide preschool education instead of child care for their children in order to prepare them for the demands and competition of later academic life. Special preschool programs, toys, computer programs, and parenting seminars such as the "Better Baby Institute" are being established by responsive entrepreneurs for parents who can pay [17].

If the evidence on early learning potential is correct, parents who do not "buy into" the early childhood education movement, because they do not believe in it or cannot afford it, deprive their children of certain academic advantages. The gap will increase between children exposed to intensive, professionally designed, "hi-tech" "space-age" equipped curricula and those from what are now called deprived environments. Compensatory education will then have to offer considerably more than its existing preschool curriculum. Perhaps the end result of the intensive early training trends will be the universalization of early childhood education programs: all children, beginning in their infancy, will be eligible, if not required, to enroll. However, at present there remain philosophical and economic barriers to the subordinating of child care policy to educational policy. If, on the other hand, the true caring for children—the feeling of care—will be replaced by purely functional educational activity, then these barriers may be protecting us.

CONSIDER THE TRADE-OFFS

These broad questions regarding the purpose are of day care and preschool closely interwoven with several basic issues pertaining to the operational design of such programs. These issues involve matters of cost versus quality, setting, regulation, and diversity.

COST VS. QUALITY

Market and political methods of service distribution have been contrasted in terms of the cost of care provided under these private and public auspices. While the political economy model of distribution may have the effect of raising the cost of care, it does not necessarily ensure a proportionate increase in quality. But quality cannot be predicted on the sole basis of the sector through which child care is allocated. For example, within both the market sector and the public sector, the characteristics of child care programs vary. Disparities in the per child cost of child care among programs may in part represent differing programmatic decisions regarding the quality versus cost trade-off.

One determinant of quality is the staff-child ratio. And one way to reduce cost is to hire fewer staff. A second influence upon the quality of care involves the caregiver's wage. Simply put, more qualified caregivers are attracted to work in programs which pay better wages. High-paying programs are few and far between. This means that well-paid child caregivers are rare. How many university professors would leave their jobs for employment in a day care or preschool program?

IN- OR OUT-OF-HOME CARE?

The quality of a dependent's child care experience is influenced by the setting in which this experience occurs. While there are many ways to categorize child care settings, the distinction between in-home and out-of-home care is among the most controversial. While the tendency is to dichotomize the choices of program design, contrasting in-home care to center care, it is important to remember that there are a range of factors that vary widely within each category. Some of these factors include the number of children or dependents in care, their hours in care, and the amount of personal attention they are provided in the particular setting.

While the highest proportion of federal child care funds has gone to out-of-home care, other settings have also been supported by federal dollars. As noted by Sheila Kamerman and Alfred Kahn, federal dollars were distributed to programs eligible for federal reimbursement (under Titles XX, IV-A, and IV-B of the Social Security Act) in a pattern which favored full-time center care. Under this distribution, center care received 55%; family day care homes, 23%; in-home care, 21%; and other care settings, 2% of federal funds [18]. While weighted in favor of out-of-home care, at least 43% of these funds were allocated to noncenter care (family day care homes' 23%, plus in-home care's 21%) [19].

Institutional settings have been criticized for various failings. During the 1940s and 1960s, a number of studies of institutionalized infants found the effects of too much institutionalized care this setting to be counterdevelopmental. In the mid-1940s, Rene Spitz examined the consequences of the effect of "continuous institutional care of infants under one year of age, for reasons other than sickness." Spitz found that children deprived of their mothers at three months and reared in an unstimulating (foundling-home) institutional environment suffered delays in their physical, behavioral, and cognitive development. In fact,

37% of these children died by the age of two [20]. While his findings provide a strong empirical argument against an existing mode of group care, it also demonstrated that institutional care need not be destructive, that the terrible effects of "hospitalism" could be prevented in a healthy group care environment which purposively encourages development [21].

Goldfarb's study in the 1940s concluded that children who survived the first three years of institutionalization were not necessarily going to be free of its scars. Indeed, a high frequency of cognitive and behavioral problems appeared several years after the children he studied had been removed from institutional care [22].

Various forms of institutional and group care have also been criticized on ideological grounds. That children should be deprived of their mother's attention, placed in the hands of the state or other authorities, and reared in an extrafamilial environment is viewed by some as un-American, undemocratic, and a threat to the American family. Yet, as Martin Wolins pointed out, "Are not the deplorable conditions of many children who live in AFDC households and the revolving-door rotation of those in foster homes a serious challenge? . . . Perhaps an asylum should not be rejected out of hand after all." Wolins suggested that the family and the asylum institution can serve one another, each by "unlock[ing] the usually well-guarded gates of the other" [23]. And possibly, an intelligently designed institutional program can enhance the lives of its wards by encouraging independence and development.

These issues have filtered into the debate over the value of part-time institutional or "day" care. The basic caring functions of the family are not so clearly usurped by the part-time out-of-home care of its dependent members as by their total institutionalization. Still, concerns about the negative consequences of institutional care, particularly for young children, cast a shadow of skepticism over the potential impact of child care. Those who are more optimistic about child care provisions sometimes point to the experiences of group child care in both the Soviet Union and Israel. In these communal settings, child care is often cited as having a positive influence on the development of children. According to kibbutz directors, an essential factor in the provision of group care is that parents and staff be "well aware of an explicit set of values and desirable traits toward which optimal development leads" [24].

Whatever impact child care services may have on children, from a policy perspective there is one clear advantage in providing these services through out-of-home group care settings rather than in private homes. Out-of-home care settings are more visible to the public and hence more amenable to quality control than in-home care.

In the in-home versus out-of-home child care debate, family day care is the compromise between extremes. Yet it poses a number of problems in the expedition of child care goals and quality controls. Family day care in the United States falls into three categories, which reflect their administrative and regulatory characteristics:

1. Unregulated providers, operating informally and not falling within any regulatory jurisdiction.
2. Regulated (by state and/or federal law) providers, operating independently.
3. Regulated providers who operate programs under the auspices of a sponsoring agency. [25]

The issue of how and when to regulate family day care is important because almost half of the children in child care in the United States are in family child care homes.

TO REGULATE OR NOT TO REGULATE?

Quality control in child care is tied to the problems of the implementation and enforcement of regulations, the existance of unregulated settings, and the difficulties of licensure.

In 1976, Title XX of the Social Security Act, for example, changed required staff-child ratios and toughened the penalty for noncompliance with the Federal Interagency Day Care Requirements (FIDCR). "Compliance" enforcement was no longer casually based upon a federal hearing which could, at worst, reduce federal funding to a noncomplying program by 3%. Under Title XX, noncompliance with FIDCR could result in a complete cutoff of child care program payments. This suggests that "federal financial participation" under Title XX was clearly aimed at promoting the health, safety, and supervision needs of children [26]. However good the intention of these requirements, their enforcement proved difficult.

Beyond the inherent shortcomings in the public sector's ability to enforce regulations and controls in publicly funded child care programs there lurks a host of obstacles to the regulation of quality in the private sector. While the proliferation of family day care homes helps to meet the demand for child care services, taking some of the burden off of the polity, it generates countless instances of unlicensed and unregulated care. Where these settings are licensed and thus amenable to regulatory activity, the cost to government of policing the quality of care provided in a myriad of small homes dispersed over a large geographical area prohibits effective enforcement.

Another dilemma posed by regulation is whether or not it should encourage costly and perhaps unnecessary professionalization. Regulations requiring that child care staff be licensed may have this effect. Thus efforts designed to guarantee the quality of care through licensure will bear scrutiny of the unanticipated consequences.

Licensure may take several forms. The first form of licensure involves a simple process of registration. Individuals engaging in a particular activity are required to list their names in an official register, and sometimes to pay a registration fee. However, there is no control over the qualifications of those on the register. Certification is a bit more demanding. It usually requires that a particular test or series of tests be passed or another demonstration of skills be completed. Licensing offers more control than registration and certification. An individual or organization must obtain a license in order to operate. The license is usually dispensed by a recognized authority and there is a penalty for practicing without it [27]. The spread of this type of licensure in child care would impose a degree of uniformity by limiting the development of many informal, family child care and even institutional care programs where most of the caregivers are untrained.

UNIFORMITY OR DIVERSITY?

The evolution of child care and early childhood education in the United States might benefit in studying the evolution of higher education. The early institutions of higher education, such as Harvard, William and Mary, and Yale, were small colleges. Although they were modeled after English universities, they did not establish clusters of colleges and remained separate centers of learning. During the nineteenth century several small American colleges evolved into universities. In addition, other institutions of higher learning were established as universities at their inception, such as Johns Hopkins University. During the late 1800s and the early 1900s, these private institutions began to compete among themselves for excellence in research and education.

About the same time, the number of public colleges and universities began to grow. Although states had supported higher education as early as 1800, it was a century later that the federal government became involved with the states through land grant legislation. Publicly supported universities sprouted in the Midwest and later in the West, offering an alternative to the elite private universities in the East. By 1900 other institutions of higher education emerged, such as teachers' colleges, public and private schools of engineering such as MIT, art schools, theological seminaries, and "short-cycle" junior colleges. All of these were supported by a wide range of public and private funds.

Eventually, as Burton Clark explains, "because the right to sponsor institutions has been so dispersed, among private as well as public hands, many kinds of postsecondary institutions have emerged, creating a bewildering array of proprietary nonprofit and specialized schools and colleges" [28]. According to Clark, the private sector today "remains enormously varied," although it now serves only one student in four. Yet diversity is not restricted to the private sector. Dispersed control in the public sector has produced a great range of programs in higher education. All this variance among and within major sectors has led to "an unparalleled national diversity" [29].

While child programs are not as established and varied as those of higher education, the child care scenario in the United States today is already quite diverse. And this diversity, similar to that of higher education, is not restricted to the private sector [30]. The positive aspects of diversity are that child care and preschool consumers are offered a variety of choices, that innovation is welcomed, and that competition may provide a healthy stimulus among competitors. The other side of the coin is that regional, economic, and cultural inequities may result in disparate opportunities for American children and their families. Along with diversity come both varied opportunity for care and differential quality of caregiving programs.

The state of child care in California offers a case in point. The proliferation of child care services in that state has resulted in tremendous diversity. As of 1987, 24,719 providers made available 349,914 licensed child care slots in child care centers and 131,375 licensed child care slots in family day care programs. Of the children filling these slots, 41,888 were under two years of age, a circumstance indicating a necessary diversity in the design of services to include the needs of a broad age range of children [31].

As child care programs in California proliferate under varying auspices, the structure and functions of the regulatory environment become more critical. The body of regulations governing child care in California is incomplete and difficult to implement. It is clear that even state subsidization cannot ensure uniformity among child care programs. In California, there are almost 1,000 child care contracts under the Department of Education Office of Child Development. While these contracts subject child care facilities to state regulations, there is great variation in the level of care and education provided by these programs [32]. Moreover, many of the child care programs in the state do not fall under regulatory jurisdiction by virtue of contract. Of course, they are subject to certain general code regulations, but compliance is more difficult to enforce in the absence of contractual obligations. Although programs which contract with the state are subject to quality assessments, rarely has one of them lost its contract because of these assessments.

Child care "quality" is difficult to legislate. An attempt has been made to legislate quality controls in public and private programs through the establishment of caregiver-child ratios. Whether or not these ratios say much about quality, they offer something relatively straightforward to measure and regulate. In child care centers the required adult-child ratio is 1 : 6; for every eighteen children there must be one credentialed teacher; and one out of three adults must have a California children's center permit issued by the State Department of Education. Family child care is also affected by adult-child ratio standards. There are two licenses which control family child care ratios. One, for settings in which there are up to six children (the provider is included), requires one adult. The other applies to settings in which there are seven to twelve children, and it requires two caregivers, one adult and one assistant age fourteen or over [33].

Such control of caregiver-child ratios leaves much room for variation in the operation of child care programs. There are many other important and often unregulated elements in the social, psychological, educational, physical, and environmental dimensions of care, which contribute to the quality of child care programs, as evidenced in the analysis of diversity, quality, and consumer ratings in six child care settings contained in the preceding chapters.

SUGGESTIONS FOR SOCIAL CHANGE

What are the implications for policy here? One approach is to suggest increased public regulation of day care programs. Practically speaking, this is difficult to implement in a mixed economy of care, marked by a large number of diverse caregivers offering a diverse range of provisions.

QUESTION INCREASED REGULATION

Even if public bodies seriously attempted to regulate day care services, consumer evaluation would remain an important indicator of the quality of child care. Public regulation of child care services, by the very nature of its detachment and objectivity, would tend to favor the functional over the affective characteristics of care. Consumers on the other hand, as evidenced by the high priority that participants in my day care consumer study placed on staff warmth, are extremely sensitive to the affective mode of care, intuitively favoring feeling over function. Can increased regulation ever really address the affective elements of care? Or will increased regulation, in its honorable drive to improve quality, merely expand the creeping domain of functional care?

INSTITUTE PUBLIC RATING SCHEMES

The provision of services as intimate and personal as the care of one's children cannot escape some form of consumer regulation. The issues raised by the findings of my study suggest the need for public efforts that would not substitute for consumer choices but enhance its effectiveness. Following this line of thought, consumer choice might be buttressed by a public rating scheme under which all child care programs would receive a score based on the type of detailed rating scale developed in Chapter 6 and Appendix B. Public and employer subsidies could be made contingent upon programs' achieving scores that do not fall below a nationally defined baseline of quality. At the same time public and private day care programs could be required to display their ratings, affording consumers a readily available basis for making comparative judgments and providing an objective indicator against which they might corroborate their intuitive assessments of program quality. Stars could be displayed. Like the current method of signifying an excellent restaurant, an excellent child care program might be labeled a five-star program. A public rating scheme of this sort would not only ensure a baseline of quality care for children, it would animate consumer choice in the face of sensitive and complex services while promoting competition and innovation in the mixed economy of care.

HIGHLIGHT QUALITY

The media are powerful communicators. Another method of enhancing the effectiveness of consumer choice can therefore be through media highlights. Day care programs rated at the highest (five-star) level can be presented on television in the form of public service announcements. Careful attention to the content of these highlights to ensure the presentation of a diverse range of positive qualities would be essential. Highlighting quality would also provide added incentive for excellence in the field of day care, as would the institution of an annual day care program awards procedure.

FUND AND SUPPORT PUBLIC EDUCATION

The late 1980s brought massive efforts at public education regarding drug abuse and AIDS contagion. The threatened welfare of preschool children, while not considered a clear and present threat to the welfare of society, is also a critical issue of our times. Public and private funding must be directed at educating parents and child care providers regarding the elements of quality in day care. Emphasis on the affect—the feeling aspects of child care—must be maintained in this effort to educate.

LIMIT SIZE AND RATIO IN CARE

A combination of state and federal regulation, a public rating scheme, rewards for program quality, and public education must emphasize the importance of small group sizes and high adult-child ratios in child care. Every effort must be made to prevent the explicit warehousing of children and any subtler versions of this warehousing.

PROVIDE GREATER INCENTIVES FOR WORKPLACE CHILD CARE

Parents who are employed outside their homes have difficulty keeping a close and watchful eye on the quality of child care their children receive. Quality, or five-star, child care must be available in or near parents' work sites. Employers must come to understand that when they hire an employee, they are hiring a whole person with a family life outside of the workplace. Employee productivity must be viewed as a product of employee welfare. In order to bring about this understanding, greater government incentives to provide workplace child care must be instituted. These incentives must be offers too wonderful to refuse.

SUPPORT PARENTHOOD

States and the federal government must seriously consider financial support for parents who stay home to care for their preschool-age children. Requirements for receiving these funds must include parents' attendance at public child care training programs. After all, parents can stand to learn as much as can other child care providers about the well-being of their children.

A UTOPIAN VISION

The tangled problem of child care has come to the attention of the media, social scientists, politicians, policymakers, employers, entrepreneurs, law enforcers, educators, social workers, psychologists, child care workers, and other participants in our complex social system. It has, most importantly, of course, come to the attention of parents and children, the people directly affected by the state of child care in America.

By achieving a center-stage position in the play of modern life, child care questions direct our attention to still larger questions which wait in the wings, hidden and as yet almost unasked. These are profound questions regarding the evolution of all human care. The questions "Who cares?" and "Why do they care?" must be asked whenever a human service is provided. What are the motivations behind the provision of human care? Is care becoming increasingly functional and economically designed? Is care increasingly mass-produced? What trade-offs are we willing to make as human care evolves? Where are we willing to leave our children while we work? What amount of humanity are we willing to trade away, and why?

This is not an indictment of child day care programs or of the parents who use them. It is, however, an indictment of our society for its unwillingness to direct large amounts of funding to improve overall care quality and to radically improve adult-child ratios, care environments, provider training, and the availability of child care. We do have a choice in the process of social evolution. We can choose to remain highly aware of the changes going on around us and within our hearts and minds. But we must always pay close attention. We must make a solid commitment not to look away. We must decide to feel, at the deepest level, the effects of our personal and our societal decisions about how to care for those who need care, about how poor a quality of care we are willing to tolerate, and about what we are actually willing to call "quality care."

Decisions about how to meet the need for child care in the United States have implications that reach far beyond the economic, social, and educational goals discussed earlier in this chapter. Moreover, the trade-offs are broader than cost vs. quality, in-home or out-of-home, to regulate or not to regulate, uniformity or diversity in child day care, as presented here. Although these trade-offs are critical questions in child care policy development, they represent only the tip of the iceberg in modern social and ethical development.

Are we willing to do whatever it takes to redirect the course of social evolution? Would we be willing to make such a major commitment if we all agreed that we had to in order to preserve our humanity? How close are we to acting like machines, making mechanical decisions about our child care services, leaving our children for practical reasons where instinct tells us not to leave them?

As a social scientist and as a mother, I detect an undercurrent of denial in child care. This denial is indicative of a broader social denial about all human care. The findings I reported in Chapter 7 indicate that parents do not necessarily admit to themselves or to others that there are areas in which their child care programs are far from their ideal. And I know from personal experience that, all too often, a parent feels that she or he has very little choice about whether or not to leave a child while she or he works. As one mother explained, "There are too many days when my child care situation does not feel right, but I have to close my eyes, grit my teeth, and go to work. I have no other option. But I feel sick inside because I just know that I am not doing right by my child." Do we, as a society, force families to close their eyes to avoid the pain resulting from their limited choices regarding the care of their dependents? Do we as a society deny that we do this?

We have all learned that the real world falls far short of ideal. Still, it is essential that we hold our ideals firmly in our minds and seek to achieve a reality close to them. We have a right to care about our children and about all of our dependents. We have a right to feel ourselves caring. We must preserve our understanding of this right and our understanding of care itself. We must be willing to recognize when we deny ourselves the right to care deeply about how our dependents are being cared for. All too often, we turn away from what our hearts tell us, thinking that we must repress these feelings in order to survive in the modern economic jungle.

Home is where the heart is. It seems to me that we are forgetting this, both away from home and at home. Although intentional public policy can move us in the direction of positive social change, it cannot reeducate our hearts. Only a new vision—one that is spiritual, philosophical, psychological, economical, and practical, one that is whole and shared among us—can provide a picture that we can develop toward.

Perhaps home is only where the heart was. Perhaps it is departing this increasingly functional world. I urge you, the reader, to scrutinize each of your personal decisions and your public votes regarding children and all of society's other dependents. Are you aware of the trade-offs between function and feeling? Are you pressured by time and money to choose function over feeling? What do your answers tell you about changes in our human ecology? Urie Bronfenbrenner spoke beautifully to this question. Note his comment regarding our ability to raise our children to become "compassionate members of our society." If we cannot pass compassion on to future generations, what will become of our humanity?

> Today we acknowledge that the massive alteration of the natural environment made possible by modern technology and industrialization can destroy the physical ecology essential to life itself. We have yet to recognize that this same awesome process now has its analogue in the social realm as well, that the unthinking exercise of massive technological power, and an unquestioning acquiescence to the demands of industrialization, can unleash forces which, if left unbridled, can destroy the human ecology— the social fabric that nurtures and sustains our capacity to live and work together effectively, and to raise our children and youth to become competent and compassionate members of our society.
>
> It is important to understand the nature of that human ecology—its structure and its scope, the processes taking place within it, how and why the structure is breaking down, and what can be done to retard or even to reverse the prevailing trends. [34]

Perhaps we can take the heart home and let it heal. We must be creative in this endeavor. For example, we can take work home along with the heart. We have entered an era when a great deal of our employment requirements can be met in the home. Let's move work into neighborhoods. Let's keep children and their working parents in neighborhood settings. Let's consider a new version of subsidized motherhood or parenthood that encourages parents of young children to work in, or very close to, their own homes. The emerging global village will allow us to return to cottage industry, this time with a higher level of communication and technology, and with a greater connection to the outside world. This and other creative solutions must be developed and funded by policymakers. I will address the need for creative solutions in a future volume.

We must speak truth to social change. This calls for continuous and honest scrutiny of old and new social policies and programs. What type of change do we want? Can we even see change? Are we blindly and idly wandering into a futuristic depersonalization of human care? We must stop ourselves while we still have selves to stop. What we teach our children about caring is what they will grow up knowing about caring. We have the power to influence the evolution of care. We have the sensitivity to keep feeling from surrendering to function. We still know the path of the heart. It is a road paved with love and care.

APPENDIXES

Appendix A

METHOD FOR THE STUDY OF VARIABILITY AND CONSUMER RATINGS OF DAY CARE

The purpose of this study was to compare the services provided by day care programs under different auspices and to discover how these programs were assessed by consumers. The study included six programs along a continuum of public- and private-sector responses to the need for care (see Table A.1) in order to capture the variations among auspices, program characteristics, consumer characteristics, and consumer ratings.

As I have modeled it in Chapter 4, direct care has five dimensions: social, psychological, educational, physical, and environmental. I have added a sixth dimension to this study design, grouping indirect care variables such as economic and administrative variables. Based upon this model of care, the following four lines of inquiry were pursued:

1. What are the fiscal and organizational differences among child day care programs?
2. What are the substantive differences among programs?

TABLE A.1
AUSPICE CONTINUUM

Public		Quasi public	Quasi private	Private	
Site 1	Site 2	Site 3	Site 4	Site 5	Site 6
State-subsidized	City-sponsored	Military	Employer-sponsored	Nonprofit	Proprietary

3. How differently do day care consumers rate their day care programs?
4. How do consumer ratings of day care programs relate to the actual substantive characteristics of these programs?

This analysis was conducted for each of six selected day care sites along the auspices continuum delineated in Table A.1.

THE INSTRUMENTS OF COMPARISON: ESTIMATING THE QUALITY OF CARE PROVIDED

To compare sites along the auspices continuum for their substantive programmatic differences, a list of day care program characteristics was developed within each dimension of direct and indirect care. In each dimension of direct care, the list of characteristics is divided into four categories: setting, protection, nurturing, and development. Each of these subdivisions is broken into quantitative and qualitative elements. In this manner I developed the "Day Care Program Characteristics Evaluation Guide" (Appendix B) as a tool for program assessment.

Because of limits of time and resources, this entire evaluation guideline was not used. Rather, in order to compare the six sites' program characteristics, I selected four elements in each of the five dimensions of care. Prior to assigning each site a score (of 1 through 5) for each element of each dimension, I observed and noted these elements at all of the study sites. This allowed me to make an informed and comparative judgment. Each site's scores for each dimension were then summed to give an overall assessment in each dimension of care. Finally, each site's scores in each dimension were totaled to yield a research assessment of the quality of care offered under different auspices. The elements of care which were rated are listed in Table A.2.

TABLE A.2
ELEMENTS OF CARE

Element of care	Score range
Social dimension	
Size/ratio	1–5
Organizational cooperation and tension management	1–5
Family involvement	1–5
Group playtime	1–5
Overall assessment	4–20
Psychological dimension	
Privacy	1–5
Responsiveness to individual needs	1–5
Identity enhancement	1–5
Planned transitions	1–5
Overall assessment	4–20
Educational dimension	
Explicit philosophy and goals	1–5
Time spent on educational activity	1–5
Verbal interaction	1–5
Sensory stimulation	1–5
Overall assessment	4–20
Physical dimension	
Health protection and sick care	1–5
Cleanliness	1–5
Nutrition	1–5
Hygiene and physical education	1–5
Overall assessment	4–20
Environmental dimension	
Neighborhood setting	1–5
Indoor space per child	1–5
Physical organization of space	1–5
Equipment	1–5
Overall assessment	4–20
Total assessments	
Social dimension	4–20
Psychological dimension	4–20
Educational dimension	4–20
Physical dimension	4–20
Environmental dimension	4–20
Research assessment	20–100

ESTIMATING THE QUALITY OF CARE RECEIVED: THE CHILD CARE CONSUMER QUESTIONNAIRE

The day care consumer questionnaire was designed to obtain three categories of data (see Table A.3): (1) background information on each respondent (child day care consumer); (2) information about consumer cost, access, and choice situations in the use of their respective care programs; and (3) consumer ratings of respective day care programs (see Appendix C).

TABLE A.3
DATA CATEGORIES

Item No.	Item
Backgound information includes:	
1.	Sex
2.	Age
3.	Marital status
4.	Educational background
5.	Spouse's educational background
6.	Racial or ethnic heritage
7.	Total number in household
8–15.	Number in household by age group
16.	Employment status
17.–19.	Occupational status
Information about consumers' cost, access, and choice situations includes:	
20.	Distance of workplace from home
21.	Distance of day care center from home
22.	Distance of day care center from workplace
23.	Family income
24.	Cost of day care to family (consumer)
25.	Important factors in consumer selection of day care
26.	Consumer alternatives to this program selection
Consumer rating information includes:	
27.	Best components of this program
28.	Components which need improvement
29.–30.	General ratings
31.–34.	Ratings of environmental dimension of care
35.–38.	Ratings of physical dimension of care
39.–42.	Ratings of social dimension of care
43.–46.	Ratings of educational dimension of care
47.–50.	Ratings of psychological dimension of care
51.–54.	Economic and administrative family impact ratings

DATA ANALYSIS

Central to the comparison of consumer ratings under different auspices was the analysis of the data provided by the consumer questionnaire. This component of the study also reveals something about the relationship between dependent consumer rating variables and independent variables such as those pertaining to auspices, socio economic characteristics of consumers and their families, and cost and the distance of the day care program being rated.

The research assumption was that the dependent variable, consumer rating, is a function of auspices as well as of several consumer characteristic variables measured by the questionnaire. These include education (questionnaire's Item 4), family income (Item 23) and the cost of the care to the family (Item 24).

Consumer ratings were obtained in Questions 29 through 54 (see pp. 258–259, Appendix C). Several dependent variables were obtained by combining the scores on question groups which provide specific ratings in each dimension, and then combining the scores of all the question groups for a "total direct care" and a "total care" rating.

In each of the six question groups, respondents were asked to rate four characteristics of the care provided within that particular dimension. These dimensions include the five direct and one indirect dimension described earlier. The four ratings with each dimension were added together to create a scale of 20 points for each dimension's rating (four rating items multiplied by the highest possible score of 5 on each). This type of dependent variable, a within-dimension consumer rating, was computed for each of the five dimensions of direct care and the one of indirect care. (It should be noted that in the calculation of ratings, the "don't know," 0 response was recoded to equal 3, because on an ideal continuum "don't know" is most like a neutral response. Refer to the instructions for Questions 29 through 54 for an explanation of the term "ideal." [1])

What informs consumer rating? In order to delve into the structure of consumers' ratings of their day care programs, a consumer rating profile can be constructed from the six subratings and the total-direct-care and total-direct-plus-indirect-care ratings.

The total care rating was computed by summing all nongeneral ratings, Items 31 through 54. The highest possible total care ratings was 120, 20 points in each of six dimensions, or 24 rating items multiplied by the highest rating of 5 on each. Table A.4 shows the dependent variables computed as such. (These total 120 because questions rating the indirect dimension of care have been added to those addressing the elements of care listed in Table A-2.)

TABLE A.4
DEPENDENT CONSUMER RATING VARIABLES

Consumer ratings	Highest score	Questions
Environmental dimension rating	20 = 4 × 5	31–34
Physical dimension rating	20 = 4 × 5	35–38
Social dimension rating	20 = 4 × 5	39–42
Psychological dimension rating	20 = 4 × 5	43–46
Educational dimension rating	20 = 4 × 5	47–50
Total direct care rating	100 = 20 × 4	31–50
Indirect dimension rating	20 = 4 × 5	51–54
Total care (direct plus indirect) rating	120 = 24 × 5	30–54

Based upon the theoretical framework which I developed, a number of descriptive and inferential analyses were conducted upon this data, as discussed in Chapters 5, 6, and 7.

METHOD OF DATA ACQUISITION

CRITERIA FOR SITE SELECTION

As I pointed out earlier, the single most important criterion for site selection is auspices. Six overlapping auspices categories were delineated, and a site was selected from each.

Other important considerations in the selection of sites were that site administrators were willing to subject themselves and their programs and clients to my observation (albeit unobtrusive) and analysis, and that the site and its enrolled persons, related families, and staff had not been "overstudied" in recent years.

COLLECTION OF DATA

Every parent or guardian (care consumer) at each site received a copy of the day care consumer questionnaire, with an attached cover letter explaining the general purpose of the study, ensuring anonymity, and asking that the questionnaire be returned as soon as possible (see Appendix C). So as not to bias my own observations, the questionnaire data were not analyzed until after all site visits were completed and all program characteristics data compiled.

Completion of the program characteristics evaluation was accomplished during five to ten visits to each site. So as not to intrude upon the atmosphere of the setting in a way which would contaminate my findings, all photographs were taken during the last visits, after all other data were collected.

An exit interview with at least one key administrator was conducted in order to collect any data still missing and to report on the course of the study. This form of "exit" will make it possible for me to return, if and when further study is desired.

While much of the information was gained through my own observations and during interviews with key functionaries, there were occasional discussions with other staff, visiting representatives of business and government, some parents and family members, and even some children. The anonymity of these informants is protected.

Appendix B

DAY CARE PROGRAM CHARACTERISTICS EVALUATION GUIDE

The following list of day care program characteristics is designed to serve as a general guideline only, and not to dictate a specific definition of quality in day care. Many of the items on the list have been included because they designate possible areas of concern rather than positive or negative program traits. Any researcher, program evaluator, or day care consumer consulting this guideline should keep in mind that there is no single combination of program traits which represents the ideal or optimal care. At best, programs can be compared for their respective abilities to efficiently combine many elements of care in a manner which is beneficial to the care receivers.

REQUISITES FOR CARE (INDIRECT ASPECTS OF CARE)

BACKGROUND FACTORS

- Auspices: Public, private.
- General characteristics of dependents in care: Infants, children, disabled or ill, frail elderly.
- Range of services other than day care available at this site.
- Licensing: Which licenses does the site have?
- Guidelines: Does the program meet any particular standards or guidelines?

1. ADMINISTRATIVE AND ORGANIZATIONAL

Program Goals

- Translating day care goals into operational and procedural terms.
- Program evaluation.
- Assessing clients' needs and capabilities.

Staff

- Staff licensing: Which licenses are held by one or more staff members?
- Staff training.
- Means of recruiting staff.
- Staff turnover rate.

Attendance

- Means of recruiting clients.
- Absenteeism rate of enrollees.

Schedule

- Operating days.
- Operating hours.

2. ECONOMIC AND FISCAL

Program Budget

- Annual overall program cost at this site for budget year 19___.

- Program budget, if different from site budget for same budget year (and number of sites operating under program budget).

Cost of Service

- Average number of enrollees at site in budget year listed above.
- Average caregiver-enrollee ratio in same budget year.
- Annual program cost per capita at site. (If different rates to provider for different enrollees, list.)
- Cost per enrollee/year or enrollee/month to consumer (to family). (If different rates for different consumers, list.)
- How is this price to consumer set?
- How does this price compare to those of other day care programs?

Wages

- Staff pay scale, by job title; caregiver wage.
- How are the caregiver wages set?
- How does this wage compare to those of other facilities?

Economic Restrictions

- Are there economic reasons for the caregiver-enrollee ratio at this site?
- Size of waiting list.

SUBSTANTIVE PROGRAM CHARACTERISTICS (DIMENSIONS OF DIRECT CARE)

GENERAL

Quantitative Data

- Number of staff.
- Number of enrollees.
- Caregiver-enrollee ratio.

Qualitative Data

- Overall quality of the care is adequate.

1. SOCIAL DIMENSION OF CARE

Setting

Quantitive Data

- Racial composition of enrollee population.
- Racial composition of staff.
- Age range of enrollees.
- Age range of caregiving staff.
- Any preenrollment screening for social characteristics (i.e., age, sex, religion)?

Qualitative Data

- Racial representations among staff and enrollee populations are similar.
- Sexes are represented similarly among staff and enrollee populations.
- Age range of staff is broad enough to meet the various demands of caregiving (from physical vigor to emotional maturity).
- Effects of preenrollment screening.

Protection

Quantitative Data

- Presence of organizational mechanisms for resolving differences among staff.
- Presence of organizational mechanisms for hearing clients' complaints.

Qualitative Data

- Cooperation among staff is apparent.
- Cooperation encouraged among enrollees.
- Low or appropriate tension level among the group of enrollees and staff.
- Effective management of interpersonal problems, disagreements.

Nurturing

Quantitative Data

- Presence of formally specified family involvement (i.e. parental involvement) in program.

Qualitative Data

- Program members (including enrollees) are involved in community activities.

- Staff-parent (or staff-guardian, staff-family) relationships appear constructive.
- Staff-enrollee relationships appear positive.
- Type of family (i.e., parent-child, guardian-enrollee) relationships encouraged by staff appear positive.
- Adequate amount of attention is given to family members (i.e., mother *and* father, guardians, siblings, etc.).
- Relationships among peers (among enrollees) are encouraged.

Development

Quantitative Data

- Amount of time spent on unstructured group play/recreation.
- Amount of time spent on structured group play/recreation.
- Holidays are observed: Which holidays?
- Rules are printed and posted in a visible place.

Qualitative Data

- Unstructured group play/recreation appears beneficial.
- Structured group play/recreation appears beneficial.
- Discipline, limits, and rules are evident.
- Expectations are expressed to enrollees.

2. PSYCHOLOGICAL DIMENSION OF CARE

Setting

Quantitative Data

- Any preenrollment psychological screening and evaluation?
- Amount of structured (planned) quiet time.

Qualitative Data

- Enrollees have enough privacy.
- Time is well organized; there is a sense that there is enough time.
- Independence of enrollees is encouraged.

Protection

Qualitative Data

- Program and staff are responsive to individual needs.

- Individual temperaments are respected.
- Program and staff are responsive to the age-related needs of enrollees.
- There is an appropriate degree of personal involvement by staff members in their caregiving activities.

Nurturing

Quantitative Data

- Individuals have (keep) objects of importance to themselves at the site.

Qualitative Data

- There is an adequate amount of one-to-one attention for enrollees.
- There is an adequate amount of undisturbed, extended time between individual enrollees and individual staff members.
- Positive close relationships are formed between enrollees and staff.
- There is appropriate affection, warmth toward enrollees.
- There is appropriate physical contact between caregivers and enrollees.
- Program generates a sense of constancy, regularity, and dependability for enrollees.
- Staff provides assistance in coping to enrollees.
- There is effective management of psychological upset or trauma.

Development

Quantitative Data

- There are planned opportunities for personal feedback from staff to enrollees.

Qualitative Data

- Transition times (arrivals and departures) between family and care setting are positive and developmental.
- Attention is given to enrollees' attitudes upon arrival at the site each day.
- Attention is given to enrollees' attitudes at departure time each day.
- Frustration levels generated appear to encourage development.

3. EDUCATIONAL DIMENSION OF CARE

Setting

Quantitative Data

- Program model.

- Program design.
- Any preenrollment screening for aptitude or educational level?

Qualitative Data

- Environment appears conducive to learning.

Protection

Quantitative Data

- Amount of time spent on practical education (survival skills) geared to current needs outside of this care setting.

Qualitative Data

- There is attention to enrollees' current needs for survival skills outside of this care setting.
- There is an adequate amount of this protective education.

Nurturing

Quantitative Data

- There is an adequate level of caregiver-enrollee verbal interaction.
- There is age-appropriate mental stimulation for enrollees.
- There is adequate sensory stimulation.
- Relationships between staff and enrollees help enrollees to learn.

Development

Quantitative Data

- Amount of time spent on educational game playing.
- Amount of time spent on instruction in academic subjects.
- Amount of time spent on practical education geared to future needs.

Qualitative Data

- There are adequate opportunities for each enrollee to act upon his or her environment.
- Enrollees' explorations and experimentations are permitted whenever appropriate.
- There is an adequate emphasis on creative development.
- There is an adequate emphasis upon education geared to future needs.
- There are adequate type(s) of academic instruction provided.

4. PHYSICAL DIMENSION OF CARE

Setting

Quantitative Data

- Any preenrollment physical screening and evaluation?

Qualitative Data

- There is suitable variation or concentration of physical capabilities or disabilities among enrollees.
- Physical health of enrollees is acceptable.

Protection

Quantitative Data

- Any diagnostic screening program at site (aimed at early recognition of illness and other health problems)?
- Any immunization program at site?
- Any sick care available at site?
- Amount of time spent on promoting cleanliness among enrollees.

Qualitative Data

- Reasonable health care is available for ill enrollees at site.
- There is adequate attention to enrollees' cleanliness (via bathing, diapering, dressing, washing hands, etc.).
- There is adequate emphasis upon safety.
- There is adequate supervision as a safeguard against accidents.

Nurturing

Quantitative Data

- Meals and snacks are provided.

Qualitative Data

- There is an adequate emphasis upon nutrition.

Development

Quantitative Data

- Amount of time spent on hygiene and health care education.
- Amount of time spent on physical education.

Qualitative Data

- There is adequate hygiene–health–care education.
- There is adequate physical education.

5. ENVIRONMENTAL DIMENSION OF CARE

Setting

Quantitative Data

- Setting.
- Zoning.
- Square footage indoors.
- Square footage of outdoor play area.
- Kitchen facilities.
- Toilet and bathing facilities.
- Equipment and supplies.

Qualitative Data

- General upkeep is good.
- Area surrounding the site is suitable.

Protection

Quantitative Data

- Physical provisions for safety.

Qualitative Data

- Setting (grounds and access) is safe.
- There are physical safeguards against accidents.
- Equipment (i.e., toys, chairs, etc.) is safe.
- There is adequate cleanliness of setting.

Nurturing

Quantitative Data

- Physical surroundings include private spaces.
- Physical surroundings provide a place for each individual's possessions.
- Special areas are designated.
- Attention to indoor air quality (ventilation and temperature).

Qualitative Data

- Physical environment is aesthetically pleasing.
- Setting is appropriate for the care provided.
- Physical surroundings contribute to the bodily comfort of enrollees.
- Physical surroundings lend a sense of neatness and order rather than confusion.
- Physical surroundings provide a sense that there is enough space.

Development

Qualitative Data

- Physical environment is supportive.
- Physical environment is challenging, encourages development.

Appendix C

DAY CARE CONSUMER QUESTIONNAIRE AND COVER LETTER

I constructed the following questionnaire for use in the study of consumer ratings described in Chapter 7. All parents at each site received the same questionnaire—with one exception: The words "day care" were replaced with "child care," "night care," "after-school care," "nursery school," and "pre-school" when the title of the program or program component in which parents enrolled their children used one of these terms in place of "day care." (This adaptation was made following a pretest in which parents who had enrolled their children in a preschool and paid a sizable tuition for it expressed displeasure at having their preschool program described as "day care.") Aside from this minor adaptation, the same questions were asked of all parents at all sites.

This questionnaire has been designed for use, with one other minor change, in day or part-time care settings for people of all ages (i.e., school-age children, the disabled, the ill, and the elderly). To use this questionnaire in settings where care is provided to other than children, simply replace "children" with "enrollees" or "family members," depending upon the syntax of the question to be reworded. When changes are made in words which (1) designate the type of care being rated (replacing "day care" with "institutional care," for example) and (2) designate the type of dependents receiving care, this questionnaire can be used in the study of consumer ratings of other forms of care.

Dear Parents, Guardians, and Family Members,

I am conducting a study on the way families view child care programs. This study will cover programs in ten different locations. My specific interests are to find what families in different circumstances want from their programs and how well these wants are satisfied.

I would greatly appreciate your participation in this study. The attached questionnaire does not ask your name. The findings based on answers to these questions will not identify any individual respondents or their children or other family members. All your replies are confidential.

The results of this study will improve our knowledge of child care services. This knowledge, hopefully, will benefit the people served by these programs in the future.

Please return this questionnaire by July 1. You can place it in the box marked "Questionnaires" at your child care site.

Thank you for your cooperation.

Sincerely,

Angela Browne

CHILD CARE CONSUMER QUESTIONNAIRE

1. Your sex:
   1. Male
   2. Female

2. Your age:
   1. 21 years and under
   2. 22–25 years
   3. 26–30 years
   4. 31–35 years
   5. 36–40 years
   6. 41–45 years
   7. 46–50 years
   8. 51–60 years

3. Your present marital status:
   1. Single
   2. Married
   3. Separated
   4. Divorced
   5. Widowed
   6. Other _____

4. Your educational background:
   1. Less than high school
   2. Some high school
   3. High school completed
   4. Vocational training
   5. Some college
   6. College degree
   7. Graduate degree/s (list)

   _____

5. Educational background of spouse or adult who lives with you:
   1. Less than high school
   2. Some high school
   3. High school completed
   4. Vocational training
   5. Some college
   6. College degree
   7. Graduate degree/s (list)

   _____

   8. Not applicable

6. What do you consider your racial/ethnic heritage?
   1. American Indian or Alaskan native
   2. Asian or Pacific Islander
   3. Black
   4. Hispanic
   5. White
   6. Other _____

7. How many people live in your household (including yourself)?

   _____

   Of these people in your household, how many are:

8. Working age adults (age 18 through 65) _____

9. Adults between the ages of 65 and 80 _____

10. Adults over the age of 80 _____

11. Young people between the ages of 12 and 18 _____

12. Children between the ages of 6 and 12 _____

13. Children between the ages of 3 and 6 _____

14. Children between the ages of 1½ and 3 _____

15. Children 18 months and younger _____

16. Are you currently employed, in school, or in job training? Circle *all* that apply:
    1. No, unemployed looking for work.
    2. No, working as a full-time homemaker in my home.
    3. No, other (please specify): _____
    4. Yes, enrolled in a part-time study or training program.
    5. Yes, enrolled in a full-time study or training program.
    6. Yes, I am employed.
       If you are employed:

17. Are you employed full time or part time?
    1. I am employed full time.
    2. I am employed part time.

18. What is your job title? _____

19. What kind of work do you do? (Please describe; for example, clerical, administrative.)

20. Where do you work, study, or receive job training?
    1. At home.
    2. Within 1 mile of home.
    3. 2–5 miles from home.
    4. 6–10 miles from home.
    4. 11–20 miles from home.
    5. Over 20 miles from home.

21. How far from your home is this child care center?
    1. In my home.
    2. Within 1 mile of home.
    3. 2–5 miles from home.
    4. 6–10 miles from home.
    5. 11–20 miles from home.
    6. Over 20 miles from home.

22. How far from your workplace is this child care center?
    1. In my workplace.
    2. Within 1 mile of work.
    3. 2–5 miles from work.
    4. 6–10 miles from work.
    5. 11–20 miles from work.
    6. Over 20 miles from work.

23. In what category is your family's yearly income?
    1. Under $8,000 a year.
    2. $8,001 to $12,000 a year.
    3. $12,001 to $18,000 a year.
    4. $18,001 to $24,000 a year.
    5. $24,001 to $30,000 a year.
    6. $30,001 to $40,000 a year.
    7. Over $40,000 a year.

24. How much do you pay for child care per month? Please state the total cost for all family members in child care:
    It costs my family _____ dollars a month altogether.
    1. Nothing—zero dollars.
    2. Under $50 per month.
    3. $51 to $100 per month.
    4. $101 to $150 per month.
    5. $151 to $200 per month.
    6. $201 to $250 per month.
    7. $251 to $300 per month.
    8. $301 to $350 per month.
    9. $351 to $400 per month.
    10. Over $400 per month.

25. When choosing a child care program, what do you consider the most important features?
    Please rank the following in order of most importance to you, from 1 (most important) to 9 (least important):
    Write your numbers here:
    _____ The educational program.
    _____ The social activities.
    _____ The physical activities.
    _____ The personal warmth of staff.
    _____ The building.
    _____ The hours that the program is open.
    _____ The distance from your home and/or work.
    _____ The cost.
    _____ Other, please specify: _____.

26. If this child care program were not available, what would you do?

27. What do you like best about this child care program?

28. If you could change anything about this child care program, what would it be?

How does this child care program compare with what you would imagine to be your ideal child care program?
Please give a score to each of the following parts of this child care program. A 1 is the lowest score, and a 5 is the highest score you can give in comparing each item below to your view of an ideal program:

	Far from ideal $\longrightarrow$ The ideal					Don't
	(Needs improvement) $\longrightarrow$ (Best possible)					know
29. How would you rate this program in general?	1	2	3	4	5	0

How would you rate:

30. The quality of the care, overall?	1	2	3	4	5	0
31. The size of the building?	1	2	3	4	5	0
32. The comfort?	1	2	3	4	5	0
33. The safety?	1	2	3	4	5	0
34. The quality of the equipment?	1	2	3	4	5	0
35. The meals and nutrition?	1	2	3	4	5	0
36. The program's health care?	1	2	3	4	5	0
37. The general health of the people enrolled in this program?	1	2	3	4	5	0
38. The time spent on physical development?	1	2	3	4	5	0
39. The ages of staff members?	1	2	3	4	5	0
40. The atmosphere of cooperation?	1	2	3	4	5	0
41. The discipline (i.e., the way rules are enforced)?	1	2	3	4	5	0
42. The opportunities for family involvement?	1	2	3	4	5	0
43. The living skills which are taught here?	1	2	3	4	5	0
44. The quality of education?	1	2	3	4	5	0

45. The amount of time spent on educational activity?	1	2	3	4	5		0
46. The educational philosophy?	1	2	3	4	5		0
47. The amount of quiet time?	1	2	3	4	5		0
48. The degree to which staff are personally involved in their work?	1	2	3	4	5		0
49. The amount of one-to-one attention from staff?	1	2	3	4	5		0
50. The way your family members who are enrolled in this program respond to this program?	1	2	3	4	5		0
51. The distance of this care from your home?	1	2	3	4	5		0
52. The distance of this care from your workplace?	1	2	3	4	5		0
53. The hours this program is open?	1	2	3	4	5		0
54. The cost of this care?	1	2	3	4	5		0

NOTES

INTRODUCTION

1. Senator Alan Cranston, quoting Department of Health and Human Services statistics; *Congressional Record,* Proceedings of the 100th Congress, First Session; Vol. 133, No. 1.; S162; Tuesday, January 6, 1987.
2. C. West Churchman, *The Systems Approach and Its Enemies* (New York: Basic Books, 1979). A detailed analysis of this problem is also presented in Angela Browne and Aaron Wildavsky, "Implementation as Adaptation," *Implementation* (Third Edition) (Berkeley: University of California Press, 1984), pp. 220–225.
3. Senator Alan Cranston, *op. cit.*
4. Angela Browne, "Mixed Economy of Child Care Policy in the United States," *International Child Welfare Review,* No. 62 (September 1984a).
5. Senator Alan Cranston, *op. cit.*
6. These data are from a study by the Bureau of Census quoted in Ramon G.

261

McLeod, "Census: Day Care Use Up 60%," *San Francisco Chronicle,* May 8, 1987, p. 38.

7. Fern Chapman Schumer, "Executive Guilt: Who's Taking Care of the Children?" *Fortune,* February 16, 1987, p. 35.
8. This question was asked of parents who participated in the author's day care consumer study. See Note 23.
9. Carol Dilks, "Employers Who Help with the Kids," *Nation's Business,* February 1984, pp. 59–60.
10. Fern Chapman Schumer, *op. cit.,* pp. 35–36.
11. See Angela Browne, "The Market Sphere: Private Responses," *Child Welfare,* July–August 1985.
12. Angela Browne, "What Purpose Is Served by Child Day Care Policy in the United States?" *International Child Welfare Review,* No. 63 (December 1984b).
13. John Gliedman and William Roth, *The Unexpected Minority: Handicapped Children in America* (New York: Harcourt, Brace, Jovanovich, 1980), p. 197.
14. David J. Armor, "White Flight and the Future of School Desegregation" (Santa Monica, CA: Rand Corporation, 1978), pp. 187–225.
15. Sylvia Ann Hewlett, "Coping with Illegal Immigrants," *Foreign Affairs,* Vol. 60 (Winter 1981–82), pp. 358–378.
16. Barbara Deane, "The Lori Nathan Case," *California Living Magazine,* March 18, 1984, pp. 10–14.
17. Stephen Magagnini and Susan Sward, "Why the State Can't Stop Day-Care Center Abuse," *San Francisco Chronicle,* November 9, 1984, pp. 1, 5, and 6.
18. Susan Cunningham, "Day Care Screening Law: More Harm Than Good?" *APA Monitor,* Vol. 16, No. 8 (August 1985), p. 18.
19. Cathy Guisewite, "Cathy" Comic Strip, *San Francisco Chronicle,* September 24, 1986.
20. "What Price Day Care?" *Newsweek,* September 10, 1984, p. 15.
21. Senator Alan Cranston, *op. cit.*
22. Nancy Chodorow, *The Reproduction of Mothering: Psychoanalysis and the Sociology of Gender* (Berkeley: University of California Press, 1978), pp. 211 and 213.
23. Angela Browne, 1984a and 1984b, *op. cit.*

CHAPTER 1

1. Philip Jacobs, *The Economics of Health and Medical Care* (Baltimore: University Park Press, 1980), pp. 91–95.

2. J. T. McLeod, "Consumer Participation, Regulation of Professions, De-centralization of Health Services" (Toronto: University of Toronto and J. T. McLeod Research Associates Ltd., August 1973), pp. 30–32. This report was submitted to the Minister of Public Health in Saskatchewan.
3. Jacobs, *op. cit.,* pp. 93–94.
4. U.S. Department of Commerce, *Pocket Data Book USA 1979* (Washington, DC: Bureau of Census, April 1980), p. 165.
5. *Ibid.,* p. 223, and U.S. Treasury Department quoted in *The World Almanac and Book of Facts 1988* (New York: Pharos Books, Scripps Howard Co., 1987), pp. 94–96.
6. *Ibid.,* pp. 93–96.
7. *Ibid.,* pp. 173 and 205.
8. McLeod, *op. cit.,* p. 42.
9. *Ibid.*
10. W. Trotter, *Collected Papers of Wilfred Trotter* (London: Oxford University Press, 1974), p. 5.
11. Mack Lipkin, *The Care of Patients: Concepts and Tactics* (New York: Oxford University Press, 1974), p. 5.
12. *Ibid.,* p. 168.
13. See Neil J. Smelser, "Vicissitudes of Work and Love in Anglo-American Society," in Neil J. Smelser and Erik H. Erikson (Eds.), *Themes of Work and Love in Adulthood* (Cambridge: Harvard University Press, 1980), pp. 105–106. See also Talcott Parsons and Edward A. Shils, "Values, Motives and Systems of Action," in Talcott Parsons et al. (Eds.), *Toward a General Theory of Action* (Cambridge: Harvard University Press, 1949).
14. *Ibid.,* Smelser, pp. 105–118.
15. Shelly Kessler, unpublished paper on the past White House Conferences on Children (New Haven, CT: Carnegie Council on Children, 1972), quoted in Hillary Rodham, "Children Under the Law," *Harvard Education Review,* Vol. 43 (November 1973), pp. 487–514.
16. Of course, the value of biological parents to children has long been contested by philosophers who find the family itself to be an obstacle to the emancipation of the individual and the restructuring of the social order. On the other hand, as Robert Nisbet points out, obscure philosopher Johannes Althusius, at the beginning of the seventeenth century, distinguished between two general "types of association: the natural and the civil, the family (and the encompassing clan) being a natural social unity" which plays an important role in the study of politics. Nisbet contends that "To more and more of those who seek the philosophical foundations of a free society, it has become apparent that the solitary individual is a precarious and insecure foundation for freedom and rights." Robert Nisbet, *The So-

cial Philosophers (New York: Washington Square Press, Simon & Schuster, 1973), pp. 181–183.

17. John Holt, *Escape from Childhood* (New York: E. P. Dutton & Co., Inc., 1974), p. 150.
18. Edith H. Grotberg, "Child Development," in Edith H. Grotberg (Ed.), *200 Years of Children* (Washington, DC: U.S. Department of Health and Human Welfare, 1976), pp. 403–405.
19. Consumer sovereignty is defined as "the conception that consumers control economic life . . . that the consumer is the ultimate ruler of economic life through his control of the market." In Harold S. Sloan and Arnold J. Zurcher, *Dictionary of Economics* (New York: Harper & Row, 1970), p. 96.
20. The proportion of children whose mothers worked increased from 38.8% in 1970 to 52.8% in 1980. For children under the age of six, these percentages were 28.5% in 1970 and 43.0% in 1980. The trend continued in the 1980s. *Children's Defense Fund, America's Children and Their Families: Key Facts* (Washington, DC: Children's Defense Fund, 1982), p. 31; and U.S. Department of Commerce, "Who's Minding the Kids?" *Household Economic Studies* Series P-70, No. 9 (Washington, DC: Bureau of the Census, May 1987), pp. 1–11.
21. C. Coelen, F. Glantz, and D. Calare, *Day Care Centers in the U.S.: A National Profile 1976–1977* (Cambridge, MA: Abt Books, 1979), p. 84.
22. See Richard C. Endsley and Marilyn R. Bradford, *Quality Day Care: A Handbook of Choices for Parents and Caregivers* (Englewood Cliffs, NJ: Prentice-Hall, 1981), pp. 22–25; G. Smith, "Perry Mendel's Golden Diapers," *Forbes*, Vol. 123, No. 13, pp. 67–69; and J. Lelyveld, "Drive-in Day Care," *New York Times Magazine*, June 5, 1977, p. 110; and *Kinder-Care Annual Report 1986* (Montgomery, AL: Kinder-Care Learning Centers, Inc., October 1986), pp. 1–5.
23. *World Almanac, op. cit.*, p. 84.
24. See Anne Shyne and Anita Shroeder, *The National Study of Social Services to Children and Their Families* (Washington, DC: U.S. Children's Bureau, 1978); and U.S. Department of Commerce; *op. cit.*, pp. 7–9.
25. Jacobs, *op. cit.*, pp. 90–91.
26. National Center for Health Statistics, U.S. Department of Health and Human Services "Home Health Care for Persons 55 Years and Over," *Vital and Health Statistics Publication: Statistical Publication Series*, Vol. 10, No. 73 (1972); cited in Neil Gilbert, *Capitalism and the Welfare State: Dilemmas of Social Benevolence* (New Haven, CT: Yale University Press, 1983), p. 121.
27. Martin Wolins and Yochanan Wozner, *Revitalizing Residential Settings* (San Francisco: Jossey-Bass, 1982), pp. 4–15.

28. Ann W. Shyne, "Who Are the Children? A National Overview of Services," *Social Work Research and Abstracts,* Vol. 16, No. 1 (Spring 1980), p. 29.

29. Wolins and Wozner, *op cit.,* p. 27.

30. *Ibid.,* pp. 15–31.

31. William Weissert, "Two Models of Geriatric Day Care: Findings from a Comparative Study," *Gerontologist,* Vol. 16 (1976), p. 420.

32. Bettleheim, Bruno, *A Home for the Heart* (New York: Alfred A. Knopf, 1974), p. 29.

CHAPTER 2

1. Angela C. Browne, "The Mixed Economy of Day Care: Consumer Versus Professional Arrangements," *Journal of Social Policy,* Vol. 13, No. 3 (1984), p. 321.

2. This estimate is based on a 2,000–hour work year for each employed parent. For number of children with employed parents, see *Employed Parents and Their Children: A Data Book* (Washington, DC: Children's Defense Fund, 1982), pp. 61, 62, and 65. See also Bureau of Labor Statistics, cited in *The World Almanac 1988* (New York: Scripps Howard Co., 1987), p. 84.

3. See Alfred H. Kahn and Sheila B. Kamerman, "Families Have Problems," in *Helping America's Families* (Philadelphia: Temple University Press, 1981); Christopher Lasch, *Haven in a Heartless World: The Family Besieged* (New York: Basic Books, 1975); White House Conference on Families, *Listening to America's Families* (Washington, DC: The White House Conference on Families, October 1980).

4. Judith S. Wallerstein and Joan Berlin Kelley, *Surviving the Breakup: How Children and Parents Cope with Divorce* (New York: Basic Books, 1980), p. 6; and "Births, Marriages, and Deaths for February 1988," *Monthly Vital Statistics Report,* Vol. 37, No. 2 (May 18, 1988), p. 3.

5. Children's Defense Fund, *op. cit.,* p. 61.

6. U.S. Department of Commerce, *Money, Income and Poverty Status of Families and Persons in the United States,* Series P-60, No. 127 (Washington, DC: Bureau of Census, August 1981), p. 7.

7. See Nathan Glazer, "The Limits of Social Policy," in Neil Gilbert and Harry Specht, *The Emergence of Social Welfare and Social Work* (Itasca, IL: F. E. Peacock, 1981), pp. 190–205.

8. Present changes in tax laws have decreased this "marriage tax" but have not eliminated it. In 1983, a dually employed married couple, together

earning $30,000 and taking $7,000 in net deductions, paid a tax of $3,868. An unmarried couple, together earning the same $30,000 with the same deductions, paid less in tax, $3,662. See Jane Bryant Quinn, "Profiting from the New 1040," *Newsweek,* February 28, 1983, p. 64.

9. *The New York Times,* December 12, 1971, p. 4.

10. See Neil Gilbert's discussion in *Capitalism and the Welfare State: Dilemmas of Social Benevolence* (New Haven, CT: Yale University Press, 1983), pp. 100–104.

11. See Barry Hindess and Paul Q. Hirst, *Pre-Capitalist Modes of Production* (London: Routledge & Kegan Paul, 1975); Carl N. Delger, *At Odds: Women and the Family in America from the Revolution to the Present* (New York: Oxford University Press, 1967); and Ruth Schwartz Cowan, *More Work for Mother* (New York: Basic Books, 1983).

12. Arlene Skolnick (Ed.), *Rethinking Childhood: Perspectives on Development and Society* (Boston: Little, Brown & Co., 1976), p. 269.

13. From an anthropological perspective, the husband, wife, and child or children are the nucleus, "the unit of structure from which a kinship is built up." The extended family is "a group founded on kinship and locality." See Felix M. Berardo, "The Anthropological Approach to the Study of the Family," in E. Ivan Nye and Felix M, Berardo (Eds.), *Emerging Conceptual Frameworks in Family Analysis* (New York: Praeger Publishers, 1981), pp. 10–51. In the jargon of family treatment and family systems a "symmetrical relationship brings together two people of equal status," as opposed to a complementary, asymmetrical relationship. See the examination of how family relationships contribute to growth and dysfunction, in Curtis Janzen and Oliver Harris, *Family Treatment in Social Work Practice* (Itasca, IL: F. E. Peacock Publishers, Inc., 1980), pp. 1–27.

14. L. Hirschorn, "Social Policy and the Life Cycle: A Developmental Perspective," *Social Service Review,* Vol. 51 (1977), pp. 434–450; and S. L. Rhodes, "A Developmental Approach to the Life Cycle of the Family," *Social Casework,* Vol. 58 (1977), pp. 301–311.

15. Margaret Mead, "What Is Happening to the American Family?" *Journal of Social Casework,* November 1947, pp. 323–330.

16. Neil Gilbert and Harry Specht, *Dimensions of Social Welfare Policy* (Englewood Cliffs, NJ: Prentice-Hall, 1974), pp. 2–6.

17. Hindess and Hirst, *op. cit.,* pp. 9 and 66.

18. Lasch, *op. cit.,* pp. 7, 25, 118, 145, and 185.

19. Richard John Neuhaus, "Renting Women, Buying Babies and Class Struggles"; Barbara Sherman Heyl, "Commercial Contracts and Human Connectedness"; and Barbara Katz Rothman, "Cheap Labor: Sex, Class,

Race—And Surrogacy," all in *Society,* Vol. 25, No. 3 (March–April 1988).

20. Glazer, *op. cit.;* Lasch, *op. cit.*
21. See Neil Gilbert's discussion of paid volunteers in his book *Capitalism and the Welfare State, op. cit.,* pp. 126–128; and Lasch, *op. cit.*
22. W. Buckley, *Sociology and Modern Systems Theory* (Englewood Cliffs, NJ: Prentice-Hall, 1967).
23. Gilbert, *op. cit.,* p. 101.
24. George Gilder, *Wealth and Poverty* (New York: Basic Books, 1981), pp. 111 and 121.
25. See Gilbert Steiner, *The Futility of Family Policy* (Washington, DC: The Brookings Institution, 1981).
26. Karl Zinsmeister, "Brave New World: How Day Care Harms Children," *Policy Review,* No. 44 (Spring 1988), p. 45.
27. Sylvia Ann Hewlett, "Child Carelessness," *Harper's,* November 1983, pp. 20–25.
28. White House Conference on Families, *Listening to America's Families* (Washington, DC: U.S. Government Printing Office, October 1980), p. 21.
29. Urie Bronfenbrenner, *The Ecology of Human Development* (Cambridge, MA: Harvard University Press, 1979), pp. 3–43.
30. See Steiner, *op. cit.,* pp. 71–102.
31. Ford Foundation, *Women, Children, and Poverty in America* (New York: Ford Foundation, January 1988), p. 8; and Children's Defense Fund, *The Child Care Handbook* (Washington, DC: Children's Defense Fund, 1981), p. 8.
32. Carolyn S. Edwards, *USDA Estimates of the Cost of Raising a Child: A Guide to Their Use and Interpretation,* Miscellaneous Publication 1411, 1981 (Washington, DC: U.S. Department of Agriculture, 1981), pp. 31–35.
33. See Bureau of Labor Statistics, *Women Who Head Families: A Socioeconomic Analysis* (Washington, DC: U.S. Department of Labor, March 1977); and Allyson Sherman Grossman, "Divorced and Separated Women in the Labor Force—An Update," *Monthly Labor Review,* October 1978, pp. 43–44.
34. U.S. Department of Commerce, *Who's Minding the Kids?* Series P-70, No. 9 (Washington, DC: Bureau of the Census, May 1987), p. 14.
35. Commerce Clearing House, *Employer-Sponsored Child Care Programs* (New York: Commerce Clearing House, 1982).
36. Grossman, *op. cit.,* pp. 43–44.
37. Ford Foundation, *op. cit.,* pp. 6 and 41–42.

38. *Ibid.*, pp. 6 and 41–42.
39. In 1986, 25% of all black women and 20% of all Hispanic women were unemployed (compared to 14% of all white women). *Ibid.*, p. 6.
40. Sheila B. Kamerman and Alfred J. Kahn, *Child Care, Family Benefits and Working Parents: A Study in Comparative Policy* (New York: Columbia University Press, 1981), pp. 246–247.
41. April von Frank, *Family Policy in the USSR Since 1944* (Palo Alto, CA: R. & E. Research Associates, 1979).
42. Von Frank, *ibid.*, provides a detailed history of Soviet family policy.
43. Neil Gilbert, "Sweden's Disturbing Family Trends," *The Wall Street Journal*, June 24, 1987, p. 23.
44. Martha Friendly and Laurel Rothman, "No Way to Bring Up Baby," (Toronto) *Globe and Mail*, January 19, 1988, p. A7.
45. Glen Collins, "U.S. Day-Care Guidelines Rekindle Controversy," *New York Times*, February 4, 1985, p. 20.
46. Warren T. Brookes, "Day Care: Is It a Real Crisis or a War over Political Turf?" *San Francisco Chronicle*, April 27, 1988, Briefing Section, p. 5.
47. Freddie H. Lucas, *Day Care Research* (New York: J. C. Penney Co., 1972).
48. General Motors, Organizational Research and Development Department, *Quality of Worklife Executive Conference, 1980: Organizational Issues and Their Potential Solutions* (General Motors, April 11, 1980).
49. James W. Ehrenstrom, "Four Cornerstones for the Effective Design of Flexible Working Hours," *Alternative World Patterns Conference Proceedings* (Atlanta: American Institute of Industrial Engineers and National Council for Alternative Work Patterns, May 1980).
50. White House Conference on Families, October 1980, *op. cit.*, p. 18.
51. J. C. Penney Company, *Work and Families: Report to Corporate Leaders on the White House Conference on Families* (Washington, DC: White House Conference on Families; and New York: J. C. Penney Co., October 22, 1980).
52. White House Conference on Families, *Business Briefing Questionnaire Summary* (unpublished) (Washington, DC: White House Conference on Families, November 1980).
53. Senator Orrin Hatch, "Seeking Political Unity for Child Care," *The Washington Times*, October 20, 1987, p. F3.
54. *Ibid.*
55. Senate Bill 1678, *Congressional Record*, Vol. 133, Washington, September 11, 1987, No. 137.
56. Senator Alan Cranston, Senate Bill 1309, "Economic Equity Act of 1987," June 2, 1987.

57. *Ibid.*
58. Mary McNamara, "At Last! A Major Push for Child Care," *Ms. Magazine,* February 1988, p. 17. For further discussion of child care controversies, see Connaught Marsher, "Socialized Motherhood: As Easy as ABC," and George Gilder, "An Open Letter to Orrin Hatch," both in *National Review,* Vol. 40, No. 9 (May 13, 1988), pp. 28–34; William J. Bennett, "The Role of the Family in the Nurture and Protection of the Young," *American Psychologist,* March 1987, pp. 246–253; and Miranda Spivak, "Political Compromise Afoot?" *Ms. Magazine,* July 1988, pp. 68–69.

CHAPTER 3

1. See Clair Vickery, "The Time-Poor: A New Look at Poverty," *The Journal of Human Resources,* Vol. 12, No. 1 (Winter 1977), pp. 27–48.
2. See Carolyn S. Edwards, *USDA Estimates of the Cost of Raising a Child: A Guide to Their Use and Interpretation* (Washington, DC: U.S. Department of Agriculture, Miscellaneous Publication 1411, 1981).
3. These figures are for the western United States and for one child in a husband-wife family with five or fewer children. Edwards, 1981, *ibid.,* p. 47.
4. U.S. Department of Commerce, *Who's Minding the Kids?* (Washington, DC: Bureau of the Census, Series P-70, No. 9, May 1987), pp. 26–34.
5. From Halcyone Bohen and Anamaria Viveros-Long, *Balancing Jobs and Family Life* (Philadelphia: Temple University Press, 1981), pp. 232–236; see also Fern Schumer Chapman, "Executive Guilt," *Fortune,* February 16, 1987, pp. 30–36; and Sally O'Neill, "Choosing Children over Careers," *San Francisco Examiner,* July 19, 1987, p. D-1.
6. Bohen and Viveros-Long, *ibid.*
7. Neil Gilbert, *Capitalism and the Welfare State: Dilemmas of Social Benevolence* (New Haven, CT: Yale University Press, 1983), p. 32; see also, as cited by Gilbert, Mary Ann Scheirer, "Program Participants' Positive Perceptions: Psychological Conflict of Interest in Social Program Evaluation," in Lee Sechrest et al. (Eds.), *Evaluation Studies Review Annual,* Vol. 4 (Beverly Hills, CA: Sage, 1979), pp. 407–424; and Malcolm Bush and Andrew Gordon, "The Advantage of Client Involvement," in Thomas Cook et al. (Eds.), *Evaluation Studies Review Annual,* Vol. 3 (Beverly Hills, CA: Sage, 1978), pp. 767–783.
8. Heidi M. Ferrar, *The Relationship Between a Working Mother's Job Satisfaction and Her Child Care Arrangements* (Pennsylvania State University,

August 1978), pp. 27–33; and Alan Andreasen, *The Disadvantaged Consumer* (New York: Free Press, 1975), pp. 13–14, 53, 234, and 333.

9. Angela C. Browne, "The Market Sphere: Private Responses to the Need for Day Care," *Child Welfare*, Vol. 54, No. 4 (1985), pp. 367–368.

10. Governor's Advisory Committee on Child Development Programs, *Employer Sponsored Child Care* (Sacramento: State of California, July 1981), p. 18.

11. A critical review of the unsuccessful implementation of these programs can be found in James Bovard, "Busy Doing Nothing: The Story of Government Job Creation," *Policy Review*, Vol. 24 (Spring 1983), pp. 87–102.

12. U.S. Department of Labor, *Summary of the Job Training Partnership Act* (Washington, DC: U.S. Department of Labor, Employment and Training Administration, Office of Strategic Planning and Policy Development, Office of Planning and Policy Analysis, October 7, 1982).

13. California State Assembly Bill (AB) 3424, Section 15073, Year 1982.

14. Reported by a PIC director, who wishes to remain anonymous, during an interview with the author, Spring 1983.

15. Governor's Advisory Committee on Child Development Programs, *op. cit.*, p. 4.

16. "Child Care Called Inadequate," *San Francisco Chronicle*, December 1, 1986, Business Section, p. 1.

17. C. Russell Hill, "Private Demand for Child Care," *Evaluation Quarterly*, Vol. 2, No. 4 (November 1978), p. 523.

18. B. Johnson, *Marital and Family Characteristics of the Labor Force*, Special Labor Force Report 237 (Washington, DC: U.S. Government Printing Office, March 1979); see also Bureau of Labor Statistics, *Children of Working Mothers*, Special Labor Force Report 217 (Washington, DC: U.S. Government Printing Office, March 1977); see also Children's Defense Fund, *Employed Parents and Their Children: A Data Book* (Washington, DC: Children's Defense Fund, 1981), p. 59.

19. Bureau of Labor Statistics, *Marital Family Characteristics of Workers: 1970–1978*, Special Labor Force Report 219 (Washington, DC: U.S. Government Printing Office, 1978).

20. Bureau of Labor Statistics, *Women Who Head Families: A Socioeconomic Analysis*, Special Labor Force Report 213 (Washington, DC: U.S. Government Printing Office, March 1979); see also U.S. Dept. of Commerce, *op. cit.*

21. *Ibid.*

22. Zale Corporation, *Zale Corporation Child Care Center* (Dallas, TX: Zale Corporation, 1980); and Honeywell Women's Task Force, *Child Care*

Recommendations for Honeywell Employees (Minneapolis: Honeywell Corporation, July 1980); see also White House Conference on Families, *Listening to America's Families* (Washington, DC: Government Printing Office, 1980); and Joyce Moscato, "The Child-Care Connection," *Union*, November–December 1987, pp. 16–19.

23. "Dad Joins Mom in Child Care Concerns," *Personal Report for the Executive*, June 1, 1987, p. 2, reporting on a recent Gallup Poll.

24. Bureau of Labor Statistics, *Absence from Work: Measuring the Hours Lost*, Special Labor Force Report 229 (Washington, DC: U.S. Government Printing Office, May 1978); see also R. Endsley and M. Bradford, *Quality Day Care: A Handbook of Choices for Parents and Caregivers* (Englewood Cliffs, NJ: Prentice-Hall, 1981).

25. Sheila Kamerman and Alfred Kahn, *Child Care, Family Benefits, and Working Parents: A Study in Comparative Policy* (New York: Columbia University Press, 1981).

26. Zale Corporation, *op. cit.*, and D. Ogilvie, *Employer Subsidized Child Care* (Washington, DC: Inner City Fund, September 1973).

27. Jane Bryant Quinn, "Day Care: The Key Job Benefit," *San Francisco Chronicle*, March 12, 1988, p. 133.

28. National Employer Supported Child Care Project, *List of Employer Supported Child Care Programs in the U.S. 1981–82* (Pasadena, CA: Child Care Information Service, 1983); see also Carol Dilks, "Employers Who Help with the Kids," *Nation's Business*, February 1984, pp. 59–60.

29. Robert B. Reich, *The Next American Frontier* (New York: Times Books, 1983), pp. 37–39.

30. "Day Care at Work Makes a Comeback," *Nation's Business*, July 1980, p. 20.

31. Cathy Trost, "Creative Child Care Programs Aid Employees Who Work Odd Hours," *Wall Street Journal*, March 18, 1988, p. 21.

32. Women's Bureau, *Employers and Child Care: Establishing Services Through the Workplace*, Pamphlet 23 (Washington, DC: U.S. Department of Labor, revised August 1982), pp. 15–16.

33. Ralph Estes, *Corporate Social Accounting* (New York: John Wiley & Sons, 1976), p. 2.

34. For a discussion of these valuation approaches, see Estes, *ibid.*, pp. 108–149.

35. Raymond A. Katzell and Daniel Yankelovich, *Work, Productivity, and Job Satisfaction: An Evaluation of Policy-Related Research* (New York: Harcourt Brace Jovanovich, 1975), p. 416.

36. Women's Bureau, August 1982, *op. cit.*, p. 5.

37. Ellen Mathia, "Corporate Day Care—Nyloncraft Frames Issue of the '80's," *South Bend Tribune,* South Bend, IN, August 1982; see also Sandra Friedland, "More Companies Offering Day Care," *New York Times,* July 20, 1980, Section 11, p. 1.

38. Edward Itwata, "Corporate Child-Care Center Debuts," *San Francisco Chronicle,* September 11, 1986.

39. Halcy Bohen, *Report on European Policies Affecting Families,* Memorandum to German Marshall Fund, June 30, 1981, p. 25.

40. *Ibid.*

41. *Ibid.,* p. 26.

42. L. A. Chung, "Ambitious Child Care Programs," *San Francisco Chronicle,* March 20, 1985, p. 4.

43. Catherine E. Born, "Proprietary Firms and Child Welfare Services: Patterns and Implications," *Child Welfare,* Vol. 62, No. 2 (March–April 1983), pp. 109–118.

44. Gordon Manser, "Further Thoughts on Purchase of Service," *Social Casework,* July 1973, pp. 421–427.

45. Born, *op. cit.,* p. 112.

46. C. Coelen, F. Glantz, and D. Colare, *Day Care Centers in the U.S.: A National Profile 1976–1977* (Cambridge, MA: Abt Books, 1978).

47. Dan Belm, "Little Kids, Big Bucks," *This World, San Francisco Chronicle,* April 26, 1987, p. 5; see also Gary Ferman, "The Kid Biz," *The Miami Herald,* June 13, 1988, p. 1BB.

48. Sharon L. Kagan and Theresa Glennon, "Considering Proprietary Child Care," in Edward F. Zigler and Edmund W. Gordon, *Day Care: Scientific and Social Policy Issues* (Boston: Auburn House, 1981), pp. 404–405.

49. *Ibid.,* p. 405.

50. R. Ruopp et al., *Children at the Center: Summary of Findings and Their Implications* (Cambridge, MA: Abt Books, 1979), quoted in *ibid.,* p. 408; see also *ibid.,* pp. 402–408.

51. Nancy J. Walker, *San Francisco's Office Affordable Childcare Program.* Memorandum 10-9-85. San Francisco Board of Supervisors.

52. L. Chung, "Ambitious Child Care Program," *San Francisco Chronicle,* March 20, 1985, p. 4.

53. Bradley Googins and Dianne Burden, "Vulnerability of Working Parents: Balancing Work and Home Rules," *Social Work,* Vol. 32, No. 4, (July–August 1987), pp. 295–300. See also Cathleen Jordan, Norman Cobb, and Rex McCully, "Clinical Issues of the Dual-Career Couple," *Social Work,* Vol. 34, No. 1, (January 1989), pp. 29–32.

CHAPTER 4

1. "A particularly high incidence of such developmental impairment has been found in urban lower socioeconomic groups. Though most of the studies concentrate on cognitive development, a few dealing with general development have arrived at similar conclusions." Roy K. Lilleskov, "Experiences with Early Childhood Intervention," in Peter B. Neubaur (Ed.), *Early Child Day Care* (New York: Jason Aronson), p. 19.

2. What are these functions? The family unit can be compared to an organizational system of action, and especially to an institutional system of action. In the words of Wolins and Wozner, "The primary components of institutions are the competencies of residents and staff and their activities or interactions." Similarly, the primary components of families can be described as the incompetencies or needs of dependents (usually children) and the competencies of other family members (usually parents) in providing care for them. The task of parents is thus to enable their children to enter adulthood with adequate psychological, social, mental, and physical competencies or "masteries." This is the "function" of care.

   On family and institutional similarities, see Martin Wolins and Yochanan Wozner, *Revitalizing Residential Settings* (San Francisco: Jossey-Bass, 1982), pp. 17–19, 75–76, and 89–90; and regarding the system of action upon which Wolins and Wozner base their model of institutional care settings, see Talcott Parsons, "The Point of View of the Author," in *The Social Theories of Talcott Parsons* (Englewood Cliffs, NJ: Prentice-Hall, 1962), p. 333.

   Regarding the differences between parents and paid caregivers, see David Elkind, *Miseducation: Preschoolers at Risk* (New York: Alfred A. Knopf, 1987), pp. 95–101.

   Familial and informal assistance are the most natural and immediate responses to the need for care. This response sphere, defined in Chapter 1, is a "first line of defense" located around the point of origin of the dependence grid, where dependence is perceived as being normal and self-limiting in duration and degree (see Figure 1.1).

3. As I pointed out in Chapter 1, good care serves as an antidote to dependence. The lessening of dependence accompanies the acquisition of the "masteries" which are promoted by developmentally oriented care. In their classification of ideal types of personal subsystems, Wolins and Wozner (cited above) define four fields of "mastery": personal-psychological, physical-behavioral, social, and cultural-valuative. In analyzing the dimensions of care, I have combined elements of Wolins and Wozner's category of cultural-valuative mastery with one which I call the social dimension of care. And I have separated some of the personal masteries

from Wolins and Wozner's category of personal-psychological mastery, to create a separate category for cognitive mastery, which I call the educational dimension of care.

4. Psychologist Ed Zigler argues that no adult should care for more than three children. See Robert J. Trotter, "Project Day-Care," *Psychology Today,* December 1987, p. 36, for further discussion. Regarding the need for consistency among caregivers, see Doris E. Durrell, *The Critical Years* (Oakland, CA: New Harbinger Publications, 1984), pp. 31–32.

5. These phrases are quoted from Martin Wolins's lectures in his course entitled "The Benevolent Asylum," offered in the School of Social Welfare at the University of California, Berkeley, Spring 1981.

6. These time spans are described by Sheila M. Pringle and Brenda E. Ramsey in *Promoting the Health of Children: A Guide for Caretakers and Health Care Professionals* (St. Louis: C. V. Mosley, 1982); see also Bernice L. Neugarten et al., "The Changing Meanings of Age," *Psychology Today,* Vol. 21, No. 5 (May 1987), pp. 29–33.

7. John Gleidman and William Roth, *The Unexpected Minority: Handicapped Children in America* (New York: Harcourt Brace Jovanovich, 1980), pp. 68–69. See also Sarah Rule, "Day Care for Handicapped Children," *Child Care Quarterly,* Vol. 15, No. 4 (Winter 1986), pp. 223–232.

8. See Constance T. Fischer, "I.Q. Enter the Child," in Gertrude J. Williams and Sol Gordon (Eds.), *Clinical Child Psychology* (New York: Behavioral Publications, 1974), p. 333; see also David Elkind, "Superkids and Super Problems," *Psychology Today,* Vol. 21, No. 5 (May 1987), p. 60.

9. Pringle and Ramsey, *op. cit.,* p. 1.

10. Henry Maier defined seven ingredients of care in his description of the "core of care." See Henry W. Maier, "The Core of Care: Essential Ingredients for the Development of Children at Home and Away from Home," *Child Care Quarterly,* Vol. 8, No. 3 (Fall 1979), pp. 161–265.

11. This section on direct care draws upon a wealth of development literature. Many specific references to the literature have been omitted because of the limitations of space. Consult the Bibliography for extended references.

12. Sibylle K. Escalona, "Developmental Issues in the Second Year of Life: Their Implications for Day Care Practices," in Neubauer, *op. cit.,* pp. 33–34; and Durrell, *op. cit.*

13. Testimony before the Governor's Commission on Child Development regarding child development curriculum frequently mentioned the need for "warmth of the familiar," including the "presence of peers and staff that speak the child's native language and share the same cultural background." *Developmental Needs of Young Bilingual Children,* Governor's Advisory Commission on Child Development, May 1982, p. 12.

14. An interesting example of developmental impetus provided by older children was reported to me by a mother who claimed that her baby had been toilet-trained only by mimicking older children.

15. Curtis Janzen and Oliver Harris, *Family Treatment in Social Work Practice* (Itasca, IL: F. E. Peacock Publishers, 1980) p. 192; see also Judith S. Wallerstein and Joan Berlin Kelly, who conceptualize "family rupture as intersecting sharply with the child's progression or developmental pathway," in *Surviving the Breakup* (New York: Basic Books, 1980), pp. 51–52.

16. This controversy is encapsulated in the Piaget/Sutton-Smith debate of the 1960s. See J. Piaget, "Response to Brian Sutton-Smith," *Psychological Review,* Vol. 73 (1966), pp. 111–112; B. Sutton-Smith, "Piaget on Play: A Critique," *Psychological Review,* Vol. 73 (1966), pp. 109–110; and "A Reply to Piaget: A Play Theory of Copy," *Psychological Review,* Vol. 73 (1966), pp. 113–114.

17. Brian Vandenberg, "Play: Dormant Issues and New Perspectives," *Human Development,* Vol. 24 (1981), p. 357.

18. Rachel M. Henry, "A Theoretical and Empirical Analysis of 'Reasoning' in the Socialization of Young Children," *Human Development,* Vol. 23 (1980), p. 108. See also the account of moral thought advanced by L. Kohlberg in "Moral Stages and Moralization: The Cognitive-Developmental Approach," in M. Lickona, *Moral Development and Behavior* (New York: Holt Rinehart & Winston, 1976).

19. See Joseph Marcus and Halbert B. Robertson, *Growing Up in Groups: The Russian Day Care Center and the Israeli Kibbutz* (New York: Gordon & Breach, 1972).

20. Sheldon White and Barbara Notkin White, *Childhood: Pathways of Discovery,* The Life Cycle Series (San Francisco: Harper & Row, Publishers, 1980), p. 81.

21. Sibylle K. Escalona, "Developmental Issues in the Second Year of Life: Their Implications for Day Care Practices," in Peter B. Neubauer (Ed.) *Early Child Care* (New York: Aaronsun, 1974).

22. Daniel Goleman, "Little Fears That Grow with Age of Child," *New York Times,* April 21, 1988, p. B9.

23. Carl Bereiter and Seigfried Engelmann, *Teaching Disadvantaged Children in Preschool* (Englewood Cliffs, NJ: Prentice-Hall, 1966). See also "Picking Up on the Beat," *The Miami Herald,* January 11, 1988, p. 2–C.

24. Summaries of many of these studies and others mentioned here can be found in Sally Ryan (Ed.), *A Report on Longitudinal Evaluations of Preschool Programs: Vol. 1. Longitudinal Evaluations.* (Washington, DC: U.S. Government Printing Office, DHEW Publications No. (OHD) 76–30024).

25. This study did state in a section entitled "Alternative Interpretations and Explanations" that "one possibility is that Head Start has actually been effective, but that the limitations of the present study design preclude detection of the full effects of Head Start." Westinghouse Learning Corporation, *The Impact of Head Start: An Evaluation of the Effects of Head Start on Children's Cognitive and Affective Development: Vol. 1. Text and Appendices A–E.* Presented to the Office of Economic Opportunity pursuant to Contract No. B89–4536 (Ohio University: Westinghouse Learning Corporation, June 12, 1969), pp. 240–245.

26. See Ryan, *op. cit.*

27. These powerful effects of care (outside the educational dimension) upon cognitive development are exemplified in the Westinghouse study of affective development versus cognitive development. Instruments measuring cognitive development were the Metropolitan Readiness Tests, Stanford Achievement Tests, and Illinois Test of Psycholinguistic Abilities. Affective development was measured against a Children's Self-Concept Index, Classroom Behavior Inventory, and Children's Attitudinal Range Indicator. Westinghouse Learning Corporation, *op. cit.*, p. 57. See also David Elkind, *Miseducation: Preschoolers at Risk* (New York: Alfred A. Knopf, 1987), pp. 60–62.

28. Ryan, *op. cit.*, p. 67.

29. "Day Care and Contagion," *The Harvard Medical School Health Letter,* Vol. 7, No. 7 (May 1983), pp. 3–4; and Gary A. Gingrich et al., "Serologic Investigation of an Outbreak of Hepatitis A in a Rural Day Care Center," *American Journal of Public Health,* Vol. 73, Number 10 (October 1983), pp. 1199–1201; "AIDS 'Hysteria' at S.F. Nursery School," *San Francisco Chronicle,* March 24, 1988, p. A-3; Rod Moser, "Keeping Kids Healthy in Day Care," *Medical Self Care,* May–June 1988, pp. 35–40.

30. Ellen Hale, "Good Nutrition for Your Growing Child," *FDA Consumer,* Vol. 21, No. 3 (April 1987), p. 23.

31. White and White, *op. cit.*, pp. 70–71. See also Ronald J. Lemire, *Normal and Abnormal Development of the Human Nervous System* (New York: Harper & Row, 1975).

32. Note that the "functional approach" to the effects of environment upon behavior regards only those stimuli which measurably affect behavior as being, conceptually, part of the environment. In this view all non-behavioral criteria for the "good environment" may be eliminated from the definition of environment. See Jacob L. Gewirtz, "On Designing the Functional Environment of the Child to Facilitate Behavioral Development," in Caroline Chandler et al. (Laura L. Dittman, Ed.), *Early Child Care: The New Perspectives,* (New York: Atherton Press, 1968) pp. 209–210.

33. Lois Barclay Murphy, "Individualism of Child Care and Its Relation to Environment," in Chandler et al., *ibid.*, pp. 69–75.
34. Constantinos A. Doxiadis, *Ekistics: An Introduction to the Science of Human Settlement* (New York: Oxford University Press, 1968), p. 327.
35. *Ibid.*, p. 29.
36. D. J. Greenberg, Ina C. Uzgiris, and J. McV. Hunt, "Attentional Preference and Experience: 3. Visual Familiarity and Looking Time," *Journal of Genetic Psychology*, Vol. 117, pp. 123–135.
37. See M. D. Ainsworth, *Maternal Deprivation* (New York: Child Welfare League of America, 1969).
38. John Newson and Elizabeth Newson, "Cultural Aspects of Childrearing," in Arlene Skolnick (Ed.), *Rethinking Childhood: Perspectives on Development and Society* (Boston: Little, Brown & Company, 1976), p. 326.
39. *Ibid.*, p. 326.
40. *Ibid.*, p. 326.
41. *Information Please Almanac 1982* (New York: Simon & Schuster, 1981), p. 776.
42. Carl N. Degler, *At Odds: Women and the Family in America from the Revolution to the Present* (New York: Oxford University Press, 1980), pp. 72–73.
43. White and White, *op. cit.*, pp. 1–20 and 81–120.
44. "Bringing Up Superbaby," *Newsweek*, March 28, 1983, pp. 62–68; and "Parents Warned to 'Let Children Be Children,'" *San Francisco Chronicle*, November 4, 1987, p. C-11.
45. Alice S. Rossi, "A Biosocial Perspective on Parenting," *Daedalus*, Vol. 106, No. 2 (1977), p. 5.
46. *Ibid.*, p. 7.
47. Note that Site 5 includes computer learning for toddlers in its early education program.
48. Brigitte Berger and Peter L. Berger, *The War over the Family: Capturing the Middle Ground* (Garden City, NY: Anchor Press/Doubleday, 1983), p. 156.

CHAPTER 5

1. The program description quoted here was printed in a statement by the county schools. The publication is not cited here, in order to protect the anonymity of the site and respondents.
2. *Ibid.*
3. Note that these services can be loosely organized into the dimensions of

direct care defined by this study: social, psychological, educational, physical, and environmental.

4. During one information-gathering visit, I was asked to "sit" in a room with fifteen children and no other adults, because one staff member was ill and another was late.

5. The Navy has demonstrated its concern for its families of all socioeconomic backgrounds who experience the special problems of military life. "The nature of our Navy does not, in general, change. Ships and squadrons will continue to deploy and people will continue to be transferred to billets where their skills are needed most. The requirements not generally imposed on nonmilitary families—coupled with the nature of our business to prepare and defend our nation—place great strains on the Navy family, even under the best circumstances." Lando W. Zech, Jr., Vice Admiral, U.S. Navy, in the introductory letter to *Navy Family Advocacy Program Training 1982* (Washington, DC: Creative Associates and U.S. Department of the Navy, 1982), p. 2.

6. It is expected that group size specifications will be issued soon.

7. The providing corporation continues to expand its child care business into geographical areas where there is a demand. To date, most of its sites are sponsored directly by the corporation as profit-making operations, instead of being employer-sponsored. In some instances, the corporation shares facilities with state-subsidized programs (an arrangement resembling, at least physically, the sharing of a school building by Site 1 and Site 2 in this study).

8. The parents of these children are among the ones who participated in the day care consumer questionnaire survey which is described in Chapter 7, Appendix A, and Appendix C. The findings of the study indicate that this group of parents were not markedly critical of this program.

CHAPTER 7

1. Neil Gilbert, *Capitalism and the Welfare State: Dilemmas of Social Benevolence* (New Haven, CT: Yale University Press, 1983), pp. 31–41.

2. Information available from the California State Commission of Child Development in Sacramento, CA. See also Cynthia Gorney, "The Baffling Case of the McMartin Preschool," *San Francisco Chronicle, This World Magazine*, June 26, 1988, pp. 10–14; and Barbara Deane, "The Lori Nathan Case," *San Francisco Sunday Examiner and Chronicle, California Living Magazine*, March 18, 1984, pp. 10–16.

3. For example, see Malcolm Bush and Andrew Gordon, "The Advantages of

Client Involvement," in Thomas Cook et al. (Eds.), *Evaluation Studies Review Annual* (Beverly Hills, CA: Sage, 1978), Vol. 3, pp. 787–783; Mary Ann Scheirer, "Program Participants' Positive Perceptions: Psychological Conflict of Interest in Social Program Evaluation," in Lee Sechrest et al. (Eds.), *Evaluation Review Annual* (Beverly Hills, CA: Sage, 1979), Vol. 4, pp. 407–424; and Brian Stipek, "Citizens' Satisfaction with Urban Services: Potential Misuse as a Performance Indicator," *Public Administration Review,* Vol. 39 (January–February 1979), pp. 46–52.

4. Donald Campbell, "Reforms as Experiments," in F. G. Cars (Ed.), *Readings in Evaluation Research* (New York: Russell Sage, 1977), pp. 172–204; Mary Ann Scheirer, *op. cit;* and Neil Gilbert and Joseph Eaton, "Who Speaks for the Poor?" *Journal of the American Institute of Planners,* Vol. 36 (November 1970), pp. 411–416.

5. In her summary of studies dealing with working mothers' satisfaction with their child care arrangements, Heidi Ferrar suggested that the positive biases of respondents may be due to social mores, guilt feelings, and a lack of knowledge about alternatives. Heidi M. Ferrar, *The Relationship Between a Working Mother's Job Satisfaction and Her Child Care Arrangements* (Philadelphia: Pennsylvania State University, August 1978), p. 33.

CONCLUSION

1. Although the variables and findings identified in Chapters 6 and 7 specifically address the characteristics of child care services and consumers, their implications extend to the broader problem of consumer choice as a regulatory mechanism in the arena of human care.

2. "The Realities and Fantasies of Industry-Related Child Care," proceedings of a symposium hosted by the University of Colorado Medical Center and funded by Office of Child Development Child Care Project Grant No. CB-248 (Denver: May 21, 1973), p. 58.

3. June H. Zeitlen and Nancy Duff Campbell, "Availability of Child Care for Low-Income Families: Strategies to Address the Impact of the Economic Recovery Tax Act of 1981 and the Omnibus Budget Reconciliation Act of 1981," *Clearinghouse Review,* Vol. 16, No. 4 (August–September 1981), p. 310.

4. *Omnibus Budget Reconciliation Act of 1981,* Pub. L. No. 97–35, 2307, 05 Stat. 357.

5. Zeitlen and Campbell, *op. cit.,* pp. 311–312.

6. Many of the phrases and numbers quoted in this discussion of tax benefits

are from *Employer-Sponsored Child Care Programs* (Commerce Clearinghouse, 1982).

7. *Ibid.*, p. 25.

8. *Ibid.*, p. 26.

9. Kenneth Keneston and the Carnegie Council on Children, *All Our Children: The American Family Under Pressure* (New York: Harcourt Brace Jovanovich, 1978), p. 23.

10. Neil Gilbert, *Capitalism and the Welfare State* (New Haven, CT: Yale University Press, 1983), p. 98.

11. Edward Zigler and Victoria Seitz, "Head Start as a National Laboratory," in William Bridgeland and Edward A. Duane (Eds.), *The Annals of the American Academy of Political and Social Science: Young Children and Social Policy,* Vol. 461 (May 1982), pp. 81–90.

12. Victoria Seitz et al., "Effects of Place of Testing on the Peabody Picture Vocabulary Test Scores of Disadvantaged Head Start and Non Head Start Children," *Child Development,* Vol. 46 (January 1975), p. 482; and Zigler and Seitz, *op. cit.,* p. 88.

13. David J. Irvine et al., "Evidence Supporting Comprehensive Early Childhood Education for Disadvantaged Children," in Bridgeland and Duane, *op. cit.,* pp. 74–80.

14. Masuru Ibuka, *Kindergarten Is Too Late* (New York: Simon & Schuster, 1977), p. 24.

15. Seymour Papert, *Mindstorms: Children, Computers and Powerful Ideas* (New York: Basic Books, 1980).

16. For example, see Maria Montessori, *The Discovery of the Child* (New York: Ballantine Books, 1967); Glenn Doman, *How to Teach Your Baby to Read: The Gentle Revolution* (New York: Random House, 1964).

17. "Bringing Up Superbaby," *Newsweek,* March 28, 1983, pp. 62–68.

18. Steven Fosburg, *Family Day Care in the United States: Summary of Findings,* Vol. 1, National Day Care Home Study, DHHS Pub. No. (OHDS) 80–30282 (Washington, DC: Abt Associates, Administration for Children, Youth and Families, Health and Human Services, September 1981), pp. 1–10.

19. Sheila B. Kamerman and Alfred J. Kahn, *Child Care, Family Benefits and Working Parents: A Study in Comparative Policy* (New York: Columbia University Press, 1981), pp. 186–187.

20. See Rene A. Spitz, "Hospitalism: An Inquiry into the Genesis of Psychiatric Conditions in Early Childhood," *Psychoanalytic Study of the Child,* Vol. 1 (1945), pp. 53–74, and Vol. 2 (1946), pp. 113–177; and R. A. Spitz, "The Role of Ecological Factors in Emotional Development in Infancy," *Child Development,* Vol. 20, No. 3 (1949), pp. 145–155.

21. "Hospitalism" refers to the physical condition of the body after a long confinement in a hospital, and also to a morbid hospital atmosphere and the effect of institutionalization on individuals.

22. W. Goldfarb, "Infant Rearing and Problem Behavior," *American Journal of Orthopsychiatry,* Vol. 13, No. 2 (1943), pp. 249–266; W. Goldfarb, "The Effects of Early Institutional Care on Adolescent Personality," *Journal of Experimental Education,* Vol. 12 (1943), pp. 106–120; and W. Goldfarb, "Psychological Privation in Infancy and Subsequent Adjustment," *American Journal of Orthopsychiatry,* Vol. 15, No. 2 (1945), pp. 247–255.

23. Martin Wolins, "Some Theoretical Observations on Group Care," in Martin Wolins (Ed.), *Successful Group Care: Explorations in the Powerful Environment* (Chicago: Aldine Publishing, 1974), pp. 8–10.

24. Halbert Robinson, quoted in Joseph Marcus and Halbert B. Robertson (Eds.), *Growing Up in Groups: The Russian Day Care Center and the Israeli Kibbutz* (New York: Gordon & Breach, 1972), p. x.

25. John R. Nelson, Jr., "The Politics of Federal Day Care Regulation," in Zigler and Gordon, *op. cit.,* pp. 284–285.

26. *Ibid.,* p. 284.

27. Milton Friedman, *Capitalism and Freedom* (Chicago: University of Chicago Press, 1982), pp. 144–145.

28. Burton R. Clark, "United States," in John H. Van de Graaf et al., *Academic Power: Patterns of Authority in Seven National Systems of Higher Education* (New York: Praeger, 1978), p. 107.

29. *Ibid.,* p. 108.

30. Moreover, even the same public program, operating under a particular set of guidelines, will be implemented differently at different sites of service delivery.

31. Much of the information and specific data in this section on California were obtained during an interview in 1983 with Jack Hailey, Director of the Governor's Advisory Committee on Child Development Programs in Sacramento, California. These data were updated in 1988. For detailed information regarding the diversity of child care in California, see the *California Inventory of Child Care Facilities* (San Francisco: California Child Care Resource and Referral Network, October 1987). See also Tanya Tull, in the Governor's Advisory Committee on Child Development Program, *Developmental Needs of Young Bilingual Children: A Report to the Governor and the Superintendent of Instruction* (Sacramento: May 1982), pp. 6–7; and Anna B. Mayer, *Day Care as a Social Instrument: A Policy Paper* (New York: Columbia University, January 1965).

32. For example, Site 1 (described in Chapters 5 and 6) operates under the

auspices of the state department of education, but it offers primarily custodial care rather than a full preschool education.

33. Refer again to sources listed in Note 31.

34. Urie Bronfenbrenner, *On Making Human Beings Human: A Curriculum for Caring*, monograph (Cornell University, 1980), p. 1.

APPENDIX A

1. In the calculation of general overall and specific dimension ratings, "don't know" was scored as a 3 on the 5-point scale, recording indecision as neutrality on all rating scales.

BIBLIOGRAPHY

THE CARE AND EDUCATION OF DEPENDENTS

CARE—GENERAL

Holt, John. *Escape from Childhood*. New York: E. P. Dutton & Co., 1974.

Jacobs, Philip. *The Economics of Health and Medical Care*. Baltimore: University Park Press, 1980.

Lipkin, Mack. *The Care of Patients: Concepts and Tactics*. New York: Oxford University Press, 1974.

Robinson, Halbert, and Joseph Marcus (Eds.). *Growing Up in Groups: The Russian Day Care Center and the Israeli Kibbutz*. New York: Gordon & Breach, 1972.

Rodham, Hillary. "Children Under the Law." *Harvard Educational Review*. Vol. 43, November 1973:487–514.

Shyne, Ann W. "Who Are the Children? A National Overview of Services." *Social Work Research and Abstracts.* Vol. 16, No. 1, Spring 1980:29–33.

Spitz, Rene A. "Hospitalism: An Inquiry into the Genesis of Psychiatric Conditions in Early Childhood." *Psychoanalytic Study of the Child.* Vol. 1, 1945:53–74, and Vol. 2, 1946:113–177.

Trotter, W. *Collected Papers of Wilfred Trotter.* London: Oxford University Press, 1941.

Weissert, William. "Two Models of Geriatric Day Care: Findings from a Comparative Study." *Gerontologist.* Vol. 16, 1976:420.

Growth and Development Issues

Beadle, Muriel. *A Child's Mind.* Garden City, NY: Doubleday, 1970.

Bettelheim, Bruno. *The Uses of Enchantment.* New York: Vintage Books, 1975.

Bettelheim, Bruno. *A Good Enough Parent: A Book on Child-Rearing.* New York: Alfred A. Knopf, 1987.

Brazelton, T. *Infants and Mothers.* New York: Delta, 1983.

Bridgeland, William, and Edward A. Duane. *The Annals of the American Academy of Political and Social Science: Young Children and Social Policy.* Vol. 461, May 1982.

"Bringing up Superbaby." *Newsweek.* March 28, 1983:62–68.

Butler, Dorothy. *Babies Need Books.* New York: Atheneum, 1985.

Churchman, Deborah, and Karen Kristy. "The Guilt-Solving Myths That Day Care Is Better." *Washington Post.* November 16, 1980.

Coles, Robert. *The Moral Life of Children.* Boston: Houghton, Mifflin, 1986.

Committee on Infant and Preschool Child. "Parenting—An Annotated Bibliography." Children's Bureau, Administration for Children, Youth and Families, Office of Human Development Services. DHEW Publication No. (OHDS) 78–30134, 1982.

Doman, Glenn. *How to Teach Your Baby to Read: The Gentle Revolution.* New York: Random House, 1964.

Durrell, Doris E. *The Critical Years.* Oakland, CA: New Harbinger Publications, 1984.

Engelmann, Siegfried, and Therese Engelmann. *Give Your Child a Superior Mind.* New York: Simon & Schuster, 1981.

Fischer, Constance T. "I.Q.: Enter the Child." *Clinical Child Psychology,* pp. 334–350. New York: Behaviorial Publications, 1974.

Goldfarb, W. "The Effects of Early Institutional Care on Adolescent Personality." *Journal of Experimental Education.* Vol. 12, 1943: 106–129.

Goldfarb, W. "Infant Rearing and Problem Behavior." *American Journal of Orthopsychiatry.* Vol. 13, No. 2, 1943:249–266.

Goldfarb, W. "Psychological Privation in Infancy and Subsequent Adjustment." *American Journal of Orthopsychiatry*. Vol. 15, No. 2, 1945:247–255.

Greenberg, D. J., Ina C. Uzgiris, and J. McV. Hunt. "Attentional Preference and Experience: 3. Visual Familiarity and Looking Time." *Journal of Genetic Psychology*. Vol. 117, 1986, 123–135.

Henry, Rachawl M. "A Theoretical and Empirical Analysis of 'Reasoning' in the Socialization of Young Children." *Human Development*. Vol. 23, 1980:108–118.

Hernstein, R. "I.Q.," *The Atlantic*. Vol. 228, 1971:43–58 and 63–64.

Ibuka, Masaru. *Kindergarten Is Too Late*. New York: Simon & Schuster, 1977.

Jensen A., "How Much Can We Boost I.Q. and Scholastic Achievement?" *Harvard Educational Review*. Vol. 39, No. 1, 1969:1–123.

Lansky, Vicki. *Feed Me! I'm Yours*. New York: Bantam Books, 1974.

Lansky, Vicki. *Practical Parenting Tips*. New York: Bantam Books, 1985.

Leach, Penelope. *The Child Care Encyclopedia*. New York: Knopf, 1987.

Liebman, Bonnie F. "Eating for Two." *Nutrition Action*. Vol. 14, No. 3, April 1987:1 and 4–6.

McCall, Robert B. "A Hard Look at Stimulating and Predicting Development: The Cases of Bonding and Screening." *Pediatrics in Review*. Vol. 3, No. 7, January 1982:205–211.

Montessori, Maria. *The Discovery of the Child*. New York: Ballantine Books, 1967.

Nadelson, Carol, and Malkah Natman. "Child Psychiatry Perspectives: Women, Work and Children." *Journal of the American Academy of Child Psychiatry*. Vol. 20, No. 4, Autumn 1981:41–48.

Neifert, Marianne. *Dr. Mom*. New York: G. P. Putnam's Sons, 1986.

Olmstead, Richard W. (Ed.). "Behavioral Pediatrics: The Newly Abbreviated and Revised Denver Development Screening Test." *The Journal of Pediatrics*. Vol. 99, No. 6:995–999.

Papert, Seymour. *Mindstorms: Children, Computers and Powerful Ideas*. New York: Basic Books, 1980.

"Parents Warned to 'Let Children Be Children'." *San Francisco Chronicle*. November 14, 1987:C11.

Piaget, Jean. *Play, Dreams and Imitation in Childhood*. New York: Norton, 1962.

Piaget, Jean. "Response to Brian Sutton-Smith." *Psychological Review*. Vol. 73, 1966:111–112.

Pilling, Doria, and Mia Kellmer Pringle. *Controversial Issues in Child Development*. London: National Children's Bureau, Sail Elk, 1978.

Pringle, Sheila M., and Brenda E. Ramsey, in *Promoting the Health of Chil-*

dren: A Guide for Caretakers and Health Care Professionals. St. Louis: C. V. Mosley, 1982.

Rutter, Michael. "The Long-Term Effects of Early Experience." *Developmental Medicine and Child Neurology.* Vol. 22, 1980:800–815.

Seitz, Victoria, et al. "Effects of Place of Testing on the Peabody Vocabulary Test Scores of Disadvantaged Head Start and non Head Start Children." *Child Development.* Vol. 46, No. 482, January 1975:36–39.

Skolnick, Arlene (Ed.). *Rethinking Childhood: Perspectives on Development and Society.* Boston: Little, Brown & Company, 1976.

Spitz, R. A. "The Role of Ecological Factors in Emotional Development in Infancy." *Child Development.* Vol. 20, No. 3, 1949:145–155.

Sutton-Smith, B. "Piaget on Play: A Critique." *Psychological Review.* Vol. 73, 1966:109–110.

Sutton-Smith, B. "A Reply to Piaget: A Play Theory of Copy." *Psychological Review.* Vol. 73, 1966:113–114.

Trotter, Robert J. "You've Come a Long Way, Baby." *Psychology Today.* Vol. 21, No. 5, May 1987:34–45.

Vandenberg, Brian. "Play: Dormant Issues and New Perspectives." *Human Development.* Vol. 24, 1981:357–365.

Westinghouse Learning Corporation. *The Impact of Head Start: An Evaluation of the effects of Head Start on Children's Cognitive and Affective Development: Volume 1: Text and Appendices A–E.* Presented to the Office of Economic Opportunity pursuant to Contract No. B89–4536. Ohio University, Westinghouse Learning Corporation, June 12, 1969.

White, Sheldon, and Barbara Notkin White. *Childhood: Pathways of Discovery.* The Life Cycle Series. San Francisco: Harper & Row, 1980.

DAY CARE POLICIES AND PROGRAMS

Administration for Children, Youth and Families, Day Care Division. *Family Day Care in the United States: Summary of Findings,* Volumes 1–7, Abt Associates, U.S. Department of Health and Human Services, Pub. No. (OHDS) 80–30282, September 1980.

Anderson, Elaine A. "Family Day Care Provision: A Legislative Response." *Child Care Quarterly.* Vol. 15, No. 1, Spring 1986:6–14.

Axelrod, Toby. "Child Care: A Complete Guide to Coast-to-Coast Resources." *Ms.,* Vol. 15, No. 9, March 1987:60–64.

Bellam, Dan. "Little Kids, Big Bucks." *This World, San Francisco Chronicle.* April 26, 1987:5–6.

Bereiter, Carl, and Seigfried Engelmann. *Teaching Disadvantaged Children in Preschool.* Englewood Cliffs, NJ: Prentice-Hall, 1966.

Biber, Barbara. "Child Development Associate: A Professional Role for Developmental Day Care." New York: Bank Street College of Education, n.d.

Browne, A. Christine. Office for Families, Administration for Children, Youth and Families. *Promising Practices, Reaching Out to Families* (with Office for Families' Staff). Washington, DC: U.S. Department of Health and Human Services, 1981.

Browne, Angela. "Mixed Economy of Child Day Care Policy in the United States," including "Supply and Demand at the National Level" and "Child Day Care in California: A Case in Point." *International Child Welfare Review.* No. 62, September 1984:29–36.

Browne, Angela. "The Mixed Economy of Day Care: Consumer Versus Professional Assessments." *Journal of Social Policy.* Vol. 13, Part 3, July 1984:321–331.

Browne, Angela. "What Purpose Is Served by Child Day Care Policy in the United States?" *International Child Welfare Review.* No. 63, December 1984:33–43.

Browne, Angela. "The Market Sphere: Private Responses." *Child Welfare.* July–August 1985:367–381.

California Child Care Resource and Referral Network (CCRRN). *California Inventory of Child Care Facilities.* San Francisco: CCRRN, February 1987.

"Caring About Child Care." *Ms.,* Vol. 15, No. 9, March 1987:31.

Chung, L. A. "Ambitious Child Care Program." *San Francisco Chronicle.* March 20, 1985:4.

Coelen, C., F. Glaantz, and D. Colare. *Day Care Centers in the U.S.: A National Profile 1976–1977.* Cambridge, MA: Abt Books, 1978.

Collins, Alice H., and Eunice L. Watson. *Family Day Care: A Practical Guide for Parents, Caregivers and Professionals.* Boston: Beacon Press, 1976.

Collins, Glenn. "U.S. Day Care Guidelines Rekindle Controversy." *New York Times.* February 4, 1985:20.

Cranston, Senator Alan. *Congressional Record.* 100th Congress, First Session. Vol. 133, No. 1, S162, January 6, 1987.

Cunningham, Susan. "Day Care Screening Law: More Harm Than Good?" *American Psychological Association (APA) Monitor.* Vol. 16, No. 8, August 1985:18 and 20.

Deane, Barbara. "The Lori Nathan Case." *California Living Magazine, San Francisco Chronicle.* March 18, 1984:10–14.

Elkind, David. *Miseducation: Preschoolers at Risk.* New York: Alfred A. Knopf, 1987.

Endsley, Richard C., and Marilyn R. Bradbard. *Quality Day Care: A Hand-*

book of Choices for Parents and Caregivers. Englewood Cliffs, NJ: Prentice-Hall, 1981.

"Family Day Care Network Creates Jobs and Day Care." *The Children's Advocate*. Berkeley, CA: Berkeley Children's Services, January–February 1981:4.

Gleidman, John, and William Roth. *The Unexpected Minority: Handicapped Children in America*. New York: Harcourt Brace Jovanovich, 1980.

Gorney, Cynthia. "How Young Is Too Young?" *Parenting*. October 1987:50–54.

Governor's Advisory Committee on Child Development Programs. *The Alternative Child Care Program (AB 3059) 1976–77*. Sacramento: State of California, July 1977.

Governor's Advisory Committee on Child Development Programs. *Voucher Payment in California: A Review of the Public Policy Issues Raised by the Use of Vouchers as a Child Care Payment System*. Sacramento: State of California, June 21, 1977.

Governor's Advisory Committee on Child Development Programs. *Annual Report: 1978*. Sacramento: State of California, 1978.

Governor's Advisory Committee on Child Development Programs. *Child Care Licensing and Regulation: A Report by the Governor's Advisory Committee on Child Development Programs*. Sacramento: State of California, February 1978; reissued February 1981.

Governor's Advisory Committee on Child Development Programs. *Child Care Allocations: A Report Guided by the Task Force on Child Development Services*. Sacramento: State of California, February 1980.

Governor's Advisory Committee on Child Development Programs. *AB 3059: A Report to the Governor on the Alternative Child Care Programs 1976–80*. Sacramento: State of California, 1980.

Hatwood Futrell, Mary. "Public Schools and Four Year Olds." *American Psychologist*. March 1987:251–253.

"Hearing Report on California's Child Care Teacher Shortage: Executive Summary." Minutes of Child Development Programs Advisory Committee Meeting. Sacramento: November 19, 1987.

Kadushin, Alfred. "Day Care Service." *Child Welfare Services,* pp. 335–391. New York: Macmillan, 1974.

Kamerman, Sheila B. "Child Care Services: National Picture," Interim Report. New York: Columbia University School of Social Work, Cross-National Studies, 1983.

Kaplan, Melissa G., and Thomas M. Buescher. "Inservice Training for Urban Day Care Centers: An Evaluation of Training Strategies." *Child Care Quarterly*. Vol. 15, No. 1, Spring 1986:33–49.

"Kinder-Care Annual Report 1985." Montgomery, AL: Kinder-Care Learning Centers, Inc., October 18, 1985.

Koppleman, Jeane. "Why Day Care Is Not Good for Kids." *Women's American Ort Reporter.* Fall 1986:7 and 10.

Magagnini, Stephen, and Susan Sword. "Why State Can't Stop Day-Care Center Abuse." *San Francisco Chronicle.* November 9, 1984:1 and 5.

Malone, Margaret. *Child Day Care: The Federal Role.* Congressional Service, Issue Brief No. 1. Washington, DC: Library of Congress, Congressional Research Service, 1981.

Malta, Stephen. "Cashing in on the Child Care Dilemma." *San Francisco Chronicle.* May 21, 1987:37 and 42.

Mauger, Sylvia. *Changing Childcare.* London: Writers and Readers Publishing, 1974.

Mayer, Anna B. *Day Care as a Social Instrument: A Policy Paper.* New York: Columbia University, 1965.

McLeod, Ramon G. "Census: Day Care Use Up 60%." *San Francisco Chronicle.* May 8, 1987:38.

Montgomery, Laurel, and Carol Seefeldt. "The Relationship Between Perceived Supervisory Behavior and Caregivers' Behavior in Child Care." *Child Care Quarterly.* Vol. 15, No. 4, Winter 1986:251–259.

Neubauer, Peter B. (Ed.). *Early Child Day Care.* New York: Aronson, 1974.

Robins, Philip K., and Samuel Weiner (Eds.). *Child Care and Public Policy: Studies of the Economic Issues.* Lexington, MA: Lexington Books, D. C. Heath & Co., 1978.

Ruben, David. "Who's Minding the Children?" *Parenting.* October 1987:55–56.

Rubin, Karen. "Whose Job Is Child Care?" *Ms.,* Vol. 15, No. 9, March 1987:32–43.

Ryan, Sally (Ed.). *A Report on Longitudinal Evaluations of Preschool Programs. Volume 1: Longitudinal Evaluations.* Washington, DC: U.S. Government Printing Office, DHEW Publication No. OHD 76–30024, 1980.

Schumer Chapman, Fern. "Executive Guilt: Who's Taking Care of the Children?" *Fortune.* February 16, 1987:30–38.

Trotter, Robert J. "Project Day-Care." *Psychology Today.* Vol. 21, No. 12, December 1987:32–41.

Walker, Nancy G. "San Francisco's Affordable Child Care Program." San Francisco: Supervisor Walker's Office, October 9, 1985.

"What Price Day Care?" *Newsweek.* September 10, 1984:15.

Wolins, Martin (Ed.). *Successful Group Care.* New York: Aldine Publishing, 1974.

Women and Family Issues Committee, Association of Labor and Management

Alcoholism Counselors and Administrators. *Child Care Resource Directory.* San Francisco: San Francisco Bay Area ALMACA and 1st Nationwide Bank, May 1987.

Yeiser, Lin. *Nannies, Au Pairs, Mothers' Helpers—Caregivers: The Complete Guide to Home Child Care.* New York: Random House, 1987.

Zeitlen, June H., and Nancy Duff Campbell. "Availability of Child Care for Low-Income Families: Strategies to Address the Impact of the Economic Recovery Tax Act of 1981 and the Omnibus Budget Reconciliation Act of 1981." *Clearinghouse Review.* Vol. 16, No. 4, August–September 1981:310–315.

Zigler, Edward F. "Formal Schooling for Four Year Olds? No." *American Psychologist.* March 1987:254–260.

STATE-SPONSORED CHILD CARE IN CALIFORNIA

Bernard, Jesse. *Women and the Public Interest.* New York: Aldine Publishing, 1971.

Cox, Irene. "The Employment of Mothers as a Means of Family Support." *Welfare in Review.* Vol. 8, No. 6, 1970:9–17.

Fine, Ronald E. *Final Report: AFDC Employment and Referral Guidelines.* Minnesota: Institute for Interdisciplinary Studies, 1972.

Garwin, Charles D., Audrey D. Smith, and William J. Reid. *The Work Incentive Experience.* New York: Universe Books, 1978.

Governor's Advisory Committee on Child Development Programs. *Developmental Needs of Young Bilingual Children: A Report to the Governor and the Superintendent of Instruction.* Sacramento: May 1982.

Mayo, Judy. *Work and Welfare: Employment and Employability of Women in the AFDC Program.* Chicago: Community and Family Study Center, 1975.

Moore, Miami. *The Woman Question in Child Care.* Day Care and Child Development Council of America, 1974.

Roby, Pamela. *Child Care—Who Cares?.* New York: Basic Books, 1973.

Smith, Audrey D., and William J. Reid. "Child Care Arrangements of AFDC Mothers in the Work Incentive Program." *Child Welfare.* Vol. 52, No. 10, 1973:651–666.

Steiner, Gilbert Y. *The State of Welfare.* Washington, DC: The Brookings Institution, 1971.

THE FAMILY AND FAMILY POLICY

HISTORY AND DESCRIPTION OF THE FAMILY

Adams, Bert N. *Kinship in an Urban Setting*. Chicago: Markham Publishing, 1968.

Aries, Philippe. *Centuries of Childhood: A Social History of Family Life*. New York: Vintage Books, 1962.

Bennett, William J. "The Role of the Family in the Nurture and Protection of the Young." *American Psychologist*. March 1987:246–250.

Burden, Susan, et al. *The Single Parent Family*. Proceedings of the Changing Family Conference V, The University of Iowa, Iowa City: University of Iowa, 1976.

Bureau of Labor Statistics. *No. 213: Women Who Head Families: A Socioeconomic Analysis*. Washington, DC: Department of Labor, March 1977.

Bureau of Labor Statistics. *No. 217: Children of Working Mothers*. Washington, DC: U.S. Department of Labor, March 1977.

Bureau of Labor Statistics. *No. 219: Marital and Family Characteristics of Workers, 1970–78*. Washington, DC: U.S. Department of Labor, 1978.

Chodorow, Nancy. *The Reproduction of Mothering: Psychoanalysis and the Sociology of Gender*. Berkeley: University of California Press, 1978.

Coser, Rose Laub (Ed.). *The Family: Its Structures and Functions*. New York: St. Martin's Press, 1974.

Degler, Carl N. *At Odds: Women and the Family in America from the Revolution to the Present*. New York: Oxford University Press, 1980.

Edwards, Carolyn S. *USDA Estimates of the Cost of Raising a Child: A Guide to Their Use and Interpretation*. Washington, DC: U.S. Department of Agriculture, Miscellaneous Publication 1411, 1981.

Grossman, Allyson Sherman. "Divorced and Separated Women in the Labor Force—An Update." *Monthly Labor Review*. October 1978:43–44.

Grotberg, Edith H. (Ed.). *200 Years of Children*. Office of Child Development, Division of Research & Evaluation. U.S. Department of Health, Education & Welfare, Office of Human Development. DHEW Publication No. (OHD) 77–30103, 1980.

Handel, Gerald. *The Psychosocial Interior of the Family*. Chicago: Aldine Publishing, 1967.

Hareven, Tamara. "Family Time and Industrial Time: Family and Work in a Planned Corporation Town, 1900–1924." *Journal of Urban History*. May 1975:365–389.

Hareven, Tamara. "Modernization and Family History: Perspectives on Social

Change." *Signs: Journal of Women in Culture and Society.* Vol. 2, No. 1, Autumn 1976:190–206.

Hindess, Barry, and Paul Q. Hirst. *Pre-Capitalist Modes of Production.* London: Routledge & Kegan Paul, 1975.

Institute for Research on Poverty. "Poverty." *Focus.* Madison: University of Wisconsin, Vol. 5, No. 2, Winter 1981–1982.

Johnson, Beverly. "Marital and Family Characteristics of Workers, 1970–78." *Monthly Labor Review.* April 1979:49.

Kephart, William M. "Experimental Family Organization: An Historico-Cultural Report on The Oneida Community." *Marriage and Family Living.* August 1963:261–271.

Leslie, Gerald R. *The Family in Social Context.* New York: Oxford University Press, 1967.

Makarenko, A. S. *The Collective Family: A Handbook for Russian Parents.* Garden City, NY: Anchor Books, 1967. (First published in USSR, 1937.) (Intro. by Urie Bronfenbrenner.)

Rossi, Alice S. "A Biosocial Perspective on Parenting." *Daedalus.* Vol. 106, No. 2, 1977:1–31.

Rubenstein, Hymie. "Conjugal Behavior and Parental Role Flexibility in an Afro-Caribbean Village." *Canadian Review of Sociology and Anthropology.* Vol. 17, No. 4, 1980:29–34.

Schusky, Ernest L. *Variation in Kinship.* New York: Holt, Rinehart & Winston, 1974.

Tilly, Louise A., and Joan W. Scott. *Woman, Work and Family.* New York: Holt, Rinehart & Winston, 1978.

U.S. Department of Commerce. *American Families and Living Arrangements.* Washington, DC: Bureau of the Census, March 1980.

FAMILY PROBLEMS

"Alcoholism and the Family: Putting the Pieces Together." *Alcoholism.* January–February 1981:19–22.

Aldoory, Shirley. "Research into Family Factors in Alcoholism." *Alcohol Health and Research World.* Vol. 3, No. 4, Summer 1979:2–6.

Black, Claudia. "Innocent Bystanders at Risk: The Children of Alcoholics." *Alcoholism.* January–February 1981:22–29.

Brieland, Donald. "Children and Families: A Forecast." *Social Work.* Vol. 19, No. 5, September 1984:568–579.

Bronfenbrenner, Urie. "Children and Families: 1984?" *Society.* Vol. 18, No. 2, Whole No. 130, January–February 1981:38–41.

"Costs of Being a Parent Keep Going Higher." *Wall Street Journal.* October 2, 1980:1.

Dulfano, Celia. "Recovering from Alcoholism: Rebuilding the Family." *Alcoholism.* January–February 1981:33–36.

Dunsing, Marilyn M. "Changes in the Economic Aspects of Family Life." University of Illinois, White House Conference on Families, Washington, DC, 1980.

Edwards, Deryl. "Justice William Rehnquist: Family Arguments Shouldn't Be an Adversary System." *Moral Majority Report,* Washington, DC. June 30, 1980:3.

Estes, Richard J., and Harold L. Wilensky. "Life Cycle Squeeze and the Morale Curve." *Social Problems.* Vol. 25, No. 3, February 1978:277–292.

Ferree, Myra Marx. "The Confused American Housewife." *Psychology Today.* September 1976: 76–80.

Flanzer, Jerry. "Alcohol-Induced Family Violence." *Alcoholism.* January–February 1981:30–32.

Furstenberg, Frank F. "Teenage Parenthood and Family Support." Presented to the National Research Forum on Family Issues, sponsored by the White House Conference on Families, Washington, DC. April 1980.

Geismar, L. L., and Michael A. LaSorte. *Understanding the Multi-Problem Family.* New York: Associated Press, 1964.

Harris, Marvin. *America Now: The Anthropology of a Changing Culture.* New York: Simon & Schuster, 1981.

Harris, Marvin. "Why It's Not the Same Old America." *Psychology Today.* August 1981:23–51.

Hill, Ruben. *Families Under Stress: Adjustment to the Crises of War Separation and Reunion.* New York: Harper & Brothers, 1949.

"Information: Key to Family Health—A Digest of the Proceedings." The General Mills American Family Forum, sponsored by General Mills, Chicago, IL. October 1979.

Joe, Tom, et al. "The Poor: Profiles of Families in Poverty." University of Chicago Center for the Study of Welfare Policy, Washington, DC. March 27, 1981.

Kellerman, Joseph. "The Spouse's Spouse: Victim or Villain?" *Alcoholism.* January–February 1981:26–29.

LaPoint, Velma. "The Impact of Incarceration on Families: Research and Family Issues." National Institute of Mental Health, Bethesda, MD, presented to Research Forum on Family Issues, National Advisory Committee on the White House Conference on Families, Washington, DC. April 1980.

Lasch, Christopher. *Haven in a Heartless World: The Family Beseiged.* New York: Basic Books, 1977.

Lichtman, Allan J., and Joan R. Challinor. *Kin and Communities: Families in America.* Washington, DC: Smithsonian Institution Press, 1979.

Lomas, Peter. *The Predicament of the Family.* New York: International Universities Press, 1967.

Mead, Margaret. "What Is Happening to the American Family?" *Journal of Social Casework.* November 1947:323–330.

Mertens, Evelyn. "Housewives or . . . House Hostages?—The Tragedy of Domestic Violence and Where to Go for Help." *Westchester.* August 1980:616–667.

Moor, Karl. "Family Rental Tax: Another I.R.S. Fiasco." *Moral Majority Report,* Washington, DC. December 15, 1980:21.

"Network News—The Newsletter of the Displaced Homemakers Network." Displaced Homemakers Network, Washington, DC. Vol. 2, No. 4, September 1980.

Nissel, Muriel. "The Family and the Welfare State." *New Society.* August 1980:259–262.

Ooms, Theodora. "Teenage Pregnancy and Family Impact: Perspectives on Policy—A Preliminary Report." Family Impact Seminar, George Washington University, Washington, DC. June 1979.

Rathbone-McCuan, Eloise. "Elderly Victims of Family Violence and Neglect." *Social Casework.* Vol. 61, No. 5, May 1980:296–304.

Rathbone-McCuan, Eloise, and Jean Triegaardt. "The Older Alcoholic and the Family." *Alcohol Health and Research World.* Vol. 3, No. 4, Summer 1979:7–12.

Rosenthal, Mitchell S. "Substance Abuse." Presented at National Research Forum on Family Issues, sponsored by the White House Conference on Families, Washington, DC. April 1980.

Vickery, Clair. "The Time-Poor: A New Look at Poverty." *The Journal of Human Resources.* Vol. 12, No. 1, Winter 1977:27–48.

Vickery, Clair. "The Changing Household: Implication for Devising an Income Support Program." *Public Policy.* Vol. 26, No. 2, Spring 1978:121–151.

Watson, Bernard. "Education and Its Impact on the American Family." Presented at the National Research Forum on Family Issues April, 1980. Philadelphia, PA: Temple University, March 1980.

Weiner, Hyman J., Sheila H. Akabas, and John J. Sommer. *Mental Health Care in the World of Work.* New York: Association Press, 1973.

Wiener, Leonard. "Easing the Pain of the 'Marriage Tax.'" *U.S. News and World Report.* August 3, 1981:53.

FAMILY-LIFE–WORK-LIFE RELATIONSHIPS

Amsden, Alice H. *The Economics of Women and Work.* New York: Penguin Books, 1980.

Bennett, Sheila Kishler, and Glen H. Elder, Jr. "Women's Work in the Family Economy: A Study of Depression Hardship in Women's Lives." *Journal of Family History.* Vol. 4, No. 2, Summer 1979:153–176.

Berk, Sarah Fernstermaker, and Catherine White Berheide. "Going Backstage: Gaining Access to Observe Household Work." *Sociology of Work and Occupations.* Vol. 4, No. 1, February 1977:27–48.

Bohen, Halcyone H., and Anamaria Viveros-Long. *Balancing Jobs and Family Life.* Family Impact Seminar Series. Philadelphia, PA: Temple University Press, 1981.

Bralove, Mary. "Problems of Two-Career Families Start Forcing Businesses to Adapt." *The Wall Street Journal.* July 15, 1981:23.

Briggs, Jean A. "How You Going to Get 'Em Back in the Kitchen? (You Aren't)." *Forbes.* November 15, 1977:13.

Brozan, Nadine. "Children, a Job and No Time." *New York Times.* August 13, 1981: C1 and C9.

Bureau of the Census. Current Population Reports, No. 117 Series P-23, *Trends in Child Care Arrangements of Working Mothers.* Washington, DC: U.S. Government Printing Office, 1982.

Butler, Peter M. "Establishments and the Work-Welfare Mix." *Canadian Review of Sociology and Anthropology.* Vol. 17, No. 2, 1980: 138–153.

Catalyst Center and Family Center. *Catalyst Career and Family Bulletin.* No. 2, May 1981.

Cowan, Bonnie. "The Legal Status of Homemakers in Tennessee." Center for Women Policy Studies, Washington, DC. March 1977.

Diebenow, Anita. "Problem-Solving with Working Mothers." *Occupational Health and Safety.* July 1981:52–55.

Elder, Betty G. "Covering the United Nations—The World Conference for Women." *Women Lawyers Journal.* 1981:46–48.

Faunee, William A. *Problems of an Industrial Society.* New York: McGraw-Hill, 1981.

Galbraith, John Kenneth. *The New Industrial State.* Boston: Houghton Mifflin, 1979.

Grossman, Allyson Sherman. "Divorced and Separated Women in the Labor Force—An Update." *Monthly Labor Review.* October 1979:43–44.

"Jobs or Babies? Japan's Women Assay Priorities." *New York Times.* December 21, 1980:11.

Johnson, Beverly. "Marital and Family Characteristics of Workers, 1970–78." *Monthly Labor Review.* April 1979:49.

Kleiman, Dena. "Many Young Women Now Say They'd Pick Family over Career." *The New York Times.* December 28, 1980:1 and 24.

Klemesrud, Judy. "Conflicts of Women with Jobs." *The New York Times.* May 7, 1981:C1 and C6.

Lucas, Freddie H. *Day Care Research.* New York: J. C. Penney Company, 1972.

Mann, Judy. "Confronting Problems of Working Women." *The Washington Post.* February 9, 1979:B1 and B5.

Mann, Judy. "Traumas of Juggling Badges and Bassinets." *The Washington Post.* March 2, 1979:B1 and B2.

Michel, Andree (Ed.). *Family Issues of Employed Women in Europe and America.* Leiden, Netherlands: E. J. Brill, 1971.

O'Neil, Sally. "Choosing Children over Careers." *San Francisco Examiner.* July 19, 1987:D-1.

Pleck, Joseph J., Graham L. Staines, and Linda Lang. "Conflicts Between Work and Family Life: A Research Summary." *Monthly Labor Review.* March 1980:29–35.

Rotbart, Dean. "Doctor's Husband: Father Quit His Job for the Family's Sake, Now Hirers Shun Him." *The Wall Street Journal.* April 13, 1981:1 and 14.

Smelser, Neil J. "Vicissitudes of Work and Love in Anglo-American Society." In *Themes of Work and Love in Adulthood,* Neil J. Smelser and Erik H. Erikson (Eds.). Cambridge: Harvard University Press, 1980.

Wilensky, Harold L. "Family Life Cycle, Work, and the Quality of Life: Reflections on the Roots of Happiness, Despair, and Indifference in Modern Society." In *Working Life: A Social Science Contribution to Work Reform,* B. Gardell and G. Johansson (Eds.). London: John Wiley & Sons, 1981.

Wilensky, Harold L., and Charles N. Lebeaux. *Industrial Society and Social Welfare.* New York: The Free Press, 1965.

"Work-to-Family Relationship Surveyed." *Findings—A Quarterly Summary of Findings from Social Policy Research.* Cambridge, Ma. Fall 1980:1

FAMILY IMPACT ANALYSIS, FAMILY POLICY, WELFARE POLICY AND RELATED ISSUES

American Families and Living Arrangements. Prepared for the White House Conference on Families. Washington, DC: U.S. Department of Commerce, Bureau of the Census. March 1980.

American Families—1980: A Summary of Findings. Princeton, NJ: The Gallup Organization. 1980.

The American Family—National Action Overview, Vol. 3, No. 5. Washington, DC: Wakefield Washington Associates, August–September 1980.

"The Anti-Family Conference." *The Moral Majority Report,* Washington, DC. March 14, 1980:14.

Axinn, June, and Mark J. Stern. "Women and the Postindustrial Welfare State." *Social Work.* Vol. 32, No. 4, July–August 1987: 282–286.

Bane, Mary Jo, and George Masnick. "The Nation's Families: 1960–1990, Diversity of Families and Households." April 10, 1980. Presented to the National Research Forum on Family Issues of the White House Conference on Families. A Summary of *The Nation's Families: 1960–1990* by George Masnick and Mary Jo Bane. Cambridge, MA: MIT/Harvard Joint Center for Urban Studies. May 1980.

Berger, Brigitte, and Peter L. Berger. *The War over the Family: Capturing the Middle Ground.* Garden City, NY: Anchor Press/Doubleday, 1983.

Bohen, Halcyone. "Report on European Policies Affecting Families." Memorandum to German Marshall Fund. Washington, DC: Children's Defense Fund, June 30, 1981.

Bohen, Halcyone, and Anamaria Viveros-Long. *Balancing Jobs and Family Life.* Philadelphia: Temple University Press, 1981.

Bronfenbrenner, Urie. *The Ecology of Human Development.* Cambridge: Harvard University Press, 1979.

"China's Birth Control Edicts Lead to Infanticide." *Fusion.* July 1981:52.

Costin, Lela B. "White House Conferences: Further Comments." *Social Work,* National Association of Social Workers. Vol. 25, No. 6, November 1980:436.

deLone, Richard H. *Small Futures: Children, Inequality, and the Limits of Reform.* New York: Harcourt Brace Jovanovich, 1979.

"Families Make America Great." *Moral Majority Report,* Washington, DC: December 15, 1980:24.

Family Impact Seminar. *Interim Report of the Family Impact Seminar.* Washington, DC: Institute for Educational Leadership, June 1978.

Family Policy Advisory Board. "Family Policy Advisory Board Report." Washington, DC, unpublished, November 1980.

"Family Program Profiles." *Alcoholism*. January–February 1981:39–47.

Federal Interagency Committee for the International Year of the Child. *Report on Federal Government Programs That Relate to Children*. Washington, DC: U.S. Department of Health and Human Services, March 5, 1979.

Feldman, Harold, and Margaret Feldman. *A Study of the Effects on the Family Due to Employment of the Welfare Mother*, Vols. 1–3. Springfield, VA: Manpower Administration, U.S. Department of Labor, National Technical Information Services, January 1972.

Gilbert, Neil. *Capitalism and the Welfare State: Dilemmas of Social Benevolence*. New Haven, CT: Yale University Press, 1983.

Gilbert, Neil. "Sweden's Disturbing Family Trends." *The Wall Street Journal*. June 24, 1987:23.

"How Child Care Works Abroad—East Germany: Parenthood Pays, France: Mama Doesn't Have to Have a Job, Sweden: Parents Say the Price Is Right." *San Francisco Chronicle*. February 24, 1981:19.

Interim Report of the Family Impact Seminar. Washington, DC: Family Impact Seminar, Institute for Educational Leadership. June 1978.

"Issue Fact Sheets." Submitted to National Advisory Committee to the White House Conference on Families by John Carr, Director, WHCF. Washington, DC: White House Conference on Families, November 26, 1980.

Sen. Roger Jepsen and Sen. Paul Laxalt. Family Protection Act. S. 1378 97th Congress, 1st Session, June 17, 1981.

Kamerman, Sheila B., and Alfred J. Kahn (Eds.). *Family Policy: Government and Families in Fourteen Countries*. New York: Columbia University Press, 1978.

Kamerman, Sheila B., and Alfred J. Kahn. *Child Care, Family Benefits and Working Parents*. New York: Columbia University Press, 1981.

Kanter, Rosabeth Moss. *Work and the Family in the United States: A Critical Review and Agenda for Research and Policy*. New York: Russell Sage Foundation, 1977.

Kellerman, Jonathan. "Big Brother and Big Mother." *Newsweek*. January 12, 1981:15.

Kroll, Woodrow Michael. "Sexual Patterns Degenerating." *Moral Majority Report*, Washington, DC. August 15, 1980:16.

"Labor: Social Policy and Human Services." *Encyclopedia of Social Work*, pp. 738–744. Washington, DC: National Association of Social Workers, 1977.

Lightfoot, Sarah Lawrence. *Worlds Apart*. New York: Basic Books, 1978.

Lipman-Blumen, Jean, and Jessie Bernard (Eds.). *Sex Roles and Social Policy*. Beverly Hills, CA: Sage, 1979.

Masnick, George, and Mary Jo Bane. *The Nation's Families 1960–1990*.

Cambridge: Joint Center for Urban Studies of MIT and Harvard University, 1980.

Miller, Dorothy C. "Children's Policy and Women's Policy: Congruence or Conflict?" *Social Work.* Vol. 32, No. 4, July–August 1987:289–292.

Money Income and Poverty Status of Families and Persons in the United States. Series P-60, No. 127. Washington, DC: U.S. Department of Commerce, Bureau of Census, August 1981.

Myrdal, Alva. *Nation and Family.* Cambridge, MA: MIT Press, 1968. (Original edition, 1941.)

"National Organizations' Issue Interest Areas—A Summary." Washington, DC: White House Conference on Families, November 1980.

Norwood, Janet L. "New Approaches to Statistics on the Family." *Monthly Labor Review.* July 1977:31–34.

Nye, F. Ivan, and Felix M. Bernardo. *Emerging Conceptual Frameworks in Family Analysis.* New York: Praeger, 1981.

"Office for Families," information memo. Washington, DC: Office for Families, Administration for Children, Youth and Families, Office of Human Development Services, FY 1980.

Off to a Good Start: A Resource for Parents, Professionals, and Volunteers. Administration for Children, Youth and Families, Office of Human Development Service, U.S. Department of Health and Human Services. DHHS Publication No. (OHDS) 81–30394. April 1981.

Proceedings of the General Council Session. Lisbon: International Union of Family Organizations, March 1980. Paris: Union Internationale des Organismes Familiaux, 1980.

"Pro-Family Conference Scheduled in Long Beach." *Moral Majority Report,* Washington, DC. June 30, 1980:14.

Promising Practices: Reaching Out to Families. Office for Families. Administration for Children, Youth and Families. Office of Human Development Services, U.S. Department of Health and Human Services, DHHS Publication No. (OHDS) 81–30324, Washington, DC. May 1981.

Ramos v. County of Madera. 4 C.3d 685, 94 Cal Rptr. 421, 484 P.2d 93.

"Recommendations to the White House Conference on Families." Family Impact Seminar, George Washington University, Washington, DC. May 1980.

Reich, Robert B. *The Next American Frontier.* New York: Times Books, 1983.

"Ronald Reagan Announces the Formation of the Family Policy Advisory Board." Arlington, VA: Reagan-Bush Committee, October 1, 1980.

Sidel, Ruth. *Women and Child Care in China.* New York: Hill & Wang, 1972.

Simons, Janet M. "Background Data for Aspen Institute Seminar: Frontiers of Corporate Competition— Linkages Between Work and Family." Aspen,

CO, August 2–8, 1981. Washington, DC: Children's Defense Fund, 1981.

The Status of Children, Youth and Families. Administration for Children, Youth and Families. DHHS Publication No. (OHDS) 80-30274. Washington, DC: U.S. Government Printing Office, 1979.

Steiner, Gilbert. *The Futility of Family Policy.* Washington, DC: The Brookings Institution, 1981.

Thompson, Rosemary. "President Carter's White House Conference on Families and Implementation via HHS Office of Families." Memo to Reagan Transition Team, from Reagan Family Policy Advisory Board, Washington, DC. November 12, 1980.

Von Frank, April A. *Family Policy in the U.S.S.R. Since 1944.* Palo Alto, CA: R. & E. Research Associates, 1979.

Weiner, Hyman J., et al. *The World of Work and Social Welfare Policy.* New York: Industrial Social Welfare Center, Columbia University School of Social Work, March 1971.

"WHCF Briefs Top Business Leaders on Improved Family Personnel Policies." *White House Conference on Families Newsletter.* Vol. 1, No. 11, November 1980.

White House Conference on Families. *Listening to America's Families: A Summary: Action for the '80's.* Washington, DC: U.S. Government Printing Office (040–000–00429–7), November 1980.

White House Conference on Families. *The Report: Listening to America's Families: Action for the 80's.* Washington, DC: U.S. Government Printing Office, October 1980.

"Work and Families: Report to Corporate Leaders on the White House Conference on Families." Prepared by J. C. Penney Company, Inc., and Public Affairs Department of the White House Conference on Families, Washington, DC. October 22, 1980.

PRIVATE-SECTOR PERSPECTIVES ON CARE

WORKPLACE AND CORPORATE POLICY—GENERAL

Akabas, Sheila (Ed.). *Labor and Industrial Settings: Sites for Social Work Practice.* New York: Councilar Social Work Education, 1979.

Bovard, James. "Busy Doing Nothing: The Story of Government Job Creation." *Policy Review.* Vol. 24, Spring 1983:87–102.

Estes, Ralph. *Corporate Social Accounting.* New York: John Wiley & Sons, 1976.

Katzell, Raymond A., and Daniel Yankelovich. *Work, Productivity, and Job Satisfaction: An Evaluation of Policy-Related Research.* New York: Harcourt Brace Jovanovich, 1975.

Omnibus Budget Reconciliation Act of 1981, Publ. L. No. 97–35, 2307, 05 Stat. 357.

"Summary of the Job Training Partnership Act." Washington, DC: U.S. Department of Labor, Employment and Training Administration, Office of Strategic Planning and Policy Development, Office of Planning and Policy Analysis, October 7, 1982.

Weiner, Hyman J., et al. *The World of Work and Social Welfare Policy.* New York: The Industrial Social Welfare Center, Columbia University School of Social Welfare, March 1971.

EMPLOYMENT-RELATED CHILD CARE

"Child Care: A Thoughtful Investment." San Francisco: Children's Rights Group, 1980.

"Child Care Referrals for Hospital Workers." *The Children's Advocate,* p. 4. Berkeley, CA: Berkeley Children's Services, January–February 1981.

Creed, Barbara, and Deene Goodlaw Solomon of the Pillsbury, Madison and Sutro Law Firm. "Summary of Federal and California Tax Provisions Relating to Child Care Before and After 1982." San Francisco: Bay Area Child Care Law Project, 1980.

"Day Care at Work Makes a Comeback." *Nation's Business.* July 1980:20.

Dilks, Carol. "Employers Who Help with the Kids." *Nation's Business.* February 1984: 59–60.

Employers and Child Care." *PAWS Newsletter 104.* New York: Pre-School Association, June 1982.

Employer-Sponsored Child Care Programs. Commerce Clearinghouse, 1982.

"Employer-Sponsored Day Care." Fact sheet produced by: The On Site Day Care: Research into the State of the Art and Models Development Project. Albany, NY: The Children's Place, December 1979.

Friedman, Dana E. "Designing a Feasibility Study: A Starting Point for Considering New Management Initiatives for Working Parents." Prepared for Conference on New Management Initiatives for Working Parents, Boston. April 1–4, 1981.

Friedland, Sandra S. "More Companies Offering Day Care." *The New York Times.* July 20, 1980:1.

Governor's Advisory Committee on Child Development Programs. *Employer Sponsored Child Care.* Sacramento: State of California, July 1981.

Governor's Advisory Committee on Child Development Programs. *Employer Sponsored Child Care: Policy Discussions, Recommendations and Bibliography.* Sacramento: State of California, July 1981.

Jaffee, Kenneth J. "Tax Incentives for Corporate Child Care." Concord, CA: Contra Costa Children's Council, 1980.

Lucas, Freddie H. *Day Care Research.* New York: J. C. Penney Co., 1972.

Mathia, Ellen. "Corporate Day Care—Nyloncraft Frames Issues of the '80's." *South Bend Tribune* (South Bend, IN). August 18, 1982.

McDonnell, Lynda. "Corporate Day-Care Programs Rise." *Minneapolis Tribune.* May 31, 1981: 1D and 7D.

Moscato, Joyce. "The Child Care Connection." *Union.* November–December 1987:16–20.

National Employer Supported Child Care Project. *List of Employer Supported Child Care Programs in the U.S. 1981–82.* Pasadena, CA: Child Care Information Service.

Parents at Work: Your Assets for the Eighties. A Conference for San Francisco Employers. San Francisco: Snider & Swift Assoc., October 29, 1981.

Patia, Raphael. *Women in the Modern World.* New York: The Free Press. London: Collier-Macmillan, 1967.

"The Realities and Fantasies of Industry-Related Child Care." Proceedings of a symposium hosted by the University of Colorado Medical Center and funded by Office of Child Development Child Care Project Grant No. CB-248, Denver, CO. May 21, 1973.

"Time Off for Child Care: Programs Vary." *New York Times.* January 27, 1981:D5.

U.S. Department of Labor, Women's Bureau. *Employers and Child Care: Establishing Services Through the Workplace.* Pamphlet 23. Washington, DC: Department of Labor, revised August 1982.

Consumer Behavior

Andreasen, Alan R. *The Disadvantaged Consumer.* New York: The Free Press, Macmillan, 1975.

Ferrar, Heidi M. "The Relationship Between a Working Mother's Job Satisfaction and Her Child Care Arrangements." Philadelphia: Pennsylvania State University, August 1978.

POLICY ANALYSIS, RESEARCH, AND EVALUATION

PROGRAM AND POLICY ANALYSIS—GENERAL

Browne, Angela, and Aaron Wildavsky. "Implementation as Exploration." In *Implementation* (3rd Edition), Jeffrey Pressman and Aaron Wildavsky (Eds.) Ch. 11. Berkeley: University of California Press, 1984.

Browne, Angela, and Aaron Wildavsky. "Implementation as Exploration." In *Implementation* (3rd Edition), Jeffrey Pressman and Aaron Wildavsky (Eds.) Ch. 10. Berkeley: University of California Press, 1984.

Browne, Angela, and Aaron Wildavsky. "What should Evaluation Mean to Implementation?" In *Implementation* (3rd Edition), Jeffrey Pressman and Aaron Wildavsky (Eds.) Ch. 9. Berkeley: University of California Press, 1984.

Charlesworth, James C. (Ed.). *Integration of the Social Sciences Through Policy Analysis*. Philadelphia: American Academy of Political and Social Science, October 1972.

Dunn, William N. *Public Policy Analysis: An Introduction*. Englewood Cliffs, NJ: Prentice-Hall, 1981.

Gilbert, Neil, and Harry Specht. *Dimensions of Social Welfare Policy*. Englewood Cliffs, NJ: Prentice-Hall, 1974.

Heclo, H. Hugh. "Review Article: Policy Analysis." *British Journal of Political Science*. Vol. 2, No. 2, January 1972:83–108.

Neiman, Max, and Catherine Lovell. "Mandating as a Policy Issue." *Policy Studies Review Annual*. Vol. 9, No. 5, Spring 1981:667–671.

Rein, Martin, and Sheldon H. White. "Policy Research: Belief and Doubt." Working Paper No. 46. Joint Center for Urban Studies of MIT and Harvard University, April 1977.

Sayer, S. T. "Macroeconomic Policy Rules Versus Discretion: Some Analytical Issues." *Journal of Public Policy*. Vol. 1, No. 4, October 1981:465–479.

Schick, Allen. "Beyond Analysis." *Public Administration Review*. Vol. 37, No. 3, May–June 1977:258–263.

Ukeles, Jacob B. "Policy Analysis: Myth or Reality?" *Public Administration Review*. Vol. 37, No. 3, May–June 1977:223–228.

Wildavsky, Aaron. *Speaking Truth to Power: The Art and Craft of Policy Analysis*. Boston: Little, Brown & Company, 1979.

RESEARCH METHODOLOGY

Becker, Thomas E., et al. "Information Resources for Program Evaluators." *Evaluation and Program Planning*. Vol. 3, 1980:25–33.

Begun, Audrey L. "Social Policy Evaluation: An Example from Drinking Age Legislation." *Evaluation and Program Planning*. Vol. 3, 1980:165–170.

Bernstein, Ilene, and Howard E. Freeman. *Academic and Entrepreneurial Research: Consequences of Diversity in Federal Evaluation Studies*. New York: Russell Sage, 1975.

Bloom, Martin, and Stephen R. Block. "Evaluating One's Own Effectiveness and Efficiency." *Social Work*. March 1977:130–136.

Brandl, John E. "Evaluation and Politics." *Evaluation*. Special Issue, 1978:6–48.

Bush, Malcolm, Andrew C. Gordon, and Robert LeBailly. "Evaluating Child Welfare Services: A Contribution from the Client." *Social Service Review*. September 1977:448–450.

Chandler, Daniel. "Evaluating California's Mental Health Programs." Prepared for Assembly Health Committee. Sacramento: Assembly Office of Research, State of California, February 1978.

Chen, Huey-Tsych, and Peter H. Rossi. "The Multi-Goal, Theory-Driven Approach to Evaluation: A Model Linking Basic and Applied Social Science." *Evaluation Studies Review Annual*. Vol. 6, 1981:38–54.

Comfort, Louise. *Education Policy and Evaluation: A Context for Change*. New York: Pergamon Press, 1982.

Connolly, Terry, and Alan L. Porter. "A User-Focused Model for the Utilization of Evaluation." *Evaluation and Program Planning*. Vol. 3, 1980:131–140.

Constable, Robert, and Rita Beck Black. "Mandates for a Changing Practice: PSRO and P.L. 94–142." *Social Service Review*. Vol. 54, No. 2:273–282.

Cook, Thomas D., and Charles Gruder. "Metaevaluation Research." *Evaluation Studies Review Annual*. Vol. 4, 1979:469–513.

Cronbach, Lee J., et al. "Our Ninety-Five Theses." *Evaluation Studies Review Annual*. Vol. 6, 1981:27–37.

Dery, David. "Evaluation and Problem Redefinition." *Journal of Public Policy*. Vol. 2, No. 1, February 1982:23–30.

Engleberg, Sydney. "Network Analysis in Evaluation: Some Words of Caution." *Evaluation and Program Planning*. Vol. 3, 1980:15–23.

Freeman, Howard E., and Marian A. Solomon. "Evaluation and the Uncertain '80's." *Evaluation Studies Review Annual*. Vol. 6, 1981:1–23.

Georgopoulos, Basil S., and Arnold S. Tannenbaum. "Subjective and Objective Output Indicators." In *Policies, Decisions and Organizations*, Fremont J. Lyden et al. (Eds.). New York: Appleton-Century-Crofts, 1969.

Glaser, Daniel. *Routinizing Evaluation: Getting Feedback on the Effectiveness of Crime and Delinquency Programs*. Rockville, MD: National Institute of Mental Health, U.S. Department of Health, Education and Welfare, 1973.

Goodsell, Charles T. "Client Evaluation of Three Welfare Programs." *Administration and Society.* Vol. 12, No. 2, August 1980:123–136.

Hatry, Harry, Richard E. Winnie, and Donald M. Fisk. *Practical Program Evaluation for State and Local Governments.* Washington, DC: Urban Institute, 1981.

Hudson, Barclay. "Domains of Evaluation." *Social Policy.* Vol. 6, No. 2, September–October 1975:79–81.

Kagle, Jill Doner. "Evaluating Social Work Practice." *Social Work.* Vol. 24, No. 4, July 1979:292–296.

Langbein, Laura Irwin. *Discovering Whether Programs Work.* Santa Monica, CA: Goodyear Publishing, 1980.

Lave, Judy R., and Lester B. Lave. "Measuring the Effectiveness of Prevention." In *Economics and Health Care,* John B. McKinlay (Ed.). Cambridge, MA: MIT Press, 1981.

Milcarek, Barry I., and Bruce G. Link. "Handling Problems of Ecological Fallacy in Program Planning and Evaluation." *Evaluation and Program Planning.* Vol. 4, 1981:23–28.

Nance, Kathy Newton, and Jolie Bain Pillsbury. "An Evaluation System for Decision Making." *Public Welfare.* Vol. 34, No. 2, Spring 1976:45–52.

Patton, Michael Quinn. *Utilization-Focused Evaluation.* Beverly Hills, CA: Sage, 1978.

Pillsbury, Jolie Bain, and Kathy Newton Nance. "An Evaluation Framework for Public Welfare Agencies." *Public Welfare.* Spring 1976: 47–51.

Rich, Robert F. *Translating Evaluation into Policy.* Beverly Hills, CA: Sage, 1979.

Rivlin, Alice M. *Systematic Thinking for Social Action.* Washington, DC: The Brookings Institution, 1971.

Rossi, Peter M., and Richard A. Berk. "An Overview of Evaluation Strategies and Procedures." *Human Organization.* Vol. 40, No. 4, Winter 1981:287– 299.

Salasian, Susan. "Evaluation as a Tool for Restoring the Mental Health of Victims." *Evaluation and Change.* Special Issue, 1980:25–30.

Scriven, Michael. "Pros and Cons About Goal-Free Evaluation." *Evaluation Comment.* Los Angeles: UCLA Center for the Study of Evaluation, December 1972.

Segal, Steven P. "Issues in the Utilization and Evaluation of Social Work Treatment." *International Social Work.* Vol. 21, No. 1, 1978:2–18.

Solomon, Marian A. "Evaluation in the U.S. Department of Health, Education and Welfare." *Evaluation and Program Planning.* Vol. 3, 1980:53–55.

Stake, Robert A. *Evaluating the Arts in Education: A Responsive Approach.* Ohio: Charles E. Merrill, 1975.

Stufflebeam, Daniel L., and William J. Webster. "An Analysis of Alternative

Approaches to Evaluation." *Evaluation Studies Review Annual*. Vol. 6, 1981:70–85.

Suchman, Edward. *Evaluative Research: Principles and Practice in Public Service and Social Action Programs*. New York: Russell Sage Foundation, 1967.

Washington, R. O. *Program Evaluation in the Human Services*. Milwaukee: University of Wisconsin, n.d.

Weiss, Carol H. *Evaluating Action Programs*. Boston: Allyn & Bacon, 1972.

Weiss, Carol H. *Evaluation Research*. Englewood Cliffs, NJ: Prentice-Hall, 1972.

Weiss, Carol H. "Alternative Models of Program Evaluation." *Social Work*. November 1974:675–681.

Wholey, J. S. "Evaluation to Improve Program Performance." *Evaluation Studies Review Annual*. Vol. 6, 1981:55–69.

EVALUATION—GENERAL

Rosenberg, Morris. *The Logic of Survey Analysis*. New York: Basic Books, 1968.

SURVEYS—CHILD CARE

"Child Care Center Survey." Boulder, CO: Boulder Memorial Hospital, 1980.

"Child Care Survey." The Child Care Committee of the Coors Women's Resource Center Task Force, Adolph Coors Company.

"Day Care Needs Assessment Survey Suggestions." Boulder, CO: Boulder Child Care Support Center, 1980.

"Fairchild Child Care Survey Summary Report." Palo Alto, CA: Palo Alto Community Child Care and Community Coordinated Child Development Council, for the Fairchild Corporation, Mountain View, CA.

MISCELLANEOUS REFERENCES

Armor, David. "White Flight and the Future of School Desegregation." Santa Monica, CA: Rand Corporation, 1978.

Clark, Buton R. "United States." In *Academic Power: Patterns of Authority in Seven National Systems of Higher Education*, John H. Van de Graaf et al. (Eds.). New York: Praeger, 1978.

Doxiadis, Constantinos A. *Ekistics: An Introduction to the Science of Human Settlement.* New York: Oxford University Press, 1968.

Friedman, Milton. *Capitalism and Freedom.* Chicago: University of Chicago Press, 1982.

Gliedman, John, and William Roth. *The Unexpected Minority: Handicapped Children in America.* New York: Harcourt Brace Jovanovich, 1980.

Hewlett, Sylvia Ann. "Coping with Illegal Immigrants." *Foreign Affairs.* Vol. 60, Winter 1981–1982:358–378.

Information Please Almanac 1982. New York: Simon & Schuster, 1981.

Sowell, Thomas. *Civil Rights: Rhetoric or Reality?* New York: William Morrow, 1984.

U.S. Bureau of the Census. *1980 Census of Population and Housing: Provisional Estimates of Social, Economic and Housing Characteristics.* PHO80–S1– 1. Washington, DC: U.S. Bureau of the Census, Government Printing Office, March 1982.

INDEX